NEA EARLY CHILDHOOD EDUCATION SERIES

Perspectives on Early Childhood Education

Growing with Young Children Toward the 21st Century

David Elkind
Editor

A NATIONAL EDUCATION ASSOCIATION PUBLICATION

Copyright © 1991
National Education Association of the United States

Printing History
　First Printing:　May 1991

Note

The opinions expressed in this publication should not be construed as representing the policy or position of the National Education Association. Materials published by the NEA Professional Library are intended to be discussion documents for educators who are concerned with specialized interests of the profession.

Library of Congress Cataloging-in-Publication Data

Perspectives on early childhood education　:　growing with young
　children toward the 21st century　/　David Elkind, editor
　　　p.　cm.—(Early childhood education series)
　Includes bibliographical references.
　"Stock no. 0351900"—Cover.
　ISBN 0-8106-0351-9
　1. Early childhood education—United States.　I. Elkind, David,
1931-　.　II. Series:　Early childhood education series (Washington D.C.)
LB1139.25.P47　1991
372.21—dc20　　　　　　　　　　　　　　　　　　90-25508
　　　　　　　　　　　　　　　　　　　　　　　　　　　CIP

CONTENTS

1. Early Childhood Education in the Postmodern Era: An Introduction, by David Elkind 3
2. AAHPERD. Physical Education and Health Education in Early Childhood, by Joel Meier, Margie R. Hanson, and Larry K. Olsen 19
3. ACEI. Present and Future Concerns for Children, by Mary Louise Hirsh-Burger 35
4. ASCA. Trends in Early Childhood Education and Counseling, by Susan Jones Sears and Doris Rhea Coy 47
5. ASCD. Early Childhood Programs: Success for All, by Patricia Cannon Conran 59
6. ATE. Critical Issues and Early Childhood Teacher Education, by Thomas J. Buttery, Edith Guyton, and John Sikula 67
7. CCSSO. Foundations for Success: Early Childhood and Family Education, by William B. Keene 77
8. CEC. Early Intervention and Family Support for Children with Special Developmental Challenges, by Crystal E. Kaiser 85
9. ECS. School Readiness and State Action, by Frank Newman 99
10. IRA. Trends and Strategies in Early Literacy Education, by Lesley Mandel Morrow, with Introduction by Dale Johnson 105
11. NABSE. The Rhetoric of Early Childhood Education Must Be Replaced by Decisive Action, by J. Jerome Harris 117
12. NAEA. The Visual Arts in Early Childhood Education, by David W. Baker 133
13. NAESP. The Critical Preschool Years, by Gary D. Salyers 141
14. NAEYC. The Implications of National Education Goals for Early Childhood Education, by Ellen Galinsky 149
15. NAME. America's Migrant Children: Most at Risk, by Al Wright 159

16. NASBE. Early Childhood Education—A Continuum, by Roseann Bentley 169
17. NASN. Health Perspectives on Early Childhood Education, by Shirley Carstens 177
18. NASP. Toward Improved Early Childhood Education in the 21st Century, by Margaret Dawson and Howard M. Knoff 189
19. NBCDI. Public School-Based Child Care and the Black Child: Building Bridges Toward Self-Sufficiency in the 21st Century, by Evelyn K. Moore 203
20. NCSS. Social Studies During the Early Childhood and Primary Years, by C. Frederick Risinger 213
21. NCTM. Engaging Young Minds in Learning Mathematics, by Shirley M. Frye and Raymond J. Brie 221
22. NEA. Early Childhood Education and the Public Schools, by Keith Geiger 227
23. NSTA. Getting Started with Science—Science Inquiry for Early Childhood Education, by Bonnie J. Brunkhorst 243
24. PTA. Early Childhood Education: The Parents' Perspective, by Ann Lynch 253
25. The Reality We Share in Common: An Afterword, by David Elkind 261

1. Early Childhood Education in the Postmodern Era: An Introduction

by David Elkind

Early childhood education in the public schools is a postmodern phenomena. While early childhood education, in the form of half-day kindergartens, was introduced in the modern era, the universality of early childhood education in our schools and its extension downward to two-, three-, and four-year-olds reflects a fundamental change in family values and institutional functions that is but one index that we are moving into a new social era. Before we look at the implications for parents and schools of this change, it is useful to put it in historical context.

HISTORICAL OVERVIEW

For purposes of discussion, we can look at the history of the family and schools in our society as evolving through three major stages. To be sure, such a description is an overgeneralization and it must be emphasized that some of the values of one stage are carried over and elaborated in the succeeding one, whereas other values are rejected from one period to the next. In general, I believe it is justifiable to speak of a new social era when there are demonstrable and major shifts in the structure, values, and functions of a society's major institutions.

The Premodern Era

The Family. The premodern era in the United States began with the establishment of the bay colonies and extended until the founding of the republic. The majority of families lived in rural communities and were engaged in farming. Parents took major responsibility for the child's religious, moral, and social upbringing. The family was also responsible for teaching children the craft skills they would need to earn a living as adults. This was done at home for young women and sometimes through the apprenticeship system for young men.

The School. Schooling during the premodern period was characterized by the predominance of locally funded and prescribed

Introduction

educational arrangements. In the south, the sons of the wealthy went to Latin schools and often to college or university in England. In New York, schools were funded jointly by the church and the community. In Massachusetts, the state required every community of 50 or more families to have a "town" school and every community of 100 or more to have a "Latin" school. On the frontier, itinerant "traveling" teachers were often all that was available to families (13).*

In the premodern era, parents paid for the education of their children, often dictated the curriculum, and looked upon the teacher and the school as in their employ.

The Modern Era

The modern era in this country began with the revolution and the founding of the republic. As often happens, major changes in social organization are accompanied by major changes in technology. The establishment of the republic was followed shortly by the industrial revolution. With the introduction of farm machinery, the need for farm labor decreased significantly while the construction of mills and factories generated a demand for factory labor. As a consequence many farm families moved to the cities. During the premodern era, some 60 percent of families lived on farms in contrast with less than 10 percent today.

A number of changes in societal values during the modern era are of importance for understanding the relations of schools and families during this period. The industrial revolution brought about a marked change in attitude toward craft skills and their products that predominated during the premodern era. These skills ranged from carpentry and quilting, to curing meats and preparing preserves. With the advent of machine-made goods, homemade ones came to be looked down upon as "primitive." Machine-made quilts were better than handmade, machine-made furniture and clothing were better than handmade, preroasted and ground coffee was better than home-roasted and ground coffee. In each case "better" meant "more efficient." Efficiency was one of the new gods of the modern era (10).

An interesting example of this valuation of anything machine-made and devaluation of anything handmade can be seen in any number of

---

*Numbers in parentheses appearing in the text refer to the References at the end of the chapter.

homes in the Midwest. These homes, built around the turn of the century, do not have wood-burning fireplaces. Instead the fireplaces have gas jets and "artificial" logs. Gas heating was more "efficient" and also much more "modern" and up-to-date than wood-burning stoves. The infatuation with the new and the rejection of the old was a very modern value.

Another value of the modern era was that "bigger is better." This value, although primarily an economic one, had family and school repercussions. In the economic realm, bigger factories, bigger machines, meant more rapid "efficient" production and hence more and bigger profits. But the bigger is better soon spread to the tallness of buildings, and became "taller is better." Skyscrapers are a uniquely modern phenomenon. So too are the supermarkets that have replaced small, "mom and pop" stores (resurrected in neighborhood chain "convenience" stores) and the shopping centers and malls that have, to some extent, replaced the "shopping streets" of small self-contained stores on city thoroughfares.

Finally, a last major new value of the modern era was consumerism. The premodern family was, of necessity, frugal. Everything was made to last and durability took precedence over fashion or style—although these values were sometimes nicely combined with durability, as in the furniture of the Shakers. Families retained their frugal values when they moved to the city. Yet an industrial society requires citizens to be consumers if the factories are to keep busy. Hence families had to be sold on the superiority of the machine-made products, the virtues of debt, and the necessity of always having the latest models and the "newest" products.

The advertising industry arose during the modern era, to foster consumerism. And, gradually, families were won over and the values of frugality were subordinated to the values of consumerism. The new values might be paraphrased as: "Debt in the service of new products is not bad and using the same product overly long is not good."

The Family. The movement of farm families to the cities brought about a major change in family structure. Families lost their self-sufficiency and came to depend upon stores for food, clothing, utensils, and furniture. Moreover, parents could no longer prepare children for

Introduction

adult vocations. Skills required for working in mills and factories were different from those required for working on the farm. Parents could no longer transmit the skills they had learned from their own parents to their offspring. A certain continuity and sharing between generations was lost as America became urban and industrial rather than rural and agricultural (11).

The Schools. It was recognized by the founding fathers, even though they themselves came from aristocratic backgrounds, that a true democracy required an educated electorate. Between 1830 and 1870 a system of schools was established to provide education for all children. One index of the shift to true democracy came with the abolition of property ownership as a condition of suffrage. Literacy, rather than wealth, emerged as the only criterion for voting in elections.

In the modern era, schools took over the preparation of youth for work in the adult world. Most schools had wood and machine shops as well as courses in mechanical drawing, typing, and sewing. Even the organization of the schools was a way of preparing youth for factory or office work. The tolling of school bells to herald the lunch period, like the factory whistles, was but one way in which schools prepared students for the routine of factory or office life.

Schools during this period also took over some of the family responsibility for child health and well-being. Children were required to be vaccinated before they entered school and most children were also screened for vision and hearing defects. Schools thus ensured that children got a minimum of health care. In providing school lunches and gym classes, schools also played a part in the nutritional and physical well-being of young people.

At the same time, schools also reflected the new values that characterized modernism. School divisions got larger (the unified school districts), as did schools (the comprehensive high school), under the dictum that "bigger is better" (16). The veneration of factory-made goods was reflected in the preference for machine-produced curriculum materials over those devised by teachers. And consumerism was reflected in schools' penchant for purchasing whatever was "new" on the market regardless of its usefulness. (Witness the numbers of overhead projectors, teaching machines, SRA kits, and so on, gathering dust in many school storerooms.)

With respect to family-school relations, the shifting of responsibilities from family to school in the areas of health and vocational training initiated a new relationship between parents, teachers, and schools. Now parents and teachers were partners, rather than employers and employees. This new relationship was evidenced in the founding, around the turn of the century, of local, state, and national Parent Teacher Associations and Organizations.

The Postmodern Era

The postmodern era was ushered in with the dropping of the atomic bombs on Nagasaki and Hiroshima that effectively ended the modern love affair with the unlimited benefits of technology. More than anything else, the atomic bomb gave brutal evidence of the dark side of technology, of its capacity to do harm as well as bring benefits. Since the 1950s we have continued to learn of the many dangers of technology. The destruction of the ozone layer by hydrocarbons, the health hazards of pesticides like DDT, and of building materials like asbestos, and of toxic wastes are but some of the perils of technology that have become part of the postmodern consciousness.

Postmodernism was furthered by the introduction of computers that quickly transformed the modern value of "bigger is better" into "smaller is better." A lap-top computer, for example, now contains more memory and speed than a whole room of earlier computing machines. Factories are becoming smaller as they become automated and robots replace workers on the assembly lines. Likewise, couples whose children have grown, are moving out of large, suburban family homes and into smaller, communal condominiums.

Finally, the emergence of Japan and other Asian countries as economic powerhouses, along with the European Economic Community that will take effect in 1992, has highlighted the dangers of a consumerism unaccompanied by an efficient and competitive industrial infrastructure. As our industries fell behind those in other countries both with respect to quality and pricing, our consumerism helped build the economies of many other countries while we became a debtor nation. Our productivity and efficiency have not kept pace with our appetite for new goods. In the

Introduction

postmodern era, we are beginning to realize that consumerism works to the benefit of our industries only if we are buying our own, not just foreign-made goods.

The Family. Trends in family life during the postmodern era continue those begun during the modern period. These trends, however, have not always followed a linear course. For example, the progressive liberation and emancipation of women that began in the nineteenth century and that resulted in women's suffrage, was set back in the middle decades of the twentieth century with the movement of families to the suburbs. In the 1960s, the women's movement was revived and sought equality in education and job opportunity. The movement of large numbers of middle-class women into the work force is thus a postmodern phenomenon that had its origin in the modern era (9).

The increase in the divorce rate is another postmodern phenomenon that began in the modern era. Around the turn of the century the divorce rate was one divorce for every seven marriages. Today the number is closer to one out of two. The increase in the divorce rate has been accompanied by an increasing secularization within the society. Marriage is a religious as well as a civil contract. Religious strictures against divorce became less effective as marriage became increasingly civil and legal, rather than religious. The prenuptial agreement is but one example of the secularization of marriage and the emphasis upon its financial obligations.

In the same way, having even young children reared by others is not new on the historical scene. This was a necessity for the children of poor families and a convenience for parents of wealth even during the premodern era. The idea that children should be reared by their parents is a middle-class, not a premodern or modern value. What has happened in the modern era, and increasingly in the postmodern period, is that middle-class parents have adopted values that once were the exclusive province of lower- or upper-class families (3).

Indeed, it is probably fair to say that much of the continued resistance to mothers working, and having children reared by others, is as much a class prejudice as it is a psychological or humanitarian concern. "Good women," that is, middle-class women, do not allow their children to be raised by others. Yet the class barriers about women's roles had already been broken by the "Playboy philosophy," which, for the first time, depicted clean-cut middle-class girls as sexual creatures. The distinction between the sacred and the profane—lower-class girls who did and middle-class girls who did not—was obliterated. To the conservative right, middle-class mothers leaving their young children to the care of others is another example of their implicit "fall" from the sacred to the profane—from middle-class virtue to lower-class vice or upper-class decadence.

One characteristic of the postmodern middle-class family, then, is that it is no longer as different, as it once was, from lower- and upper-income families. The middle-class family is no longer, as Lasch put it so well, "A Haven in a Heartless World" (8). In this respect, although capitalism seems to have won over communism, our society is nonetheless becoming more socialistic. The recent advocacy of the American Medical Association for a system of national health insurance is but another evidence of our movement toward a more egalitarian society. Social Security, Medicare, unemployment insurance, provision for the education of the disabled, are but some of the ways in which our society is beginning to look after all its citizens.

As middle-income families become more like lower-income families—with more divorce, more single parenting, more two-parent working families—they are becoming more like lower-income parents in still another way. Like low-income parents, middle-class parents are becoming increasingly dependent upon outside social institutions to aid them in their child rearing. Whereas, however, the low-income families looked to social welfare, middle-income parents are looking to the schools and to industry (parental leave, on-site child care) for support in fulfilling their parenting function.

The Schools. Schools in the postmodern era will begin to reflect the postmodern values. Some reform initiatives already embody the "smaller is better" value as they strive to provide "bottom-up" rather than "top-down" administration (e.g., experiments in Chicago and Rochester, New York). It is likely, too, that school systems will eliminate many budget-consuming middle-management positions in the same way that industry has. While schools hopefully will not get "meaner," they will get "leaner." The new distrust of technology and concerns with the

Introduction

environment will also be reflected in the schools. This value will appear not only in the curriculum (both in courses and course content), but also in institutional practice. Many schools are recycling materials and using teacher-obtained or -made materials as well as purchased curriculum materials. School buildings will increasingly be used both before and after school as well as on weekends. Conservation will begin to compete with unbridled consumerism as the dominant societal value.

Finally, schools will carry forward the trend begun in the modern era, of taking over more child rearing functions. This is already happening as many school systems provide full-day kindergartens, before-and-after school programs, school health clinics, and courses in sex, drug, and driver education. In contrast to the modern era, in which parents and schools were partners, schools will begin to take a leadership role. This is already apparent in those communities where the schools are providing courses in parent education, support groups for children of divorce and of alcoholic parents, as well as child care for teenage mothers continuing their education.

HISTORY OF EARLY CHILDHOOD EDUCATION

We can now look at the history of early childhood education in the context of these social changes and see why it is truly a postmodern phenomenon. Clearly, there was little early childhood education of the formal variety during the premodern era when the population was primarily rural and the city dwellers were engaged in light industry and commerce. Schooling in general was not as necessary as it became in modern and postmodern times and was not even thought of for younger children.

The foundations for early childhood education were laid in the modern era beginning with the writings of Pestalozzi and Froebel.

Heinrich Pestalozzi (1746-1826)

Pestalozzi was a Swiss educator who extended some of the ideas of the Enlightenment to early childhood education (7). The spirit of the Enlightenment was to look to experience, rather than to authority, for true knowledge. Pestalozzi began several schools for children whom today we would call disadvantaged. None of these schools was very successful nor lasted very long. This was probably more a result of Pestalozzi's limitations as an administrator than of the programs he initiated.

Pestalozzi was, nonetheless, a prolific writer, and in his many books gave what is perhaps the first systematic approach to the education of infants and young children. In his most famous book, *Gertrude Teaches Her Children*, which takes the form of a series of letters to mothers, he described many exercises the mother could engage in with her child. These exercises were aimed at helping children develop their intellectual and physical abilities. Moreover, these exercises were revolutionary in the sense that they took account of child development and catered to it. Up until that time young children were taught what adults thought they ought to know, namely, the catechism.

Although he was personally not successful in maintaining a school run according to his own principles, Pestalozzi did influence many parents and other educators who also began to look at what children needed to learn rather than at what adults wanted them to know.

Friedrich Wilhelm Froebel (1782-1852)

Froebel is generally regarded as the originator of early childhood education as a distinct field of pedagogy (6). He believed that children could and should be taught outside the home as well as within it and that such education should be provided by trained teachers. He developed not only a curriculum for young children but also a training school to prepare teachers to work with young children.

Perhaps Froebel is best known for his introduction of the *Kindergarten*, children's garden, where children could learn through activity. Recognizing the educational value of certain toys, Froebel advocated toys and play as the appropriate way of instructing young children. His kindergarten curriculum included blocks, pets, and simple games. The toys that Froebel introduced for educational purposes, such as a ball, he termed "gifts." He believed that children could not only learn simple ideas such as "roundness" from playing with the ball, but they could also begin to comprehend the shape of the earth and the concept of unity implicit in the sphere.

Introduction

Maria Montessori (1870-1952)

The first woman in Italy to gain admittance to and graduate from medical school, Montessori laid the foundations for early childhood education as we know it today (12). After graduating from medical school, Montessori worked with retarded children for whom she designed some innovative learning materials. She was then invited to set up an educational program for young children in a low-income housing project. Using untrained teachers and modifications of the materials she had devised for retarded children, she created what we now know as Montessori education.

Like Pestalozzi and Froebel, Montessori began with observations of how children engage in learning on their own. From these observations she was able to both choose material that were uniquely suited to the intellectual needs of young children, and describe some general principles of early childhood education. For example, Montessori believed that young children should always be exposed to the object, property, or quality before they were given the name for that object, property, or quality. Put differently, she believed that sensory learning should precede symbolic learning.

Many of Montessori's innovations have become part of the conventional wisdom of early childhood teaching practice. For example, the child-sized chairs, tables, eating and cooking utensils that she introduced are now standard furnishings in all early childhood settings. Some of her other curriculum innovations such as the button board, sandpaper letters, and square blocks of different sizes have been less widely disseminated. Montessori emphasized curriculum materials because she believed that if the environment was properly "prepared," then children would be able to spontaneously learn from it through their self-guided activity.

Unlike her curriculum materials, Montessori's teacher training methods have not been widely used outside the Montessori teacher training schools. Like Froebel, Montessori believed that early childhood teachers had to be specially trained and she worked out an elaborate training program of teacher preparation. Today, Montessori-oriented teacher training is one of the more rigorous early childhood teacher training programs in this country and abroad. Montessori teachers are particularly well schooled in the use of manipulative materials with young children.

John Dewey (1858-1952)

Although trained as a philosopher, Dewey became America's first original educator. Like Pestalozzi, Froebel, and Montessori, Dewey believed that childhood was a unique stage of life that should not be rushed. In addition he believed that education should be practical—his brand of educational philosophy has been called *Functionalism*—and should prepare children for the life they will experience outside school. While Dewey was not opposed to classical education at some levels, he believed that children should also learn many practical skills (2).

In addition to his contributions to educational philosophy, Dewey also introduced instructional innovations. Perhaps the most well known is what has come to be called the *project* method. Rather than teach subjects as separate and apart from one another, Dewey believed they could be taught in an integrated way if children were engaged in producing a product. In the process of building a boat, for example, young people would learn the vocabulary of boat building, would read about the history of the boat they were constructing, and might read books about the sea. When engaged in such a project, young people would learn knowledge and skills in many different subjects in an integrated, interesting, and rewarding way.

Dewey's ideas and methods became a major movement in the United States that lasted until the mid-1950s; it was called "Progressive Education." It disappeared from the American educational scene for many different reasons, not the least of which in distorted form it had become associated with "permissiveness"(1).

Sigmund Freud (1856-1939)

Freud created a new theory of psychopathology, a method of investigating it, and therapeutic procedures for treating mental illness. His writings continue to have a major impact in all facets of social science. His work has also had an important impact on early childhood education. Freud's discoveries of infant sexuality, the stages of psychosexual development, and of the Oedipus complex have altered the way in which we think about young children (5). Although most of what

Introduction

Freud had to say about early childhood dealt with parent-child relationships, there were some implications for out-of-home care as well. This is particularly true with respect to children's play.

Whereas writers such as Froebel and Montessori saw play as an all-important mode of learning for young children, Freud saw play as comparable to a dream. Like a dream, play has both a *manifest* and a *latent* content. Children's play can reflect inner complexes and conflicts and also be a way of working them out. A child who has just returned from the doctor, for example, may play at being doctor as a way of relieving some of the anxiety aroused by that visit. The technique of play therapy has grown out of this recognition that children's play can have symbolic meaning. It is now generally recognized that the play of young children has both cognitive *and* affective value.

Erik Erikson (1902-   )

Erikson was trained as a child analyst but has departed significantly from analytic theory (4). In his writings, Erikson has focused upon the social dimensions of development and the evolution of such social orientations as trust and identity. Four of Erikson's eight stages of development occur in early childhood.

In Erikson's view we are born with a number of social potentials. How these potentials are realized depends very much upon the sort of experiences to which we are exposed as well as on our own unique characteristics. Each potential exists as a kind of polarity and has a particular time when the balance between the two opposing tendencies will be determined. Although whatever balance is attained can be modified later, it is always more difficult than during the "critical period" for those polarities.

To illustrate the relevance of the Eriksonian stages for early childhood education, we can look at the stage of initiative versus guilt, which has its critical time around the age of four and five. If children are given the opportunity to explore the world, undertake projects on their own, they will develop a sense of initiative that is stronger than the sense of guilt. In contrast, if children are constantly told what to do, corrected if they make mistakes, they will acquire a sense of guilt that is greater than their sense of initiative.

Erikson's theory, then, has rather direct implications for the practice of early education as well as for child rearing.

Jean Piaget (1896-1980)

Although he was trained as a philosopher and biologist, Piaget's greatest contributions were to developmental psychology. Piaget elaborated a theory of intellectual development that has impacted many different disciplines, including early childhood education. While Piaget himself wrote about education in general terms (15), his work has had a major impact upon the theory and practice of early childhood education. From a theoretical point of view, Piaget's work has emphasized the importance of development, and of the limits that it sets upon learning. Learning cannot accelerate growth. Piaget's theoretical work has been a major factor in the current effort by early childhood educators to get schools to provide "developmentally appropriate" practice for young children (14). In addition, Piaget's work on the development of children's understanding of different conceptions, such as number, have led to major curriculum innovations.

EARLY CHILDHOOD EDUCATION IN THE POSTMODERN ERA

The conceptual work done by writers of the modern era set the stage for early childhood education by revealing the unique ways in which young children learn and the curriculum and educational settings best suited to their needs. This knowledge grew side by side with the societal changes that moved us into the postmodern era and the readiness of parents to put their young children in out-of-home educational settings. One of our major tasks is to build our knowledge of sound early childhood education into the many programs now serving this age group.

Another challenge will be to deal with the new conflicts of the postmodern era as they impact upon education in general and early childhood education in particular. For example, in the postmodern world the battle between communism and capitalism of the modern era has been replaced by the battle between humanitarianism and capitalism. Conflicts about the building of nuclear plants, the drilling of oil wells, the control of industrial pollution and unbridled development, as well as

Introduction

about cigarette advertising, all reflect the new tensions between capitalistic and humanitarian goals.

With respect to early childhood education, this conflict can be seen in the reluctance to adequately fund early childhood programs in both the private and public sectors. The humanitarian needs of young children are today in conflict with the other economic demands upon public budgets and the profitability of private companies. There are no simple answers to these questions. Both sides have solid arguments. Unlike retired persons, however, who have effectively organized to have their financial and medical needs recognized, young children cannot organize, and parents and early childhood educators must advocate for them.

The task, then, in the postmodern era will be to provide high-quality programs for young children both in the public and the private sector. The economic demands of early childhood education will thus come into conflict with the demands of other groups and functions for public funding and with the profit motive of private business organizations. In the postmodern world, therefore, the battle in early childhood education, as in the rest of the society, will be between the need to be economically competitive and the humanitarian need for social and environmental betterment.

The chapters in this book address this postmodern issue in a variety of ways and from many different directions. But all reiterate the underlying theme that adequate funding, training, and staffing for early childhood education is a necessary, essential, and immediate social need that must be given a high priority by government as well as by industry.

REFERENCES

1. Cremin L. *The Transformation of the Schools.* New York: Vintage, 1961.
2. Dewey, J. *Democracy in Education* New York: McMillan, 1916, p. 7.
3. Elkind, D. *The Hurried Child.* Reading, Mass. Addison-Wesley, 1981/1988.
4. Erikson, E. *Childhood and Society.* New York: Norton, 1950.
5. Freud, S. "Infantile Sexuality." *The Basic Writings of Sigmund Freud.* New York: Random House, 1938, pp. 580-603.
6. Froebel, F. *The Education of Man.* New York: D. Appleton and Co., 1904.
7. Green, J. A. *The Educational Ideas of Pestalozzi.* New York: Greenwood, 1914.

8. Lasch, C. *Haven in a Heartless World.* New York: Basic Books, 1977.
9. Masnick, G. and Bane, M. J. *The Nation's Families.* Boston: Auburn House, 1980.
10. Matthews, G. *Just a Housewife.* New York: Oxford University Press, 1987.
11. Mead, M. *Culture and Commitment.* New York: American Museum of Modern History, 1970.
12. Montessori, M. *The Montessori Method.* York: Schocken, 1967. (First printed in 1912.)
13. Mulhern, J. *A History of Education.* New York: Ronald Press, 1946.
14. Piaget, J. *The Psychology of Intelligence.* London: Routledge and Kegan Paul, 1950.
15. _____. *Science of Education and Psychology of the Child.* New York: Orion, 1970.
16. Ravitch, D. *The Troubled Crusade.* New York: Basic Books, 1983.

The Editor

David Elkind is Professor of Child Study at Tufts University. He is the author of numerous books, including *The Hurried Child, All Grown Up and No Place to Go, Miseducation,* and *Grandparenting: Understanding Today's Children.*

Dr. Elkind is a consultant to state education departments, clinics and mental health centers, government agencies, and private foundations. He lectures extensively in the United States, Canada, and abroad.

AAHPERD

American Alliance for
Health, Physical Education, Recreation and Dance

2. Physical Education and Health Education in Early Childhood

by **Joel Meier 1989-90 President,** *American Alliance for Health, Physical Education, Recreation and Dance;* **Margie R. Hanson,** *Vice President, and Consultant for Children, AAHPERD, and* **Larry K. Olsen,** *Association for the Advancement of Health Education, and Professor and Coordinator of Graduate Studies, The Pennsylvania State University, University Park. AAHPERD has a membership of 34,000 with headquarters at 1900 Association Drive, Reston, Virginia 22091.*

The American Alliance for Health, Physical Education, Recreation and Dance is an organization of six associations, all of which evolved from the parent association, the Association for the Advancement of Physical Education, founded in 1885. Each of the Associations has a special identity, but with a common bond in their interests in health and movement-related activities.

In this chapter I have asked Margie R. Hanson to address the dance, fitness, physical education, and recreation aspects of the Alliance and its concerns for children, and Larry K. Olsen to address the health education aspects.

—Joel Meier

MOVING: A CHILD'S WAY OF LEARNING

When there is so much homelessness, hunger, child abuse, plus the pressures for teaching science, mathematics, and reading skills, how can educators support physical education, dance, and play as essential to the curriculum? Children love to move. It is a fundamental function of life. Children move to learn and learn to move. For them moving is being and time to be must include time to move.

Historically, people have always believed that movement made a significant contribution to development and learning. This belief can be cited as far back as Plato's *Republic*; it has been continuously documented throughout the centuries to follow by writers such as Comenius, Pestalozzi, Froebel, Piaget, and a host of others. In American education, however, play and instruction in motor development have been considered frivolous by many because of the long-prevailing philosophy of a mind-body dualism and because our puritan ethic prizes work and believes play should be reserved for leisure outside school.

Currently, there is increasing recognition of the need to provide children with a wide range of sensory and social experiences to facilitate learning and total development. In the past we have tended to divide the child into three domains—the physical, mental, and social-emotional. Now it is clear that these domains are intrinsically interwoven and that by facilitating one we will enhance another. Early childhood educators have been leaders in this thought and practice, especially at the prekindergarten level.

Within these domains it has become increasingly evident that physical activity is a wonderful way to enrich the lives of children, not only physiologically but also affectively and cognitively. The early childhood educator has always believed that children move to learn. The physical educator and dance teacher focus on teaching children to learn to move better. Both goals are important for the child, and they can happen simultaneously.

The mutual task of physical and early childhood educators is to share their beliefs and knowledge. The need for physical activity for children is well documented in the research in terms of their growth and fitness needs. There is increasing evidence that the nation's children lack cardiovascular fitness, strength, and flexibility. Many are overweight. To have a healthy, productive nation, fitness habits and knowledge need to be established early. We also know that the early ages are golden years for skill learning, and certain manipulative patterns such as striking and throwing emerge as early as three years of age. We need to capitalize on these innate abilities and help to develop and refine basic motor skills. These skills can lead to increased confidence and provide more autonomy for children to explore their environment and learn from the world about them, as well as to provide a foundation for a lifetime of enjoyable physical activity. Recognizing these needs, the 97th U.S.

Congress passed a joint resolution recommending daily physical education for all children in K–12.

The Moving Curriculum

Over the past 20 years significant change has taken place in physical education curricula for the young child. These curricula have undergone various emphases such as movement education, perceptual-motor development, personalized learning, and integrated learnings. Current thrusts center on developmentally appropriate activities.

Great leaps in knowledge have occurred about the nature of movement and the motor development of the human being from infancy to adult. This has resulted in an understanding and a sharpened focus on basic elements of movement such as space, time, force flow, and fundamental skills.

Just as there are basics in reading and mathematics, there are basics for movement. For the young child, emphasis is based on locomotor skills: running, jumping, sliding, hopping, galloping; nonlocomotor skills: pushing, pulling, reaching, lifting; manipulative activities: striking, throwing, kicking. In addition, balance, control, and coordination are all-important factors to help children better manage their own bodies in all life situations—not just sports and games. Well-developed motor skills are important for a fully functioning human being.

Fitness is an important outcome of the child's play and planned physical education instructional programs. These programs should include vigorous activities, with each child participating fully; each child with a ball, rope or hoop; all children moving simultaneously on various pieces of equipment or in a game. It simply is not acceptable to place children in long lines waiting to take turns, to seat them in circle games with only one or two children moving, or to force them to perform beyond their immediate abilities. Fitness exercises given on command often result in total dislike for the class. Activities should be interesting, challenging, and varied. Children need to develop skills for an enjoyable pursuit of a lifetime of physical activity. Certainly health and fitness are proven national objectives.

Children's love of movement and creativity make dance an important and logical element of early education. Dance can and should be more than musical games or mere imitation of animals, birds, or flowers. Simple folk dances with and without partners are appropriate and enjoyable ways of facilitating multicultural education. Today there are numerous opportunities to call on parents and the community as resources for teaching multicultural games and dance.

Dance is an excellent vehicle for young children to explore their worlds, to discover what they can do and to be creative. All dance is movement, but not all creative movement is dance. Well-nurtured and well-taught, creative dance has the added aesthetic dimension of expressing ideas and feelings. Although music and art are standard activities in the school curriculum, creative dance is a neglected art form that can enrich the lives of children. Through dance children can explore various movements. The skilled teacher can help children develop sensory awareness, nurture their movements from simple to complex, and "help give depth, richness, and texture to children's pictures (creative thoughts) . . . to help them find the 'magic' of dance."

Play is natural for all children, and it takes many forms. Play experiences are truly the center of a prekindergarten program. Here again, through play, children move to learn and learn to move. Play experiences in prekindergarten classrooms as well as on the primary playground should include activities that encompass the development of large and small muscles of the body. To be appropriate, equipment should differ in size between prekindergarten and the primary unit. As important as free play itself, safe varied indoor and outdoor environments should be planned to meet the needs of small children. Playgrounds for these two age groups should have separate spaces. Play is the child's business, and it should be facilitated in every way.

Cognitive and Affective Values

In the past 25 years movement education as a method of teaching physical education has contributed significantly to a new look. It focuses largely on themes of learning to manage one's body in various forms of moving, adapting to equipment with a problem-solving approach, and emphasizing discovery, critical thinking, decision making, and creativity. The teaching of creative dance also focuses on these factors, and play naturally encompasses these ways of thinking. Thus all the child's learning and thinking processes are truly enhanced by this way of teaching physical education. Forming solutions to movement problems also contributes to the development of reasoning and deductive and inductive thinking.

Physical activity not only contributes to physiological development of motor skills and fitness, but it is also a laboratory for many types of cognitive learning. According to Piaget, early opportunities for a variety of practical, concrete experiences provide a sound basis for more abstract forms of later cognition. Through appropriately designed environments and planned instruction, children acquire concepts such as strong, weak, fast, slow, up, down, around, through, over, under, forward, back, sideways, high, and low. They learn to judge space, distance, direction, speed, force, as well as to anticipate the action of others. They learn in a laboratory of "doing"—how to listen, follow directions, communicate, categorize, order, compare, synthesize, and evaluate. Cognitive learnings through physical activity are far more than learning the rules of a game, taking turns, or keeping scores.

Consider also that children develop affectively in good programs by learning to value, interact, observe, think, create, and express their ideas and feelings through movement and enriched vocabulary. They learn to cooperate and to compete. They learn to relate to peers as well as to adults. They recreate and they re-create. They develop new skills and understandings that enhance their poise and self-confidence. Planned experiences focus on success rather than failure and on cooperation rather than competition to improve a child's self-esteem. These experiences also help to develop independence and responsibility, as well as a sense of caring and appreciation for others, which leads to knowledge, attitudes, and values for decision making.

In summary, the early childhood curriculum, including fundamental skills and fitness through vigorous activity, is generally classified into three components: educational gymnastics (not formal), educational games (not team sports), and educational dance (not performances). Where possible, aquatics is also included. Just as the elementary schools should not have a watered-down secondary curriculum, the prekindergarten program should not be a watered-down primary program. A prekindergarten program should be far less formal than the primary. Although it appears informal, it should be well-planned in relation to the environment, equipment, goals, and outcomes. The primary program needs to be an extension of preprimary. It needs to be more open, more free than is generally practiced. Movement programs should be equitable for all children, regardless of race, creed, gender or special needs.

Assessment

Early childhood educators, physical educators, and dance educators all face the same dilemma regarding assessment. Yet assessment is vital if educators are to be accountable. In the physical education field there are some national criteria-referenced fitness norms for primary grades. Methods of assessing fitness and child development for prekindergarten, other than testing, are now being developed—for example, checklists, observation and screening devices. In general, the test scores of young children are not reliable enough to be used as the sole basis of assessment. Dance and arts educators are reluctant to test, as are play leaders. Learning to observe children in movement is a special skill. Answers to simple questions—Are they energetic, slow, shy, strong, weak, cooperative, competitive, courageous, coordinated?—can reveal much about children's progress. Additionally, when one knows the sequence of motor skill development, it is easy to observe, for instance, if the child throws with forearm only, whole arm, rotates the trunk, steps forward with the opposite foot. In creative dance, does the child show evidence of having ideas to present? using a variety of movements? expressing feelings? having a flow to the movement? Answers to these questions will help the teacher assess the children's development.

Teacher Dilemma

Since prekindergarten programs do not yet have specialists—nor in many instances do programs for primary grades—it is essential that teacher preparation institutions offer courses in movement, dance, and play for young children. Departments of physical education, dance, and recreation need to coordinate with early childhood departments to offer specialized courses.

The teacher preparation problem is further pronounced in that the specialized departments, such as physical education, have limited offerings for teaching at the elementary level and practically none to prepare teachers for the very young child. For example, there are about

750 teacher preparation institutions in physical education in the United States; not more than 150 offer in-depth training for teaching elementary physical education. All offer a course or two, but that does not prepare a teacher adequately for working with these children. Many times, these course offerings are very weak, known facetiously as "Little Games and Little Dances for Little People."

In dance, the dilemma is even greater. For the most part, dance in the public schools is taught by physical educators who seldom have experience in creative dance. At the college level, as dance moves out of physical education departments into the performing arts, there are very few people left in education to prepare teachers of dance. One must also consider the many studios offering dance to children. Many of these are managed by inadequately prepared teachers who have limited knowledge of how children learn and develop. Thus we see a plethora of recitals and performances of routines imitating the adult world.

In recreation, the professional preparation dilemma is somewhat the same. Most recreation leaders focus heavily on administration; thus leaders on community playgrounds seldom have background in children's play. In addition, leaders on playgrounds are often young adults without degrees.

Therefore, early childhood educators need specialized courses in movement, dance, and play for children, while specialists need courses in early childhood development, as well as more preparation within their own disciplines.

Florida is one state where progress can be seen. Physical educators there must be certified in K-6 *(not* K-12 unless this certification meets all the requirements of K-6). The plan was implemented in 1984 by enlightened physical educators, a commissioner of education, and a governor who wanted better-prepared elementary physical education teachers to work with children. They were seeking a child-oriented teacher in addition to a skill-oriented teacher. Florida physical education teachers also take courses in teaching reading and mathematics. This helps them understand the elementary school program and enables them to make career changes in later years if they wish to do so.

Because more three- and four-year olds are entering the public school, there is now a demand for in-service training to help physical educators work with very young children. Conference workshops, summer college courses, and resource materials for this age level are needed throughout the United States. Specialists familiar with working with young children need to reach out to local and state early childhood groups to assist in this area. In addition, a credentialing process needs to be developed for degreed elementary teachers to enhance their working knowledge of the very young child. The American Alliance for Health, Physical Education, Recreation and Dance has developed some resource materials and is conducting conferences and workshops. It stands ready to help at your request.

—Margie R. Hanson

HEALTH EDUCATION IN EARLY CHILDHOOD

Children begin making decisions relative to many aspects of their health at increasingly young ages. If a child makes unhealthy decisions and her or his health status suffers as a consequence, that child may begin to develop a poor self-concept that could affect the behavior of the child and ultimately the ability of the child to learn. Clearly it is easier to encourage positive health habits during initial behavior development than it is to try to alter existing behavior. (18).

"Let us remember that infants do not smoke, do not take drugs, do not deliberately risk their health for pleasure or convenience. Changes in these behaviors occur much later in their lives. Our task is . . . to prevent these behaviors from changing" (7, p. 127). The early years of education are crucial, for it is then that children "gain the essential skills, knowledge, and dispositions critical to later school success" (16, p. 7). Education for decision-making that will lead to maintaining healthy lifestyles should begin at the earliest age possible. However, this education must be planned, sequential, and appropriate to the developmental level of the child. "Letting parents take care of it is no longer feasible. A comprehensive program bridges the gap between what students need and want" (17, p. 46).

> The fact is that many diverse processes intervene between people's exposure to our educational efforts and any behavioral outcome. We may instruct our children about good health; we may help them clarify their value system; we may use behavior modification techniques; and

Perspectives on Early Childhood Education

we may use any of the many methods from the arsenal of the education profession. We may do so very effectively. But, a host of other influences over which we have little or no control may impinge on these children. There is the influence of others, parents, peers, and so on. There are the children's predisposing personalities. There are situational factors that may facilitate or inhibit certain behaviors. And there are always the unpredictable idiosyncrasies that make every child and every adult into a human individual with a will of his or her own. (7, p. 128)

Nevertheless, the questions of what should be taught, how should it be taught, and who should teach health education still loom large.

What Should Be Taught?

To attempt to answer the question of what should be taught, one must first understand the concept of a comprehensive school health program. Within that context, it is also important to understand what is meant by a comprehensive health education program as well.

Traditionally, the comprehensive school health program consisted of school health services, a healthful school environment, and health instruction. More recently this tripartite model has been expanded to include five additional components: school psychology/counseling, food service, school site health promotion for faculty and staff, physical education, and an integrated school/community program (1). Within this extended framework, it is important to understand that the "comprehensive health education program includes a planned and sequential prekindergarten-12 curriculum that addresses the physical, mental, emotional, and social dimensions of health . . . [it] is integrated with the other seven components . . . and provides opportunities for students to develop and demonstrate increasingly sophisticated health-related knowledge, attitudes, skills, and practices" (13).

Comprehensive health education is fast becoming a basic in education. Prevention of health problems has captured the imagination of people in every walk of life and schools need to take advantage of the opportunity to improve health education programs (11, p. 30). Health education must also reach beyond classrooms. It must be full of interconnecting activities, highly visible in the schools and the community, and strong enough to take on the controversies that surround its very purpose (8, p. 31).

How to Teach Health

In general, the scope of the comprehensive school health education program includes community health, consumer health, environmental health, family life, growth and development, nutrition, personal health, disease prevention and control, safety and accident prevention, and substance use and abuse (drugs, alcohol, and tobacco). To be most effective, particularly at the lower grades, it is important to integrate the content of health education across many areas of the curriculum.

Unfortunately, although health education programs have been developed for the preschool student, the multiplicity of settings appears to have become a formidable barrier to any sort of standardization of those programs, and relatively comprehensive programs are even more difficult to identify. In fact, Hendricks et al. (6) identified only three curricula for early childhood that were considered comprehensive. Nevertheless, the basic purpose of health education for preschoolers should be to "lay the foundation for the kinds of adult behaviors and lifestyles that promote health and decrease risk of disease and disability" (2, p. 150). Children between the ages of three and five are beginning the cognitive development preoperational stage and are beginning to "accumulate a knowledge base which will become part [of their] future belief systems" (12, p. 138). Unfortunately, when it comes to the health education of young children, "too little comes too late" (9, p. 82).

Because health habits begin to be formed early in life and a child's knowledge base is shaped by numerous, often untoward messages, we, as educators, can no longer neglect the preschool years as a time for formal health education to begin. We must develop positive programs that are comprehensive in scope, yet flexible enough to take into consideration the individual differences of children in varied locations and settings. These curricula should provide the teacher with a myriad of methodologies from which to choose to best meet the needs of their students.

The direct teaching of health as a separate subject must receive priority as the best method of providing health instruction. However, the concepts of integrating health with other topics in the curriculum and the opportunities for informal instruction must not be overlooked. Regardless of the pattern of instruction that is utilized, curricular activities should promote not only healthful behavior and contribute to the development of a sound knowledge and attitude base, but also should promote the development of fine and gross motor skills, language abilities, cognitive orientations, self-help abilities, and social skills (6, p. 392).

The introduction of programs in early education and day care settings has resulted in new opportunities for health-related education for over 3 million pupils: we should take full advantage of these opportunities as we move toward trying to attain the Year 2000 Health Goals for the Nation. For the time-pressed practitioner, however, it is much easier to emulate or adapt a best practice than to design one (8, p. 32). Effective programs require a commitment of time, energy, and resources. Teachers need to be involved in the planning. Health is an appropriate topic for interdisciplinary study (5) and is too important to be left to chance. Advances in medical technology and health practices project a longer and healthier life span for today's youth, provided they take advantage of the alternatives that lead to healthy lifestyles (14, p. 35). We must use every educational strategy available to see that an integrated, sequentially arranged, comprehensive health education program is available to children of all ages. In the words of Dr. James O. Mason (10, p. 289) "I firmly believe that individuals taught and motivated to protect and enhance their own health can prevent unnecessary illness and injury and premature death .... Let's make sure that by the Year 2000, vigorous Health Education classes promoting healthy living for children and adults are offered ... in every school in the country." To advance health education will require more than behavior-based research aimed at improved understanding of the learner. It will also require a concomitant thrust in the areas of program development, the educational process, program implementation, and program evaluation (15, p. 11).

Who Should Teach Health Education?

An adequately prepared teacher is the cornerstone of the successful comprehensive health education program. It is the responsibility of the educational system to assure that the teacher has the opportunity to obtain adequate preparation. It is the responsibility of the state to assure that in certifying the teacher as a content specialist he or she has actually obtained course work in the specified content (9, p. 10).

In a recent American Association of School Administrators survey, respondents often reported that they had trouble finding qualified staff in health education; therefore teachers who are not qualified must be trained for the task. This is compounded by the fact that even more scarce are persons qualified as comprehensive health coordinators with even a limited background in administration. (4, p. 50)

Herein also lies the great paradox and chasm within the profession. It is the belief of many that since health education is such an important part of the total education of children of all ages, there should be a health education specialist within each school. However, the economic reality is that even if such persons were available, it is questionable that they would be hired, particularly in small schools or in the myriad of settings where young children often begin their formal educational experiences. What might be a more logical and rational approach is to see that a trained (and perhaps National Commission for Health Education Credentialing certified) health education specialist is available within each school district to assist in planning educationally sound and scientifically correct comprehensive health programs for the optimal development of the young child. This individual would be instrumental in planning and conducting appropriate in-service programs for staff, for assisting staff with obtaining resources for effective instruction, and for evaluating, over a continuing basis, the total health instruction program so that revisions of the instructional program could be made as needed.

Unfortunately, there are more unqualified teachers teaching health than any other subject. This is because of the assumption, by some educators, that any teacher, with or without a strong background, can handle health education. (4, p. 51). Clearly, this is not the case and must not continue. It is critical for administrators to understand that by assuming this standard, schools deprive students of education that could have a positive impact on them for the rest of their lives.

The other side of the paradox is the fact that at young ages, and especially in formal, elementary school levels, health instruction might be best conducted by the classroom teacher. It would be unrealistic to expect each classroom teacher to be a health education specialist. Through an extensive and effective in-service education program, however, the classroom teacher can gain an understanding of and appreciation for the nature and process of health education, as well as for the total school health program. (3, p. 166) The regular classroom teacher who is with the students every day thus has an excellent opportunity not only to engage in direct health instruction, but also to integrate health concepts into the other components of the curriculum. The classroom teacher can also take advantage of the myriad opportunities to engage in informal health instruction, an opportunity not afforded a specialist who might see the children only intermittently throughout a school year.

It is also important to integrate the services of the nurse into the classroom setting, if a nurse is available within the district. Nurses can provide a valuable resource to the classroom teacher. Although some nurses possess the necessary credentials to teach, for them to serve on a full-time basis and in all classes, would be logistically impossible. Further, since most nurses are involved in numerous aspects of the total school health program, spending full-time in the classroom might not be the best use of their valuable time (3, p. 166).

The critical component of who should teach health education is to be sure that (1) it is done competently, (2) the individual or individuals who have this responsibility want to teach health education, (3) the individuals feel comfortable with the subject matter, and (4) adequate resources are available for the teacher, including well-developed in-service opportunities in a variety of content areas.

As noted earlier, involved teachers in the planning and development of the health education program provides them with a sense of ownership. Naturally, parents and community members should also be involved, especially when dealing with such controversial areas as family life education and drug education. In addition, the planning process provides a perfect opportunity for informal education, not only of teachers, but also of parents and community members as well.

Summary

The planning, implementation, and evaluation of effective health education programs for young children is a process that requires the commitment of time, energy, and resources. One might liken the process to a triangle: there must be dedicated professionals committed to action; there must be a well-developed curriculum; and there must be adequate resources, financial and otherwise. If any one of the components is missing, the program will most likely be less than successful.

AAHPERD

Is the provision of a comprehensive school health program worth the time, energy, and resources necessary for a successful program? If preparing healthy, well-educated boys and girls for the 21st century is our goal, the answer is a resounding yes (14, p. 35), but these programs will not occur in the absence of commitment from all sectors of the population, educators, parents, and the community at large. These programs are in their infancy, but, in the words of Toffler, "We have in our power to shape change. We may choose one future over another. We cannot, however, maintain the past. In our family forms as in our economics, science technology, and social relationships, we shall be forced to deal with the new." Let's every one of us make the commitment to have a healthier generation, but now and in the future. Remember, children are our nation's most precious resource.

—Larry K. Olsen

BIBLIOGRAPHY (Moving: A Child's Way of Learning)

1. American Alliance for Health, Physical Education, Recreation and Dance (AAHPERD), Advisory Committee. *McDonald's Moving Learning Action Pack*. McDonald's (out of print), 1979.

2. American Alliance for Health, Physical Education, Recreation and Dance (AAHPERD). *Physical Best* (health related physical fitness tests K-12). Reston, Va.: AAHPERD, 1989.

3. Boucher, A., ed. "Early Childhood Physical Education." JOPERD (September 1988): 42-72.

4. Bruya, L. D., and Langerdorfer, S. J. eds. *Where Our Children Play: Elementary School Playground Equipment*. Vol. I. Reston, Va.: AAHPERD, 1988.

5. Bruya, L. D. ed. *Play Spaces for Children*. Vol. II, Reston, Va.: AAHPERD, 1988.

6. Curtis, D., ed. "The Young Child: The Significance of Motor Development." JOHPER (May 1971): 29-35.

7. Holt/Hale, S., ed. *Movement Program for Young Children*. Position paper developed by the Council on Physical Education for Children (COPEC). Reston, Va.: AAHPERD, 1986.

8. Gallahue, D. L. and Benham, T., eds. *Physical Education for Children: Professional Preparation of the Teacher Specialist.* Position paper developed by COPEC. Reston, Va.: AAHPERD, 1990.

9. Seefeldt, V., and Vogel, P. eds. *The Value of Physical Activity.* Reston, Va.: AAHPERD, 1986.

10. Stinson, S., ed. *Dance Guidelines for Curriculum and Assessment for Ages 3-8.* Position paper developed by the National Dance Association (NDA). Reston, Va.: AAHPERD, 1990.

11. Stinson, S. *Dance for Young Children, Finding the Magic in Movement.* Reston, Va.: AAHPERD, 1988.

12. Stinson, W. J. ed. "Moving and Learning for the Young Child." *Proceedings from the International Early Childhood Conference.* Reston, Va.: AAHPERD, December 1988.

13. Thompson, D., and Bowers, L. eds. *Where Our Children Play: Community Park Playground Equipment.* Reston, Va.: AAHPERD, 1989.

14. Wortham, S., and Frost, J. eds. *Playgrounds for Young Children: American Survey and Perspectives.* Reston, Va.: AAHPERD, in press.

REFERENCES (Health Education in Early Childhood)

1. Allensworth, D., and Kolbe, L., "The Comprehensive School Health Program: Exploring an Expanded Concept." *Journal of School Health* 57 (1987) 409-12.

2. Bruhn, J.; Murray J.; and Parcel, G. "Preschool Health Education Program (P.H.E.P.): Analysis of Educational and Behavioral Outcomes." *Health Education Quarterly 10* (1984): 149-71.

3. Cornacchia, H.; Olsen, L.; and Nickerson, C. *Health in Elementary Schools.* 7th ed. St. Louis: Times Mirror/Mosby College Publishing, 1988.

4. Deputat, Z. and Pavlovich, M. "School Health Programs: A Comprehensive Plan for Implementation." *Health Education* 19 (1988): 47-53.

5. Frank, C., and Goldman, L. "Growing Healthy in New York City." *Phi Delta Kappan* (February 1988): 454-55.

6. Hendricks, C.; Echols, D.; and Nelson, G. "The Impact of a Preschool Health Curriculum on Children's Health Knowledge." *Journal of School Health* 59 (1989): 389-92.

7. Hochbaum, G.: "Behavior Change as the Goal of Health Education." *Eta*

Sigma Gamman (1981, Fall/Winter): 127-30.

8. Joki, R.A. "Health Education: Program Development and Implementation." *Health Education* 19 (1988): 31-33.

9. Lloyd, J., and Combes, G. "What Do Children Know?" *Health Education Journal* 47 (1988): 81-83.

10. Mason, J. O. "Dr. Mason Outlines Goals for Improving the Nation's Health." *Journal of School Health* 59, no. 7 (1989): 289-90.

11. Miller, R. "Forward from the Fourth Delbert Oberteuffer Symposium: Administrative Aspects of School Health Education." *Health Education* 19 (1988): 30.

12. Natapoff, J. "A Developmental Analysis of Children's Ideas of Health." *Health Education Quarterly* 9 (1982): 130-41.

13. National Professional School Health Education Organizations. "Comprehensive School Health Education." *Journal of School Health* 54 (1984): 312-15.

14. Nelson, B. "Principal's Commitment: A Key to Success." *Health Education* 19 (1989): 34-35.

15. O'Rourke, T. "Reflections on Directions in Health Education: Implications for Policy and Practice." *Health Education* 20 (1989): 4-14.

16. Schultz, T., and Lombardi, J. "Right from the Start: The Report on the NASBE Task Force on Early Childhood Education." *Young Children* (January 1989): 6-10.

17. Schuman, L. "When Wellness Drives the Health Curriculum." *Health Education* 19, no. 5 (1988): 45-46.

18. Vance, B. *Teaching the Pre-kindergarten Child: Instruction Design and Curriculum.* Monterey, Calif.: Brooks/Cole Publishing Co., 1983.

19. Varnes, J.; Bolin, S.; Waters, M.; and Beach, K. "Health Education Teacher Certification in the United States." *Health Education* 20, no. 4 (1989): 8-10.

ACEI
Association for Childhood Education International

3. Present and Future Concerns for Children

by **Mary Louise Hirsh-Burger, 1989-91 President,** *Association for Childhood Education International. ACEI has a membership of 15,000, with headquarters at 11141 Georgia Avenue, Suite 200, Wheaton, Maryland 20902.*

The Association for Childhood Education International (ACEI) is a nonprofit professional membership organization that will celebrate its 100th anniversary in 1992. The Association's members come from every segment of the preschool, elementary, and middle school fields; they include child care providers, teachers, teachers-in-training, administrators, researchers, teacher educators, and institutional subscribers. During its long and distinguished history, ACEI has provided continuous and substantive support to children and to individuals and institutions who work with children in education and allied professions. The Association works to establish and maintain the highest standards for child growth, development, and learning. Among other goals, the Infancy, Early Childhood and Later Childhood/Early Adolescence Committees work to ensure developmental continuity for children from birth through 15 years of age.

The purposes of ACEI internationally are to promote the inherent rights, education, and well-being of all children; to work for desirable conditions, programs, and practices for all children; to bring into active cooperation all those concerned with children; to raise the standard of preparation for those actively involved with the care and development of children; to encourage continuous professional growth; and to focus the attention of the public on the rights and needs of children and the ways various programs must be adjusted to fit those rights and needs.

Guided by these constitutionally defined purposes, the Association regularly identifies current issues and concerns that require attention in its program of action for children.

PRESSURES FOR EARLY ACADEMIC ACHIEVEMENT

Throughout its history ACEI has been concerned with the issue of play and its importance to child development. "As programs for young children have become more highly structured and adult-centered, and as more parents expect early instruction and formal academic activities for young children, early childhood educators at all levels have to . . . persuasively defend the developmental, educational and therapeutic uses of play in the programs" (20, p.5).

Further support for the value of play may be found in an ACEI position paper, which "recognizes the need for children of all ages to play and affirms the essential role of play in healthy development." As our children go forward to the 21st century, they will "continue to experience pressure to succeed," making the necessity for play more critical. "ACEI supports those who respect and understand the power of play in children's lives and who use their knowledge about how children play at different ages to guide their practices with children. These beliefs are rooted in research, theory and exemplary practice" (5, pp. 138-45).

It has also been found that children learn to think best through direct encounters with their world; overreliance on textbooks encourages children to seek simplistic answers to complex problems (26). Similar observations have been made by Froebel, Montessori, Piaget (23, 24), Elkind (16), and others. The evidence indicates that children must touch, smell, taste, and hear objects when learning about concrete items. It is only after long and continued experimentation (play) that the child is ready for another stage of play utilizing the semiconcrete; finally, words become meaningful because of these experiences.

Yet, in spite of our best knowledge, young children today are experiencing ever-increasing pressure for academic achievement. In the call for education reform, schools have responded with "pushed-down" curricula, developmentally inappropriate kindergartens, four-year-old programs, and early testing and retention practices. Pressure for academic instruction in the "basics" and for standardized testing is coming from many sources, including the business community. ACEI takes issue with this emphasis, believing that young children need a balanced program of developmentally appropriate curricula and instruction. Acknowledging the power of play as a natural behavior contributing to young children's development, ACEI contends that no program of adult instruction can substitute for children's unstructured experiential observations and activities. Admittedly, reform is needed to revitalize education, but not with programs that compromise these basic principles of growth and development.

In its position paper "The Child-Centered Kindergarten" (3), the Association decries the misdirection of today's kindergarten programs brought about by those unmindful of the needs of children. Emphasizing the importance of nurturing the whole child—emotionally, physically, and intellectually—ACEI advocates "child-centered kindergarten programs that encourage active experiential learning, are developmentally appropriate, increase independence and promote joy in learning" (p. 242).

Parents, motivated by genuine concern, frequently raise many questions about the kindergarten program; e.g., "When will my child learn to read?" "Isn't there a great deal of time spent playing games?" "Shouldn't school time be devoted to academic learning?" Perceiving parents as important contributors to their children's education, Simmons and Brewer (29) attempt to answer these and other questions. These authors emphasize the teacher's responsibility to educate parents about the value of play and meaningful activities in their child's development.

CHILDREN AND FAMILIES AT RISK

According to a report prepared by the Census Bureau for the House Select Committee on Children, Youth and Families, U.S. children are at greater risk for social, economic, and health problems than are children in other developed nations. Released on March 18, 1990, the study reports that the greatest disparities are evident in the numbers of children affected by poverty and divorce. The United States also has higher rates of youth homicide, infant mortality, and teenage pregnancy (30). These findings underscore the urgent need for education and public policy that strengthens the family and helps eradicate substance abuse, disease, crime and violence, poverty, and homelessness.

Substance abuse and violence are penetrating deeply into the fabric of society at all levels, causing great concern for children's quality of life and development. The increasing use of drugs is the biggest international problem facing young people today. Fortunately, many schools offer programs designed to emphasize prevention and inform students about the hazards of drugs. Some of these efforts also focus on the harmful effects of alcohol, the most commonly used drug among U.S. children. Relatively few school-based programs, however, are directed to young children, who are also vulnerable to substance abuse.

Creative educational programs emphasizing prevention are also needed to help reduce the incidence of teenage pregnancy. Parent involvement is critical to the success of these programs, which are planned around a sex education and family life curriculum (33).

Still another critical issue deals with the growing problem of child abuse, both physical and emotional. Unless abused children receive adequate treatment, they run the risk of not developing "the social, psychological, intellectual and emotional skills needed to be happy, healthy, productive members of society" (22, p. 5). Also needed are school and community prevention programs aimed at children and families before they are in crisis.

Child abuse also manifests itself in schools that discipline children with corporal punishment. ACEI has taken a strong stand against this practice: "Corporal punishment must be BANNED in child care, school and other educative settings. It is a barbaric practice that has many negative implications, and does not respect individual rights." Further, it "teaches by example that the infliction of pain on others is permissible" (2).

In addressing all these problems, the total child in his/her environment—family, school, community—must be considered. To become productive citizens who contribute to society, children need an extraschool environment that is conducive to healthy growth and development. Children entering school already have an orientation toward success or failure. Those who come from homes where acceptance, mutual respect, confidence, and compatibility prevail are better adjusted and more independent than children coming from homes with discord. Consequently, they have a more positive self-image (9).

Additionally, business must continue, in fact increase, its involvement in the education of children. Moreover, Head Start should be fully funded by the 21st century. Designed to serve economically disadvantaged at-risk children three to five years of age, Head Start currently reaches fewer than 20 percent of eligible children (Select Committee on Children, Youth and Families, cited in Chafel [13, p. 242]). Yet the overwhelming evidence after 25 years is that the program works for both children and parents. This was recognized by President Bush in his 1990 budget message when he proposed a 36 percent increase in funding.

CHILD CARE: AN URGENT PRIORITY

As increasing numbers of mothers and single parents enter the workforce, the demand for quality child care has far exceeded availability. It is not surprising, therefore, that child care has been identified as an urgent priority not only by parents and educators, but also by business groups, government agencies, religious institutions, and service organizations. Unfortunately, in spite of this heightened awareness, the U.S. Congress has yet to enact comprehensive child care legislation that would benefit children and families. On the other hand, many countries throughout the world provide free, government-sponsored child care. In Belgium, for example, child care is publicly financed; in private denominational schools, it is supported by the central or local government (10).

The need for child care in the United States is not confined to any one socioeconomic group. Both low- and middle-income parents are desperately seeking quality child care for their young children. Additionally, in many families school-age latchkey children return to an empty home at the end of the school day, exposing them to considerable risk. For families living in poverty, "the absence of affordable child care is possibly the single most critical factor hindering parents from overcoming their dependency and entering the workplace" (Weissbourd and Emig, cited in Chafel [13, p. 242]).

Responding to this growing crisis, ACEI issued a position paper in 1988 entitled "The Right to Quality Child Care" (4). The Association recommends concerted and decisive action, affirming that "the first duty of family and society is to protect, guide and give care to the young. . . . We must as a society of caring people answer the cry, 'Who will care for

ACEI

the children--indeed, who if not ourselves?' " (p. 268).

Further, the Association strongly urges thoughtful attention to the many complex issues in child care, among them affordability, quality, education, reliability, accessibility, safety, nutrition, health care, licensing, staffing, and professional standards. On the issue of education, ACEI cautions that, while an educational emphasis in child care is important, it "must not become a blindly applied goal that attempts to make the entire day resemble the operation of an elementary classroom" (Zigler, cited in ACEI/Gotts, [4, p. 271]).

TEACHER PREPARATION AND PROFESSIONAL DEVELOPMENT

Believing that strong and unequivocal support for classroom teaching is urgently needed, ACEI advocates a multifaceted approach that emphasizes teacher preparation and continuous professional development. Concerted effort is needed to

1. Strengthen the teacher education programs offered in colleges and universities by rigorous application of the accreditation process currently conducted by the National Council for Accreditation of Teacher Education (NCATE).
2. Support the development of national standards for voluntary teacher certification currently being developed by the National Board for Professional Teaching Standards (NBPTS).
3. Encourage the recruitment of more minority people into the profession.
4. Expand in-service programs for active teachers so they can strengthen and upgrade the skills needed to meet the constant challenges of a very demanding profession.
5. Promote equitable salary and benefit scales commensurate with the demands placed on classroom teachers and comparable to what professionals in other disciplines receive.
6. Empower teachers to be active decision makers responsible for children's learning, not mere technicians.
7. Raise the level of respect accorded front-line classroom teachers

through information and awareness programs designed to improve the public's perception of the teaching profession.

An ACEI position paper reaffirms the need for early childhood teachers to interact successfully with children, parents, guardians, social service personnel, and school administrators. To accomplish this they need knowledge, competence, and sensitivity, as well as understanding of the broad spectrum of prenatal, infant/toddler, preprimary, primary, and elementary education (1). Preparation of teachers should therefore include liberal education, child development theory and research, group dynamics, curriculum development, methods, evaluation models, and clinical experiences with children in a variety of educational settings. Only qualified early childhood specialists should teach in preprimary through primary grades. To reinforce concepts and make learning more meaningful, the early childhood curricular areas need to be integrated. The project method as described by Short and Burger (27) has proved effective with various age levels.

Consistent with ACEI's international charter, the 1989 Annual Theme Issue of *Childhood Education* focuses on "the problems and promises of preparing teachers of young children and adolescents throughout the world" (18, p. 261). Entitled "Who Will Be Teaching the World's Children?" the issue provides a global view of teacher preparation in the United States, the People's Republic of China, the Soviet Union, Nigeria, Finland, Hong Kong, Italy, and Thailand. In giving the U.S. perspective, James Raths addresses the critical need for more ethnically varied teachers:

> Reformers are keenly aware of the divisions in society along racial and ethnic lines, and how the composition of the students in public schools is changing [Holmes Group, 1986, p.66]. In almost all the rhetoric for reform, prominent among the lists of "needs" for the profession is that of recruiting minority people into teaching (25, pp. 264-65).

But it is not enough to seek a change in the composition of teacher education candidates, Raths cautions. "Teacher educators must learn how to work with the teacher candidates entering the workforce, to provide for them, whoever they are, the best possible teacher education program" (p. 267).

LITERACY

As First Lady Barbara Bush has stated, "We must attack the problem of a more literate America through the family." To help eradicate illiteracy by the year 2000, the United Nations has declared 1990 to be International Literacy Year. ACEI lends its support to this important effort, acknowledging reading as a critical skill for children growing up in the modern world. In 1988 the Association collaborated with five other professional organizations to issue a position statement on *Literacy Development and Prefirst Grade,* prepared by the Early Childhood and Literacy Development Committee of the International Reading Association (15). The statement urges teachers of young children to "involve children actively in many meaningful, functional language experiences, including speaking, listening, writing and reading." Concern is expressed about the increasing number of rigid, formal prereading programs that focus on isolated skill development and employ standardized testing to measure children's reading and writing skills.

The statement also recommends that teachers "make parents aware of the reasons for a broader language program at school and provide them with ideas for activities to carry out at home." It has been found that parents who use print while children are present to record messages, write lists, and keep calendars encourage children to understand the importance of the written word. Parents who reward language learning, reading, and good school behavior have an important impact on their child's school achievement and self-esteem (9). Considerable research indicates that parents of children who achieve well in reading play an active role in the process. These parents talk with their children, listen to them, help them set goals, select materials, provide a print-rich environment, and directly instruct their children (28, 31, 32). The evidence confirms that children who learn to read early and enjoy reading tend to have parents who model the reading process (17, 21) and that the mother's verbal interaction with her child affects the child's linguistic/cognitive skills important for reading (8, 34).

CRITICAL THINKING AND PROBLEM SOLVING

"Teaching for thinking has become the new focus in education," promoting schools to design programs that "assist teachers in facilitating development of children's higher-order thinking skills" (7, p.67). Indeed, in this increasingly complex age, it is vital that teachers help their students to question, to analyze, to probe (12, p. 69). For example, teachers can engage young children in discussions of everyday problems and even such global concerns as conserving natural resources, finding cures for debilitating diseases, assisting the less fortunate, preventing war, feeding the world's hungry, and dealing with natural catastrophe.

Children must learn to make appropriate decisions at the earliest level of their development. It is in the practice of this skill that they will develop into adult problem solvers. While emphasizing problem solving, teachers and parents can be instrumental in nurturing children's creativity and imagination (11). In its most recent position paper, "The Child's Right to the Expressive Arts" (6), the Association reaffirms the need to nurture children's imagination as well as intellect. Advocating curricular reform that acknowledges the importance of imaginative expression, the paper states:

> We must refashion our schools for the 21st century. School reform must, in the view of the National Education Association, recognize that the Industrial Model is obsolescent in our Information Age.... As a society, we must go beyond tolerating imagination and begin to value and educate it. In schools for the 21st century, children must learn to make decisions [and] to reflect upon experience. (p. 200)

CULTURAL DIVERSITY IN THE CLASSROOM

As the United States becomes an increasingly pluralistic society, teachers must be prepared to teach in classrooms populated by ethnically and racially diverse students. This calls for greater sensitivity to the social conventions that characterize the varied cultures represented in their classrooms. Teachers are challenged to seek information about the social world that is unique to their students' cultural background, not only foods and holidays but also "concepts of family, morality, rules, time and sex-roles" (14, p. 31).

Moreover, teachers must also prepare children to live and work in culturally diverse settings. All areas of the curriculum can include developmentally appropriate multicultural activities designed to increase children's understanding of human behavior and "how and why groups of people differ from one another in their customs, habits and traditions" (19, p. 88). According to Williams (35), such learning environments can be further enriched and energized by "the gifts of social knowledge that the children [themselves] bring to the classroom" (p. 2). But first, Williams advises, teachers need a broadened concept of "culture" to include all the experiences that impart meaning to one's life. "Children derive their identities as worthy human beings, as capable learners, as problem solvers, as aesthetic judges, from their own particular combinations of significant people, objects and events, some of which are expressive of larger cultural perspectives" (p. 3).

CONCLUSION

Pressures for early academic achievement, children and families at risk, child care, teacher preparation and professional development, literacy, critical thinking and problem solving, cultural diversity in the classroom—all demand the most enlightened thinking of educators, policymakers, parents, and other caregivers. A well-thought-out, broadly based attack on these complex issues is essential as we seek responsible action for children now and in the 21st century.

REFERENCES

1. Association for Childhood Education International, Teacher Education Committee. Position paper. "Preparation of Early Childhood Teachers." *Childhood Education* 59, (1983): 303-6.
2. Association for Childhood Education International Cryan, J. R. Position paper. "The Banning of Corporal Punishment: In Child Care, School and Other Educative Settings in the U.S." *Childhood Education* 63 (1987): 145-53.
3. Association for Childhood Education International Moyer, J.; Egertson, H.; and Isenberg, J. Position Paper. "The Child-Centered Kindergarten." *Childhood Education* 63 (1987): 235-42.
4. Association for Childhood Education International Gotts, E. E. Position paper. "The Right to Quality Child Care." *Childhood Education* 64 (1988): 268-75.
5. Association for Childhood Education International Isenberg, J., and Quisenberry, N. Position paper. "Play: A Necessity for All Children."

Childhood Education 64 (1988): 138-45.

6. Association for Childhood Education International Jalongo, M. R. Position paper. "The Child's Right to the Expressive Arts: Nurturing the Imagination as Well as the Intellect." *Childhood Education* 66 (1990): 195-201.

7. Barbour, N. H. "Can We Prepackage Thinking?" *Childhood Education* 65 (1988): 67-68.

8. Burger, M. L. "A Comparative Study of Self-Esteem Among Young Black, Spanish, and White Children." Ph.D. diss., Northern Illinois University, De Kalb, 1973.

9. ____. "Developing Self-Esteem in Young Children." *ACEI Exchange* (May 1983): 3.

10. ____. "Is There a New Move in Child Care?" *ACEI Exchange* (March 1984): 3.

11. ____. "Creativity: Can It Be Taught?" *ACEI Exchange* (June 1985): 2.

12. Carr, K. S. "How Can We Teach Critical Thinking?" *Childhood Education* 65 (1988): 69-73.

13. Chafel, J. A. "Needed: A Legislative Agenda for Children at Risk." *Childhood Education* 66 (1990): 241-42.

14. DiMartino, E. C. "Understanding Children from Other Cultures." *Childhood Education* 66 (1989): 30-32.

15. Early Childhood and Literacy Development Committee of the International Reading Association. *Literacy Development and Prefirst Grade*. Newark, Del.: IRA, 1988.

16. Elkind, D. *Miseducation of Children: Super Kids at Risk*. New York: Knopf, 1987.

17. Gearney, V. "Parental Influence on Reading." *Reading Teacher* 39 (1986): 813-18.

18. Hoot, J. L. "Teachers of Tomorrow's Children: A Global Perspective." *Childhood Education* 65 (1989): 261-62.

19. Little Soldier, L. M. "Children as Cultural Anthropologists." *Childhood Education* 66 (1989): 88-91.

20. McKee, J. S., ed. *Play: Working Partner of Growth*. Wheaton, Md.: Association for Childhood Education International, 1987.

21. Morrow, L. "Home and School Correlates of Early Interest in Literature." *Journal of Educational Research* 76 (1983): 221-30.

22. O'Brien, S. *Child Abuse and Neglect: Everyone's Problem*. Wheaton, Md:

Association for Childhood Education International, 1984.

23. Piaget, J. *The Moral Judgment of the Child.* London: Routedge and Kegan, Paul, 1932.

24. ____. *The Origins of Intelligence in Children. (M. Cook, Trans.)* New York: Norton, 1952. (Original work published in 1936)

25. Raths, J. "Reformers" Visions of Tomorrow's Teachers: A U.S.A. Perspective." *Childhood Education* 65 (1989): 263-67.

26. Short, V. M. *Childhood Education in the Changing World.* Research Report No. 6. Carrollton, Ga.: West Georgia College, May 1989.

27. Short, V. M., and Burger, M. L. "The English Infant/Primary School Revisited." *Childhood Education* 64 (1987): 75-79.

28. Silvern, S. "Parent Involvement and Reading Achievement: A Review of Research and Implications for Practice." *Childhood Education* 62 (1985): 44-49.

29. Simmons, B., and Brewer, J. "When Parents of Kindergartners Ask Why?" *Childhood Education* 61 (1985): 177-84.

30. Swoboda, F. "Study Finds U.S. Youth at Greater Risk: Global Data on Status of Children Compared." *Washington Post,* A8, March 19, 1990.

31. Teale, W. H. "Positive Environments for Learning to Read: What Studies of Early Readers Tell Us." *Language Arts* 55 (1978): 922-31.

32. ____. "Reading to Young Children: Its Significance for Literacy Development." In *Awakening to Literacy,* edited by Goelman and Oberg, Victoria, B. C.: Hunemann Education Books, 1984.

33. Theriot, R., and Bruce, B. "Teenage Pregnancy: A Family Life Curriculum." *Childhood Education* 64 (1988): 276-79.

34. White, B., et al. *Experience and Environment: Major Influences on the Development of the Young Child.* Vol. 1. Englewood Cliffs, N.J.: Prentice-Hall, 1973.

35. Williams, L. R. "Diverse Gifts: Multicultural Education in the Kindergarten." *Childhood Education* 66 (1989): 2-3.

ASCA
American School Counselor Association

4. Trends in Early Childhood Education and Counseling

by **Susan Jones Sears,** *ASCA Public Relations Chair, and* **Doris Rhea Coy, 1989-90 President,** *American School Counselor Association. ASCA has a membership of 12,500, with headquarters at 5999 Stevenson Avenue, Alexandria, Virginia 22304.*

As we approach the 21st century, our complex culture is characterized by diverse and ever-changing values in the home, community, and school. Societal-based problems are worse and this is reflected in increases in substance abuse, suicide, child abuse, teen pregnancy, school violence, and school dropouts.

School counselors are being asked to assume a greater role in the lives of their students and the students' families. The demand for counselors by both parents and teachers has led to mandated elementary counseling in states like West Virginia and North Carolina. Those elementary counselors already in the schools find themselves working more and more with prekindergarten students, latchkey programs designed to prepare children for school, and with parents. Clearly, public interest in early childhood education has increased interest in early childhood and elementary counseling.

TRENDS

A review of counseling journals suggests that several trends related to early childhood counseling and education have developed and will probably continue throughout the next decade. This chapter describes each trend briefly and also discusses actions that counselors can take to meet the challenges presented by these trends.

Children Have More Serious Problems

Increasing numbers of children experience dysfunctional family lives; as a result, they are bringing more serious problems to school. For example, children of divorce immediately undergo major changes in their daily lives. The emotional distress and conflict at home frequently impacts the children. Children's distress often manifests itself in poor concentration and underachievement as well as withdrawn or aggressive behavior. Some experts suggest that for many children the period of mourning or grief during a divorce, while not as intense, mirrors the stages children experience when a parent dies (9). First, the child cannot believe the parents are separating. This belief is followed by sadness, because the children know they will miss the parent. Feelings of anger and guilt follow. Unfortunately, it is not uncommon for children to blame themselves for the divorce, at least initially. After divorce, children may fear the future and feel insecure. They may begin to worry or feel jealous if their mothers or fathers feel insecure. They may begin to worry or feel jealous if their mothers or fathers begin to date.

Children of Alcoholic Parents. More than 10 percent of the population of the United States is being raised or was raised in an alcoholic home (1). There may be harmonious periods in these homes but generally the atmosphere is disruptive with confusion and constant stress (7). In a classroom of 25 students, four to six students are children of alcoholics (11). Studies suggest that children of alcoholics have a greater incidence of emotional, behavioral, and developmental disorders when compared to children of nonalcoholic parents. They have fewer positive peer relationships and a higher truancy rate (4). They know their home is different and become reluctant to bring friends home because they do not know what to expect.

Abused Children. The House Select Committee on Children, Families, and Youth reported in March 1987 that 1.9 million cases of child abuse occur each year. Since many cases go unreported to proper authorities, as many as one in every ten children may be abused or neglected each year. Surprisingly, parents are responsible for 80 percent of the abuse and 1 in 25 parents admit to having severely abused a child.

Child sexual abuse is particularly disturbing. Sexual abuse and molestation refer to the exploitation of a child for the sexual gratification of an adult. By conservative estimates, a child is sexually abused in America every two minutes and 4,000 children die annually as a result of sexual abuse (5).

Children Are Taking More Responsibility for Their Own Care

Because the term "latchkey" has negative connotations, the term "children in self-care" is being used to describe children who spend time alone at home and who are responsible for their own care. During the past 10 years, the number of children in self-care has increased (12), and this trend will probably continue. More and more schools are developing after-school programs to provide safe havens for these children. However, adequate child-care facilities are not currently available and nothing suggests that situation will change in the near future. Therefore, schools are becoming aware of the need to teach children how to take care of themselves.

Parents Expect More Than the 3 Rs

Parents are looking to the school for more help with the care of their children. The growth of latchkey programs is just one example of how the school can help parents, particularly those who feel overwhelmed or overburdened. School personnel are also beginning to recognize the importance of involving parents in the education and development of their children. Parent groups in which parents are shown how to employ more effective parenting skills have become popular again. Some innovative preschool programs utilizing parents as teachers have been successful in better preparing young children for school. Even more parent involvement in schools is expected in the 1990s.

The Community Is Becoming More Involved in the Schools

The problems children are facing today often require help beyond what school personnel can provide. Local mental health and social agencies are becoming more involved with the education of children. In some instances, clinics have been built near or adjacent to schools and provide comprehensive health care to low-income children and families. Mental health agencies have hired personnel to work with schools to better meet the mental health needs of children. Alcohol and other drug prevention program personnel based in the community are delivering services in schools. Because of the complexity of the problems facing children and families, community involvement in the school will probably grow during the next decade.

WHAT CAN SCHOOL COUNSELORS DO?

Given the trends just discussed, many educators want to know what early childhood or elementary counselors can do to help children, parents, and teachers with the challenges they face. While some of the middle or high school counselor's work is remedial or occurs after problems have developed, early childhood or elementary counselors engage primarily in preventative or developmental counseling. A counselor who engages in developmental counseling is one who is deeply committed to facilitating positive growth in students, and has as a goal the highest possible level of human effectiveness for each student in preschool or school. A central characteristic of developmental counselors would be their understanding of the processes of human development and their commitment to organizing and patterning the experiences and activities in the school in the best possible way to foster or facilitate these developmental processes. If counselors are truly committed to this approach, the activities in which they are engaged will be designed to meet the developmental needs of children. In addition, these counselors will be encouraging teachers to become developmental teachers or helpers also interested in fostering positive growth in their students.

Developmental Tasks of Early Childhood. As suggested, early childhood counselors are concerned with helping children master the central development tasks of early childhood:

- developing a sense of autonomy
- developing a sense of belonging and mutuality with others
- learning to manage aggression and frustration in reasonable ways
- learning to follow verbal instructions
- learning to focus attention and concentration
- learning to become reasonably independent in self-care (washing, dressing, toilet functions, etc.)
- developing realistic concepts of the physical and social world (time, space, distance, relationships, authority, etc.) (3).

If counselors are to help children achieve these developmental tasks in order to be ready to move on to the next developmental stage, they will need to work not only with the children themselves but also with parents, teachers, and the community. Historically, early childhood or elementary counselors have consulted with parents and educators in their work with children, but given current trends, counselors will have to accelerate their efforts.

What are the specific activities that school counselors do? A discussion of the type of activities that counselors engage in to help young children achieve the developmental tasks of early childhood follows. This discussion should help teachers and principals understand the scope of practice of the school counselor.

Work with Children Directly

Listen to Children. This sounds so simple but unfortunately adults do not take childhood problems seriously. Children need a nonjudgmental adult like the counselor to listen to them. In effect, the counselor is a role model for a caring adult.

Help Children Belong. Many children feel powerless at school. They may not be achieving, or have friends, or get along with their teachers. Counselors can build informal support groups for children who appear to be alienated or alone. Group counseling sessions or even informal lunch groups help children feel as if they belong.

Help Children Learn Problem Solving. Learning problem-solving skills gives children and youth a feeling of having some control over their surroundings. The following is an example of a problem-solving model counselor might use:

Steps in Problem Solving

Helping children—

- Realize there is a problem
- Stop and think. Carefully decide exactly what the problem is.
- Decide on a goal (related to the problem).
- Think of possible solutions.
- Think about the consequences of each solution.
- Choose the best solution.
- Make a plan for carrying out the solution.

If children have opportunities to learn and to practice the skills necessary to solve problems in real-life situations (i.e., what to do if I'm scared and home alone), then we are giving them tools to use both in and out of school.

Help Children Learn Self-Control. Children who can control their own emotions feel more competent. Part of self-control is knowing the rules to which one's behavior should conform. Another part is understanding social scripts: knowing how to make introductions, answer a telephone, or knowing appropriate table manners. If children are able to exercise or practice self-control, their self-control appears to improve.

Help Children Gain Effective Communication Skills . Knowing how to communicate and cooperate with others are important skills. Children who do not possess these skills are very likely to have poor peer relationships. Children with poor peer relationships are more likely to get into trouble at school, feel as if they do not belong, attend less, achieve less, and the cycle goes on. Teaching communication, cooperation, and conflict resolutions skills to four-, five-, and six-year-olds and then reinforcing them throughout elementary school is one way of helping children gain skills needed for success at school (and later in life).

Help Children Learn to Relax and Manage Stress. As Elkind (6) has pointed out, many of today's children have become the unwilling, unintended victims of overwhelming stress. Much of this stress comes from the rapid and bewildering social change and rising expectations of modern day society. Even parents are hurrying the growing-up process by treating children as adults and by burdening them with worry and anxiety, expecting them to assist adults in carrying life's load. In addition, schools have become so product-oriented that they hurry children in attempts to create better products (brighter students). The renewed emphasis on achievement and test scores has to increase the stress children experience at school. Many counselors have begun to teach relaxation methods to small groups of children. Guided fantasy is one stress management technique that can be taught to preschool and elementary-age children. Guided fantasy involves encouraging the children to imagine themselves in situations that portray feelings of comfort and calmness. The three phases used in this approach are relaxing, fantasizing, and processing (13). In the first or relaxing stage, the counselor asks the children to assume a comfortable position and to close their eyes because they are going to play an imagination game similar to watching television inside your head. During the fantasy phase, the counselor suggests that the children imagine different scenes that can continue for a longer period of time. For example, they might imagine themselves floating on a nice comfortable cloud traveling around Disney World. As they float on the cloud, the sun begins to warm their face, their shoulders, arms, etc., until they feel warm, cozy, and relaxed. At the end of the fantasy phase, the counselor suggests to the children that when they return from their fantasy trip, they can enjoy the same kind of comfort and calmness again by closing their eyes, taking some deep breaths, and using their fantasy to relax again. This processing of the experience is the third phase of guided fantasy. It helps children realize they can relax themselves when they need to do so. Of course, other stress reduction techniques can be used. Providing quiet times to draw pictures, listen to music, dance or engage in other physical exercise, and listen to stories are all strategies to help children relax.

Promote Daily School Attendance. Regular school attendance helps children keep up with classroom learning and assignments and feel a part of the school. Young children who have erratic attendance patterns are often those who drop out later. By identifying students with attendance problems early (in kindergarten and first grade), counselors can provide small group counseling to help these children feel as if they belong at school and, if necessary, teach them how to establish positive peer relationships.

Help Children Learn Study and Test-Taking Skills. Educational counseling is one of the most important activities of school counselors. Helping children begin to master memory, organization, and test-taking skills in the primary grades can only be helpful to them as they progress to more difficult academic assignments. For example, using imagery or mental pictures to remember facts or tying new information to old (association) are only two of the many memory techniques that counselors can teach children.

Enhance the Self-Esteem of Children. Self-esteem comes from children's feelings about all the things they are. Children with high self-esteem are considered to have "healthy" views of themselves. That is, the children's views are ones that realistically see shortcomings but are not overly critical of themselves. Although self-esteem is a complex concept, positive self-esteem does seem to be central to good social-emotional adjustment and appears to be associated with academic adjustment. By helping children to solve problems, to exercise self-control, and to communicate effectively (as suggested above), counselors are assisting children in gaining the skills to help them feel competent and confident in school. If children can acquire these skills, the foundation for positive self-esteem has been laid.

Work with Teachers and Principals

Conduct In-Service Training with Staff to Improve School Atmosphere. The competitive climate of many schools makes them unhappy and unproductive places for many children. Counselors can remind teachers, through regular in-service, of the developmental needs of early childhood. They can suggest activities to teachers to strengthen the self-esteem of their students, to foster cooperation among their students, and to help students appreciate individual differences. Teachers should be able to count on their counselors for current information on the personal-social development of children and for the latest techniques and strategies to foster such development.

Organize Crisis Management Teams. School counselors, because of their education and training, can organize "crisis management" teams. These teams, often consisting of selected teachers, counselors, parents, school psychologists, administrators, and sometimes nurses, are trained to deal with any of the various crises that might arise at school. Crisis management teams have been used in secondary school for many years to deal with suicide or drug-related problems. Because of the changing nature of our society, even elementary schools must be prepared for the unexpected.

Work with Parents/Families

Conduct Parent Groups. Today's parents face challenges also. Many women (and some men) find themselves rearing their children alone. Single female parents frequently experience excessive stress because of financial and child-care worries. They are, to a greater degree than ever, looking to the school for help in developing parenting skills. Counselors can conduct groups designed to teach effective parenting skills and, at the same time, provide a supportive environment for parents who are doing their best to rear their children. These groups are usually offered in the evening, and increasingly schools are arranging for child care so that the parents are able to attend. In a few communities, counselors work from noon to 8:00 p.m. in order to work more with parents and families.

Work with the Community

Work Closely with Local Mental Health and Social Agencies. Families of today can benefit from various resources within the community. Local mental health and social agencies can provide services that may not be available in the school. Counselors will need to refer both children and families to agencies within the community that are capable of providing long-term counseling.

In addition, counselors need to reach out to and coordinate the efforts of those in the community who wish to help with concerns or problems at school. It is common for local groups to come into elementary schools with sexual assault prevention or drug prevention programs. If these programs are to be successful, they must be integrated into and reinforced by the existing counseling program. Otherwise, they become one-time events with no long-term effects.

Work with Business and Industry. Counselors have always attempted to facilitate the career development of students. If current research is accurate (8), counselors need to be introducing four-, five-, and six-year-olds to the world of work. They can help children learn to appreciate the contributions of all workers and can broaden the horizons of children by introducing them to role models in nontraditional careers. Given current projections outlined in *Workforce 200* (10), female and minority children must be encouraged to develop their full potential if the United States is to remain a world leader.

TRENDS IN THE COUNSELING PROFESSION

If the public interest in early childhood education continues, and there is no reason to expect otherwise, counselors will have to become more knowledgeable about the developmental stages of infancy (birth to three years) and early childhood (three to six years). Just like elementary teachers, elementary counselors have been content to start with kindergarten. Clearly, starting with kindergarten is not soon enough.

The American School Counselor Association (ASCA), which represents roughly 13,000 school counselors throughout the United States, has renewed its interest in developmental counseling and early childhood counseling. ASCA is engaged in a nationwide effort to help counselors design counseling programs that include prekindergarten children. The success of early childhood education must be assured if we are to survive as a democratic society. The contributions of school counselors to that success were the focus of this chapter.

REFERENCES

1. Ackerman, R. J. *A Guidebook for Educators, Therapists, and Parents.* Indiana, Penna.: Learning Publications, 1983.

2. Angus, S. F. "Three Approaches to Stress Management for Children." *Elementary School Guidance and Counseling Journal* 9 (1989): 14-21.

3. Blocher, D. H. *Developmental Counseling.* New York: Ronald Press Co., 1966.

4. Bosma, W. G. H. "Children of Alcoholics--A Hidden Tragedy." *Maryland State Medical Journal* 1 (1972): 34-36.

5. Child Assault Prevention Project. *Safe, Strong, and Free.* Columbus, Ohio: The Project, 1985.

6. Elkind, D. *The Hurried Child: Growing Up too Fast too Soon.* Reading, Mass.: Addison-Wesley, 1981.

7. Fine, E. W. "Alcoholic Family Dynamics and Their Effects on the Children." Paper presented at the annual conference of the National Council on Alcoholism, Milwaukee, Wis., April 1975.

8. Gottfredson, L. "Circumscription and Compromise: A Developmental Theory of Vocational Aspirations." *Journal of Counseling Psychology* 28 (1981): 545-79.

9. Hyde, M. O. *My Friend Has Four Parents.* New York: McGraw-Hill Book Co., 1981.

10. Johnston, W. B. *Workforce 2000: Work and Workers for the 21st Century.* Indianapolis: Hudson Institute, 1989.

11. Morehouse, E. R., and Scola, C. M. *Children of Alcoholics: Meeting the Needs of the Young COA in the School Setting.* South Laguna, Calif.: National Association for Children of Alcoholics, 1986.

12. Pitney, M. "Children in Self-Care." In *Counseling Young Students At Risk: Resources for Elementary Guidance Counselors,* edited by J. C. Bleuer and P. A. Schreiber. Ann Arbor, Mich.: ERIC Counseling and Personnel Services Clearinghouse, 1989.

13. Singer, J. L. "Fantasy: The Foundation of Serenity." *Psychology Today,* July 1976.

ASCD
Association for Supervision and Curriculum Development

5. Early Childhood Programs: Success for All

by **Patricia Cannon Conran, 1989-90 President,** *Association for Supervision and Curriculum Development. ASCD has a membership of 138,000, with headquarters at 125 North West Street, Alexandria, Virginia 22314.*

Success for all and the concept of lifelong learning are the foundations for early childhood programs. In 1988, the Association for Supervision and Curriculum Development (ASCD) published *A Resource Guide to Public School Early Childhood Programs* (16). The Guide included the Association's policy analysis in the area of early childhood education (1, p. 99-115). ASCD's position is that high-quality public school programs need to be provided for four-and five-year-old children.

Four- and five- year-olds are the most recent entrants into public schools. ASCD recognizes the urgency in formulating "appropriate, carefully conceived, and forward-looking policy" (1, p. 99) for the four- and five-year-olds in response to society's trends and needs. The greatest impetus for preschool education has come from child development research findings on the importance of the preschool years as formative ones for both intellectual and social growth (12). In addition, the effects of the scientific and technological explosion of the past century have caused us to view learning as continuous, or lifelong. Early childhood education, then, is *the* foundation for lifelong learning (3).

ASCD believes there is a "clear and compelling demand for the public schools to respond to the need for early childhood programs" (1, p. 100). Former ASCD President, Barbara Day, has summarized the current social, demographic, and economic trends, as well as empirical research data regarding the effectiveness of early childhood programs with two words: "growth" and "uncertainty." Professor Day identified the many critical issues to be resolved as follows: "What will be the goals, content, and process of programs for both four- and five-year-olds; how will we fund, deliver, and determine who attends new programs for four-year olds; and how will we ensure quality in our early childhood programs?"

ASCD

(4, pp. 27-28). Professor Day advocates focusing on the possibilities, rather than the problem, to provide optimal services for our children.

American public schools have the ability to develop high-quality early childhood programs, including resources, the knowledge base about young children, facilities, organizational systems and procedures for staffing. In most cases, the public schools have credibility in the community and connections with other agencies to provide services under an umbrella of wellness.

ASCD has considered the tremendous challenge of providing successful and worthwhile early childhood programs. The Association's policy analysis panel examined several controversial issues and aspects of planning and decision making. A brief commentary on the issues follows.

Scope of the Program

School-day length is a major factor in determining scope of program for four- and five-year-olds. Presently, kindergarten children attend an average of 3.5 hours per day, and there has been substantial discussion to the effect that five-year-olds in kindergarten should receive greater service prior to serving four-year-olds.

The question of mission surfaces when discussing length of day. For example, is the mission of early childhood programs to provide education, child care, or both? ASCD has examined narrow definitions of both education and child care (academic skills instruction and custodial and protective services, respectively). Pointing out that public schools already provide many services beyond the narrow definition of education, the Association concludes, "The more useful consideration is to provide appropriate education and care for children, regardless of the setting" (1, p. 101).

In defining the scope of early childhood programs, ASCD advocates "an experience-based program that includes individual and group activities, structured and unstructured play, time for listening, sharing stories, resting, and the opportunity to be in a safe and stimulating environment for as long as their parents are at work" (1, p. 102).

Who Should Attend

Determining whether all children or only children at risk—those economically disadvantaged or those having special needs—should

Perspectives on Early Childhood Education

attend early childhood programs is a key issue. The majority of public school programs are presently for at-risk students. The present system creates equity questions since special-needs children are usually not mainstreamed or integrated with other children not having special needs. And the economically disadvantaged are frequently segregated by class or race.

Researchers have been demonstrating the positive effects of heterogeneous groupings. It is, therefore, not surprising that early childhood educators call for *all* children to be included in programs. As Grubb has written, "The best programs provide an integrated setting with children of various racial and socioeconomic backgrounds, rather than segregating at-risk children from others" (6).

ASCD's position may be inferred to favor early childhood programs that include all children in heterogeneous groupings, not merely programs for at-risk students or programs that serve children in homogeneous groupings. On a secondary issue, that of voluntary or mandatory attendance in prekindergarten programs, ASCD favors parental choice.

Evaluation of Children

Testing of children is a long-standing, controversial issue among educators and others. Success in the early prevention of school failure has gained credibility for testing young children. Development and use of multiple measures that include, but are not limited to, tests have added to the credibility of assessment. Gadson has indicated that no one test is adequate to diagnose the strengths and needs of a young child or to determine readiness or eligibility for school enrollment (5).

One syndrome that must be avoided in early childhood programs is what Goodlad refers to as CMD, or chronic measurement disease. Goodlad says we are preoccupied with pulling up plants to look at them before the roots take hold.

ASCD advocates that "test results, teacher observation, parent-provided information, and data from other professionals (e.g., medical history) should be combined to create a profile for determining how best to meet a child's needs" (1, p. 103). Ideally, information obtained will be used to challenge at a success level and prevent having too high or too low expectations that either frustrate or thwart growth.

ASCD

Funding Sources

A fundamental issue is, "Who will pay?" Research has demonstrated that we all pay, now or later. The question, then, is who pays for what, when, and how much?

Barnett has demonstrated that the Perry Preschool Program (Ypsilanti, Michigan) expenditures for early childhood programs are cost beneficial. Monies spent in serving young children have been shown to save dollars later in preventing remediation and dropouts, crime, abuse, welfare, and other social ills (2). Other researchers have shown similar cost benefits to be derived from early childhood programs. Lazar reported the results of a longitudinal meta-analysis of the effects of preschool programs on low-income children. The research group found that, regardless of curriculum model, high-quality programs can lead to lasting gains in achievement for disadvantaged children and can affect parents' values and expectations for their children's education (9). Similarly, Miller and Bizzell reported findings that showed positive and lasting effects of four different preschool programs on the academic and intellectual performance of sixth-, seventh-, and eighth-grade students (10).

Presently, primarily government funding sources support programs for at-risk young children. Private enterprise and parent fees support programs for children not at risk.

ASCD's position is that collaboration among public schools, child care programs, and other services in planning, funding, and using resources efficiently will be essential if we are to reach families who want and need high-quality early education and care for their children. ASCD also advocates complementing and not supplanting family responsibility, suggesting a sliding-fee scale to determine cost.

Curriculum Design and Implementation

The formal and hidden curricula become divisive issues in determining early childhood education. Which goals and content? What structure and strategies? Academic or developmental?

Balance in the curriculum has always been a value of ASCD. The Association advocates a high-quality early childhood program that "supports the growth of academic skills as an integrated part of the child's total development" (1, p. 105).

The philosophical undergirding of any particular program will be debatable, with programshaving definitive orientations, depending on whether planners and consumers are Deweyan, instrumentalist, or critical theorists. ASCD's description of an academically oriented program is more instrumentalist in orientation, with instruction being deliberate and systematic and teacher-directed activities sequenced and designed to build a hierarchy of competencies.

In a developmentally oriented program, the developmental interests, needs, abilities, and interests of individual children shape the activities. The developmental focus utilizes a constructivist view of meaning and stresses the importance of collaboration for cognitive and social growth. In developmental programs, academic skills are developed within an experiential framework whereby the teacher is facilitator of child-initiated activity.

A subset issue in the curriculum is whether or not to teach reading and writing. Today, literacy is the basis for minimizing at-risk behaviors. Since the ability to read requires a solid foundation of oral language, young children can benefit from learning oral language components, such as "communication, expression, and reasoning" (7, pp. 32-52).

ASCD advocates a variety of approaches, academic and developmental, chosen to meet individuals' needs. It is generally acknowledged that young children think differently from older learners. It follows that "unique educational practices should be adopted . . . to foster meaningful development and to lay the groundwork for later, more abstract learning" (12). ASCD also advocates deferring learning to read until preparatory skills, such as fine motor skills and socialization, have been mastered. If the early childhood program includes the teaching of reading, ASCD posits three goals as requirements for learner outcomes: " the ability to read independently, the ability to understand and analyze stories, and the development of a positive disposition toward reading" (1, p. 109).

Teacher Preparation

Necessary qualifications of early childhood teachers are being debated. The majority of states require training or specialization in the area of early childhood. Research studies have shown the key variable to program effectiveness to be the amount of early childhood training.

The effective preschool teacher is portrayed in Phi Delta Kappa literature as "noncontrolling, positive, responsive, and verbal" (12). The theory of young children learning by doing, with the result that teachers are like guides or facilitators, is supported by the National Association for the Education of Young Children (11, pp. 20 to 21). This is in contrast to the popular practice of "hothousing"—the practice of pressuring children to perform at levels typical of later stages of development (14, p.212). Early childhood training can help to facilitate effective teaching practices. Lay-Dopyera and Dopyera advocate developing a repertoire of various teaching situations and, then, undertaking reflection-in-action. For example, "Teachers may choose whether to establish warm, supportive relationships with children or remain more distant, hoping not to interfere with children's autonomy and integrity; whether to provide attention freely or contingently; and what degree of structuring to provide" (8, p. 29).

ASCD advocates selecting teachers for early childhood programs who hold comparable status with other teachers: a four-year degree and teaching credentials. ASCD writes, "It is essential that early childhood teachers have specific training in early childhood education/child development, and supervised practical experiences with young children" (1, p. 110).

Growth of early childhood programs will continue. Decisions to provide an extended kindergarten day and prekindergarten programs for four-year-olds may be influenced by our belief that to do so is cost beneficial. High-quality early childhood education can aid social and economic development and accrue financial and societal benefits. There appears to be more consensus for increased early childhood programming than for what the optimal combination of teaching/learning approaches may be. The one exception is that "there is universal agreement that language development is of utmost importance" (1, p. 111).

ASCD states optimistically that when high-quality, early childhood programs are provided for all children, "Perhaps then it will be possible to fulfill our belief that all children can learn and become productive adults" (1, p. 112).

Perspectives on Early Childhood Education

The value underlying early childhood programs is success for all. That is, certain children are assumed to be at risk and such children are the target consumers of early childhood programs. ASCD's position is that intervention is not enough. Sound, effective early childhood programs are believed to increase the chances of success for at-risk students throughout life. While it is not specifically advocated by ASCD, the author believes ASCD supports continuation of a "Success for All" programming for children through age eight. Robert Slavin has designed and is implementing such a program in public schools in various states. The "Success for All" program objective is to ensure that virtually every student will reach the third grade on time with adequate basic skills, that no student will be allowed to "fall between the cracks" (15). Research has shown that preventing failure early on, not only ensures success throughout life, but provides enduring benefits for society as well.

REFERENCES

1. Association for Supervision and Curriculum Development Early Childhood Education Policy Panel. "Analysis of Issues Concerning Public School Involvement in Early Childhood Education." Chapter 6 in *A Resource Guide to Public School Early Childhood Programs*, edited by Cynthia Warger. Alexandria, Va.: ASCD, 1988.
2. Barnett, W. *The Perry Preschool Program and Its Long-term Effects: A Benefit-Cost Analysis.* High/Scope Early Childhood Policy Papers, No. 2. Ypsilanti, Mich.: High/Scope Press, 1985.
3. Cryan, J. R., and Surbeck, E. *Early Childhood Education: Foundations for Lifelong Learning.* Bloomington, Ind.: Phi Delta Kappa Educational Foundation, 1979.
4. Day, B. D. "What's Happening in Early Childhood Programs Across the United States." Chapter 1 in *A Resource Guide to Public School Early Childhood Programs*, edited by C. Warger. Alexandria, Va.: Association for Supervision and Curriculum Development, 1988.
5. Gadson, M. *Testing Young Children.* Tallahassee: Florida Department of Education, 1980.
6. Grubb, N. W. *Young Children Face the States: Issues and Options for Early Childhood Programs.* New Brunswick, N. J.: Center for Policy Research in Education, 1987.
7. Katz, L. G. "Engaging Children's Minds: The Implications of Research for Early Childhood Education." Chapter 2 in *A Resource Guide to Public*

School Early Childhood Programs, edited by C. Warger. Alexandria, Va.: Association for Supervision and Curriculum Development, 1988.

8. Lay-Dopyera, M., and Dopyera, J. E. "Strategies for Teaching." In *The Early Childhood Curriculum: A Review of Current Research*, edited by C. Seefeldt, 13-33. New York: Teachers College Press, 1987.

9. Lazar, I. "Measuring the Effects of Early Childhood Programs." *Community Education Journal* 15 (1988): 8-11.

10. Miller, L. B., and Bizzell, R. P. "Long-Term Effects of Four Preschool Programs: Sixth, Seventh, and Eighth Grades." *Child Development* 54, (1983): 727-41.

11. National Association for the Education of Young Children. "Position Statement on Developmentally Appropriate Practice in Programs for Four- and Five-Year-Olds." *Young Children* 40 (1986): 20-29.

12. Phi Delta Kappa Center on Evaluation, Development, Research. *Preschool Education*. Bloomington, Ind.: Phi Delta Kappa, 1989.

13. Schweinhart, L. J.; Weikart, D. P.; and Larner, M. B. "Consequences of Three Preschool Curriculum Models Through Age 15." *Early Childhood Research Quarterly* 1 (1986): 15-45.

14. Sigel, I. E. "Does Hothousing Rob Children of Their Childhood?" *Early Childhood Research Quarterly* 2 (1987): 211-25.

15. Slavin, R. Report on "Success for All" program given at ASCD Urban Curriculum Leaders' Conference, Miami, Florida, December 7, 1989.

16. Warger, C., ed. *A Resource Guide to Public School Early Childhood Programs*. Alexandria, Va.: Association for Supervision and Curriculum Development, 1988.

ATE

Association of Teacher Educators

6. Critical Issues and Early Childhood Teacher Education

by **Thomas J. Buttery,** *Professor and Chair, Elementary and Middle Grades Education, School of Education, East Carolina University, Greenville;* **Edith Guyton,** *Associate Professor, Early Childhood Education, College of Education, Georgia State University, Atlanta; and* **John Sikula, 1989-90 President,** *Association of Teacher Educators. ATE has a membership of 4,000, with headquarters at 1900 Association Drive, Reston, Virginia 22091-1599.*

The Association of Teacher Educators (ATE) recognizes and supports the proposition that the education of young children needs to be a national priority. The Association has taken two significant steps to affirm this commitment to the early childhood years. The first action was to appoint a commission on Early Childhood Teacher Education. This is a cooperative endeavor with the National Association for the Education of Young Children (NAEYC) to study and prepare guidelines for certifying teachers of young children; it is chaired by James M. Johnson of Memphis State University. The second salient project is to develop a new text to be entitled *Family Ties.* Leonard Kaplan of Wayne State University will edit this volume dedicated to the study of the interaction of educators and the families with which they work.

The membership of ATE is sensitive to and concerned about the number of U.S. children, as well as children worldwide, living in poverty. More than 20 percent of all children live in poverty, with approximately 25 percent under six years of age. For minority children the problem is even more critical: 46.2 percent Black and 38.7 percent Hispanic compared to 16.1 percent of white children exist in poverty. In addition, 50 percent of children living in female-headed, single-parent families exist in poverty compared to 12.5 percent of other children (9). The increasing rate of teenage pregnancy creates the double problem of children raising children while also living in poverty.

According to Clark and Astuto (8), the condition of urban poverty for children is out of control. They indicate that the condition is so pervasive that we are no longer stunned by poverty statistics. ATE's First Annual Survey of Critical Issues in Teacher Education (6) found that ATE members are sensitive to the need for teacher education to occur in multicultural settings. They do not believe that this is being adequately done within the structure of present programs.

Decker and Decker (9) posit that many parents are incapable of providing a stimulating and enriched home environment for their children. They believe that early childhood programs are no longer perceived as dispossessing mothers of their nurturing functions, usurping family rights, or creating institutionalized children. Rather, compensatory programs can offer essential services to families and a positive environment for children. Early childhood programs are influenced by today's social problems. While one chapter cannot adequately address the full scope of this interaction, it is imperative that it is acknowledged.

This chapter is delimited to selected variables that are particularly important to early childhood teacher education. The authors acknowledge that space limitations preclude a comprehensive review. The topics covered include licensure versus certification, patterns of certification, federal influences on early childhood education, the relationship between liberal arts and teacher education, and alternate certification.

LICENSURE VERSUS CERTIFICATION

The world of early childhood education is constantly changing and perhaps best described as fluid. NAEYC defines early childhood as birth through age eight. However, McCarthy (13) and Decker and Decker (9) acknowledge that this definition is not uniformly accepted. Various synonyms and different chronological ages are used to record developmental milestones.

Preschool programs in private control, for example, nurseries, parent cooperatives, and business-operated day-care programs are required to have a license to operate. The requirements for licensing vary in each state, but they usually include requirements about space, staff-pupil ratio, and health and safety regulations. However, licensure programs are generally not subject to review for program quality. The staff of these licensure programs, although frequently called "teachers," are not required to hold certification. Our review of early childhood education is delimited to programs that require certification of teachers. However, it is important to acknowledge the large number of children involved in these types of licensure programs and the influence that these programs have on the curriculum for the following years of education.

PATTERNS OF CERTIFICATION

A kaleidoscope of patterns exists to certify early childhood teachers. Patterns vary from those that explicitly certify early childhood teachers, to various types of add-on endorsements, to programs of elementary education. McCarthy (13) prepared an analysis of state certification patterns for early childhood teachers and found the following information. Twenty-three states and the District of Columbia have certification identified as "Early Childhood." The programs that reflect this certification prepare candidates who are authorized to teach nine different configurations of age or grade levels. The most common pattern shared by only six states, permits the teaching of children from three to eight years of age. However, some states have title-specific programs (N-6 Certification), which are very similar to those identified as "Early Childhood Education." The combination of certification patterns denoted as explicitly "Early Childhood Education" and title-specific certification programs totals 32. An alternate pattern of certification is an early childhood endorsement added to an elementary education program for grades 1-6 or 1-8. Thirteen states have this type of endorsement. Another configuration of certification includes kindergarten in elementary certification; 19 states have this pattern.

Four states have no certification for teaching kindergarten or younger children. Elementary teachers are considered qualified to teach kindergarten in these four states.

McCarthy (13) concludes that with such a lack of commonality regarding nomenclature and accepted scope of service to be certified, it is clear why states cannot reach consensus about professional preparation. She observes that a lack of common language makes communication across state lines very difficult.

FEDERAL INFLUENCE ON EARLY CHILDHOOD EDUCATION

In his 1990 state of the union address, President Bush focused on education and stated the importance of the early childhood years. Optimists might expect from his statements that financial support would be forthcoming. However, other economic issues have educators very concerned.

The collapse of so many eastern bloc Communist governments and the change of government in Nicaragua, among other events, are placing heavy strains on our foreign aid budget and overall national budget. Despite the Bush claim to advocate improvement in education, the best prediction for federal educational policy, programs, and funds over the next decade is to expect a relatively low priority, few initiatives, and most significantly, declining fiscal support (8). This is not a new trend. Since 1981 the budget for the Department of Education has dropped from 0.6 percent to 0.4 percent of the GNP, decreased from 2.5 percent to 1.8 percent of the federal budget, and reduced the federal contribution to elementary and secondary education from 8.7 percent to 6.2 percent (8). Verstegen and Clark (17) report that during the Reagan years, Congress appropriated $135.6 billion for education. Had the Department of Education budget been frozen at the 1980 level with no enhancements except for inflation, the spending on education would have amounted to $150.4 billion.

Clark and Astuto (8) believe that three basic economic tenets will place a continuing constraint on federal education initiatives: (1) the budget has to be balanced, (2) the deficit has to be reduced, and (3) there will be no new taxes. A fourth tenet should be considered—foreign aid may need to be increased. In this season of reform, increased expenditures for elementary and secondary education have been the responsibility of the states. Unfortunately, many states, required to operate with a balanced budget, are experiencing difficulty in funding reforms, especially in light of decreased federal aid. Clark and Astuto (8) caution that states have already paid out significantly for reform and may well have difficulty covering the cost of the next level of improvement, which includes better preparation and development of teachers and administrators.

Questions emerge—What should a teacher be prepared to do? How should colleges and universities go about preparing them? What can school administrators do to help?

LIBERAL ARTS AND TEACHER EDUCATION

Few would disagree that early childhood teachers should be liberally educated. But what should be the focus of this liberal education? Both the Carnegie Corporation Task Force on Teaching as a Profession (7), and the Holmes Group (11) advocate the elimination of undergraduate education majors. Their belief is that individuals preparing to teach children need to learn subject matter in depth.

These recommendations have not been made capriciously, but they have no empirical base and raise particular problems for early childhood teachers. Nussel (15) observes that by eliminating the undergraduate major in education, the question of how to prepare early childhood teachers in all the subjects areas of the self-contained classroom is raised and typically left unanswered.

A major concentration in a content area would not automatically solve problems of preparation in subject matter for teachers. The Carnegie report and the Association of American Colleges (AAC) report (4) castigated higher education for compartmentalizing and teaching subjects to the detriment of coherent, integrated experiences. Yet further separation of the learning of content (baccalaureate) from learning about teaching (graduate) is an additional compartmentalization that might lead to early childhood teachers who fail to see relationships between how and what they were taught in undergraduate school and how and what they teach to children. The concept of teacher education often is misconstrued as only pedagogical education. It must be understood that the whole college experience of prospective teachers influences what and how they teach.

The Holmes Group is emphatic that simply eliminating undergraduate education majors is not sufficient. General education must be reformed so that it has greater coherence. Discipline-oriented courses and majors and minors must be reconstituted so they are more concept and methodology-oriented (the "structure of the discipline" notion of knowledge). General studies, majors, and minors must engage students in an inquiry process, not simply an exercise in the mastery of certain content. Instructors who are responsible for general studies and majors and minors should be better models of the teaching behaviors we want teachers of children to utilize.

The AAC (4) report also addresses the entire college curriculum and emphasizes the need for more interdisciplinary efforts. It states that "coverage" is no longer possible and that the emphasis should be on how to learn, not what to learn. "The problem with the American college curriculum is not that it has failed to offer up knowledge. The problem is that it offers to much knowledge with little attention to how the knowledge has been created and what methods and styles of inquiry have led to its creation," (p. 24). The report advocates nine elements essential to a sound education, including opportunities for inquiry and abstract logical thinking, development of historical consciousness, opportunities for students to use their values, and "access to the diversity of cultures and experiences that define U.S. American society and the contemporary world," (p. 21). The report recommends interdisciplinary studies and studies focused on world problems to meet these goals.

Accreditation standards are rather vague regarding knowledge of content of subjects taught and of general education. "The unit ensures that education students attain a high level of academic competence and understanding in the areas in which they plan to teach or work" (14, p. 39). "The unit ensures that education students receive appropriate depth and breadth in an integrated course of study that is offered by faculty in the liberal arts and other general studies" (14, p. 38). The American Association of Colleges for Teacher Education (AACTE) Early Childhood Teacher Education Guidelines do not call for a subject matter concentration in the program objectives but only for general education and professional studies. "General education provides knowledge and understanding of the liberal arts, humanities, and social, biological, and physical sciences" (3, p. 1).

A common thread in the literature is that all teachers, including teachers of young children, need a concentration in one or more content areas and a good general education. The consensus seems to be that if early childhood teachers were well educated and were taught how to learn and approached new knowledge through their general education and specialty studies, they should be better able to teach the early childhood curriculum. Child guidance and understanding are seemingly overlooked. Challenges for early childhood teacher education are what and how much content, and when they should be delivered.

Both the Carnegie and Holmes education reports advocate differentiated staffing for schools. It may be that advanced early childhood education degrees could include a cognate area, a minor, a content area, and that "lead teachers" or "career professional teachers" could provide leadership in the area(s) of the major. By delaying the choice of a major for teachers of young children until after they have had teaching experience, it is more likely that a teacher would have identified interests and talents and might be able to apply the content knowledge to teaching. A plan of this sort also addresses the difficulty of every teacher having a major in every subject taught. If implemented, the major should concentrate on the content emphasized in the early childhood curriculum. For example, an early childhood teacher might have an interdisciplinary major in sociology/psychology/anthropology and be the lead teacher of social studies education.

An additional perspective needs to be considered. Many early childhood educators are leery about the "departmentalization" of the primary grades. They believe that a teacher needs to have sustained working periods with each child to know him or her as an individual. Subject specialization could lead to a different teacher for each subject. The whole child concept believes that each child has various strengths on which to build and limitations to ameliorate. When a teacher works with a child for only one subject, it is often difficult to see the strengths, weaknesses, and personal needs of the whole child and to provide the type of comprehensive guidance that is necessary.

ALTERNATE CERTIFICATION

An issue related to content preparation for teachers is alternative certification. Adelman, Michie, and Bogart (1) defined alternative certification programs as teacher preparation programs that enroll noncertified individuals with at least a bachelor's degree in a specific subject area; and that offer shortcuts, special assistance, and/or unique curricula leading to eligibility for a standard teaching credential. Alternative certification (AC) programs bypass the traditional undergraduate education programs and tend to decrease entry requirements into the teaching profession. These programs typically require fewer education courses for certification, and/or permit alternative methods for meeting specified competencies. In addition, states that have alternative certification programs generally require internship periods of varying lengths.

Some AC programs have proven effective (1, 10, 12, 16). These programs were designed mainly for secondary teachers who have a major in the subject they will teach. Alternative certification for early childhood teachers is more complex since no one major can be assumed to be adequate for or sufficiently facilitative of good teaching.

Additionally, AC programs generally have combined reduced professional preparation and supervised on-the-job training. Teacher educators are less comfortable with these aspects for early childhood teachers, since early childhood programs generally have more education courses than their secondary counterparts (child psychology, child development, methods courses in all subject areas, as well as art and music courses). Also, for many, it is more acceptable for teachers of older children to "learn from their mistakes" than it is for a teacher to practice on first graders. Just the fact that the early childhood teacher spends all day with one group of children makes the impact of mistakes much more powerful. It also is more difficult for experienced early childhood teachers to leave their classrooms to be mentors/supervisors for AC interns.

The addition of four-year-old programs, and the lengthening of kindergarten to a full day in primary schools will increase the demand for early childhood teachers. The fact exists that a shortage of appropriately trained early childhood teachers may occur. In all likelihood, one solution that will be offered is AC programs. These programs were largely developed in response to a need for secondary teachers of science and mathematics. Early childhood teacher educators must be watchful and ensure that such programs meet standards set by the Association of Teacher Educators (5) and the American Association of Colleges for Teacher Education (2). The profession should not and cannot allow inadequately prepared individuals into early childhood classrooms to learn how to teach using groups of young children as guinea pigs.

CONCLUSION

A tremendous challenge exists to make early childhood education and teacher preparation more effective and meaningful. Debate and research about the issues presented here must continue. The process of reform will not be inexpensive, and early childhood educators should not apologize for demanding additional funding. The problems that American society and its educational system in this and other areas are expensive. The solutions to the problems require a change in societal priorities and modification of funding patterns currently inadequate to address a failing system.

REFERENCES

1. Adelman, N.E.; Michie, J.; and Bogart, J. *An Exploratory Study of Teacher Alternative Certification and Retraining Programs.* Washington, D.C.: Department of Education, Office of Planning, Budget, and Education, 1986.
2. American Association of Colleges for Teacher Education "Alternative Certification: A Position Statement of AACTE." *Journal of Teacher Education* 36, no. 3 (1985): 24.
3. ____. "Early Childhood Teacher Education Guidelines." Paper presented at the meeting of the American Association of Colleges for Teacher Education, Anaheim, California, 1989.
4. Association of American Colleges. "Integrity in the College Curriculum: A Report to the Academic Community." *Chronicle of Higher Education* 29, no. 22 (1985): 12-30.
5. Association of Teacher Educators. *Minimum Standards for Alternative Teacher Certification Programs.* Reston, Va.: ATE, 1989.
6. Buttery, T.J.; Haberman, M.; and Houston, W.R. *First Annual Survey of Critical Issues in Teacher Education.* Washington, D.C.: Association for Teacher Educators, 1990.
7. Carnegie Corporation Task Force on Teaching as a Profession. *A Nation Prepared: Teachers for the Twenty-First Century.* New York: Carnegie Forum on Education and the Economy, Carnegie Corporation of New York, 1986.
8. Clark, D.L., and Astuto, T.A. "The Disjunction of Federal Education Policy and Educational Needs in the 1990s." *Journal of Education Policy* 4, no. 5 (1989): 11-26.
9. Decker, C.A., and Decker, J.R. *Planning and Administering Early Childhood Programs.* Columbus, Ohio: Merrill Publishing Co., *1988.*

10. Guyton, E. *The 1988-89 Georgia Alternative Preparation Program Research Report.* Atlanta: Georgia Department of Education, 1989.
11. Holmes Group. *Tomorrow's Teachers.* East Lansing, Mich.: Holmes Group, Inc, 1986.
12. Hutton, J.B. *Alternative Teacher Certification: Its Policy Implications for Classroom and Personal Practice.* Commerce, Texas: East Texas State University, 1987.
13. McCarthy, J. *State Certification of Early Childhood Teachers: An Analysis of the 50 States and the District of Columbia.* Washington, D.C.: National Association for the Education of Young Children, 1988.
14. National Council for Accreditation of Teacher Education. *Standards, Procedures, and Policies for the Accreditation of Professional Education Units.* Washington, D.C.: NCATE, 1987.
15. Nussel, E.J. "What the Holmes Group Report Doesn't Say." *Phi Delta Kappan* 68, no. 1 (1986): 36-38.
16. Schecter, E.; Rorro, C.; Osander, J.; and Chmara, D. *The New Jersey Professional Teacher Program: A Third-Year Report.* Trenton: New Jersey State Department of Education, 1987.
17. Verstegen, D.A., and Clark, D.L. "The Administration in Federal Expenditures for Education During the Reagan Administration." *Phi Delta Kappan* 70, no. 2 (1988): 134-38.

CCSSO
Council of Chief State School Officers

7. Foundations for Success: Early Childhood and Family Education

by **William B. Keene, 1989-90 President,** *Council of Chief State School Officers. CCSSO has a membership of 57, with headquarters at 400 North Capitol Street, N.W., Suite 379, Washington, DC 20001-1511.*

CALL FOR ACTION

Our concern is for young children and what society must do to assist them in developing their infinite capacities. Our focus is on the partnership of family, health and other care givers, and educators who need to help each child develop those capacities. Our challenge is to assure the partnership is in place and prepared to nurture each child from the earliest moments of life.

Our commitment as educators addresses our colleagues who teach; policymakers in localities, states, and the nation; those who provide education and other caring services; and leaders of community, business, and labor. We must come together at a time of profoundly changed and changing family and societal patterns to create new ways of supporting families and assuring that each child's earliest years provide the foundation for a creative life.

THE IMPERATIVE

There is no more essential or more sensitive challenge before us than to create new partnerships and shared responsibilities for the development of young children. No participant can be successful alone in this task, but each has obligations and opportunities.

Families are the first and most continuous teachers. In the past, children entered the formal education system when it was believed they were ready to leave the constant care of parents and were prepared for an expanded learning environment. During the child's earliest years, the parents' role and the attention of schools existed independent of each other.

The world of children has changed in many ways. The time available to families for nurturing their children has diminished dramatically. Economic pressures on families cause young children to be placed in other care-giving environments much earlier. Further, much more is now known about patterns and periods of early learning and what stimulations and directions are most appropriate.

The dichotomy between nurturing and education has been blurred beyond distinction both because of the unprecedented societal changes affecting the very young and because we know good care for young children promotes learning and good learning experiences are caring and nurturing. We know families never cease being teachers; we also have learned that teachers must consider the total well-being of the children they teach.

Our values and institutions hold that each child should have the opportunity to develop to his or her fullest. That vision remains clear. That opportunity, however, is imperiled. Our society must strengthen its commitments and change its services and institutions to address the realities facing our children and families.

The realities for the nearly four million infants born in the late 1980s and early 1990s are as follows:

- Fifty percent will have mothers entering or reentering the work force before their babies are one-year-old;
- Seventy percent will receive some or much of their care outside their homes by the time they are three-years-old;
- Twenty-five percent will begin their lives already at risk of personal and educational failure because of the poverty and stress in their families; and
- Those at risk economically will have less opportunity to participate in high-quality early childhood programs, thus widening the chasm between the disadvantaged and those more fortunate.

For all children, and especially for the many in peril, support for both them and their families is essential. Providing this support would not only help individual families but also would be sound national policy because of

Perspectives on Early Childhood Education

- Inability of children to benefit fully from their education because of poor health or lack of family stability;
- Loss of individual potential when early interventions are not available to children at crucial points in their development or to their families when experiencing distress and dysfunction;
- Cost to society of remediation, special education, welfare services, adjudication, and rehabilitation resulting from a lack of early interventions; and
- Loss of productivity to the work force by family members who cannot work because of the lack of proper child-care arrangements.

This call to action is for direct, creative, and expanded assistance to young children and their families. They would benefit directly; we would all gain.

PRINCIPLES

The strategies for Chief State School Officers' call to action are based on these principles:

- All children, regardless of race, ethnic background, home language, religion, family income, disability, or gender must have equal access to high-quality early childhood programs and services.
- All families must have access to assistance that will help them (a) care for and educate their children; and (b) develop the skills, knowledge, and attitudes essential for family functioning.
- Early childhood programs must assist each child to develop a full range of fundamental social, emotional, physical, and cognitive abilities.
- The developmental programs of the early childhood years must be extended into and integrated with education at the elementary school level.
- Resources and programs for young children and families must be coordinated to assure availability, effectiveness, and comprehensiveness.

STRATEGIES FOR CHANGE

Health, education, social, economic, and family policy goals must be one and the same for young children. The educational and developmental aspects of such integrated policy should include these strategies.

Universally Available High-Quality Early Childhood Services for All Children with Concentration of Public Resources on Early Childhood Programs for Children at Risk

The evidence demonstrates that high-quality early childhood programs are dramatically beneficial to young children. It is not as important where programs are available, under either public or private auspices, as their accessibility to the families that need them. Parts of a fabric of early childhood education programs already exist; those parts need to be woven together to reach all who need them and want to be covered.

We know that children at risk who participate in high-quality early childhood programs will increase substantially their likelihood of success in school. Yet, while families with annual incomes above $20,000 enroll their children in preschool at a rate of 52 percent, the enrollment rate for families with annual incomes below $10,000 is only 29 percent. Our society cannot afford to deny any child the opportunity to participate in a program that will have long-lasting positive benefits, both for that child and for society.

In a fragmented way, public policy already directs that the available and limited public funding for early childhood programs be concentrated on special populations, such as through Head Start and programs to reach young handicapped children. These efforts need to be blended into an overall policy to help those families most in need.

In 1987, our Council adopted the position that all four-year-old children at risk of later school failure should be guaranteed an opportunity for prekindergarten programs through public funding. Ideally, these programs would be available by the age of three. Prekindergarten programs should be accompanied by publicly supported child care to assure full-day attention where needed. The providers of prekindergarten programs may be multiple—public and private agencies—with the overall governance of public funds under the direction of the appropriate state and local education agencies.

Perspectives on Early Childhood Education

Strengthening Capacities of Families

The family is the focal point in fostering and sustaining a child's positive growth and development. The family "curriculum" in the earliest years is more important than the school curriculum. However, increasing numbers of families need assistance in providing experiences that lead to positive development of children.

Developing attitudes, values, and expectations, and learning to succeed in school are not separate entities for young children—they are pieces of the total nurturing and care they receive at home and away from home. The results of the best programs for young children are only, in part, increases in their cognitive skills. The stronger result is in the positive effects of their families. In the long run, this will have a greater impact on a child's life chances than higher school test scores. Many families need help in developing their capacities, including:

- Programs that reach new parents—particularly at the prenatal period through age two—to establish early, supportive partnerships to help their children;
- Support in fulfilling family roles at home, with appropriate strategies such as home-based programs for families of the very young and networking for families of older children;
- Assurances that the patterns and scheduling of formal schooling, once it begins, will be consonant with the experiences that have benefited their children in early childhood programs; and
- Sensitivity to the culture of the family, with full recognition of the desire and ability of families to help their children.

Assuring Standards of Quality for Early Childhood Programs

The positive effects of high-quality programs for young children and their families are so strong and consistent as to be powerfully convincing. Public policy must incorporate the best of what we know about caring for and educating young children by requiring high standards of quality.

Children who view themselves as competent, worthwhile individuals are more likely to experience success in life than those who do not. Educators can help children feel worthwhile by providing supportive learning environments that build upon the individual child's strengths and by recognizing the different learning rates and styles of children. Because young children learn best through active manipulation of the environment, concrete experiences, and communicating with peers and adults, programs must be designed to emphasize these elements.

Basically, quality programs require:

- A child development approach that exemplifies what is known about how very young children learn in an environment uniquely fashioned to their needs for physical, emotional, social, and intellectual growth;
- Staff prepared for the special field of early childhood education and benefiting from networks and supervision that provide constant renewal;
- Adult-child ratios appropriate for the age and needs of the child and meeting standards established in the child development field;
- A length of program day and year and the provision of a continuous learning environment matched to family need; and
- Evaluations, both of programs and the progress of individual children, that are based on developmental goals and reflective of the uniqueness of early childhood education.

Wherever a child is educated or cared for in a formal arrangement outside the home, minimum standards of safety and program suitability must be required. Even more important, however, are standards of quality set through informed and bold public policy that will lead to success for all children.

Broad and Deep Collaboration for Comprehensive Services to Young Children and Families

Initiatives for interagency collaboration on early childhood programs exist in almost every state, either from the impetus of federal programs or state executive directive. States and localities should build upon those initiatives. Interagency and intergovernmental forums should be used to further attract attention and support of the public and policymakers, to establish clear goals and solutions for children's needs, to implement services jointly, and to provide continual evaluation of progress.

Families need more help than ever in connecting to multiple social services. While local, state, and federal resources are available, access to them often is difficult for those families most in need. By working with other resource providers, schools have a unique opportunity to help make these connections. Cooperation must be required in statutory provisions, and funds must be provided to assure they work.

CONCLUSION

Our nation critically needs to strengthen its public commitments to young children and families so that they may adjust to the demands and stresses of changed social and economic conditions.

The Council of Chief State School Officers made a commitment in 1987 to assure each student the full range of opportunities for successful graduation from high school. To fulfill that commitment, the Council called for the establishment of 11 state guarantees for at-risk children and youth, including provision of early childhood and parent education programs. The Council believes the single most important investment to be made in education is the provision of high-quality programs for the nation's youngest children, especially for those who are most at risk and for their families. This investment must be accompanied by strategies for strong standards of quality and the assurance of broad and deep collaboration among agencies at each governmental level and across levels.

Chief state school officers are ready, state by state, and nationwide, to join with families, colleagues, policymakers, and the public to implement these strategies. Our children will bring joy and pride to themselves, their families, and their country only to the extent to which we help them do so. For our society to neglect or shortchange their potential and their opportunity is intolerable. We must act together, now.

NOTE

This statement of the Council was approved unanimously by its members in November 1988. The statement resulted from a two-year review of early childhood education policy. The Council of Chief State School Officers (CCSSO) is a nationwide nonprofit organization of the 57 public officials who head departments of public education in every state, the District of Columbia,

CCSSO

the Department of Defense Dependents Schools, and five extra-state jurisdictions. CCSSO seeks its members' consensus on major education issues and expresses their views to civic and professional organizations, to federal agencies, to Congress, and to the public.

CEC
Council for Exceptional Children

8. Early Intervention and Family Support for Children with Special Developmental Challenges

by **Crystal E. Kaiser 1989-90 President,** *International Division for Early Childhood of the Council for Exceptional Children. CEC has a membership of 54,000, with headquarters at 1920 Association Drive, Reston, Virginia 22091.*

INTRODUCTION TO EARLY INTERVENTION IN THE NINETIES

The decade of the nineties has been christened the "Decade of Early Intervention" and holds great promise for the realization of dreams long held by those who have cared deeply about the nurturance of our youngest citizens who have handicapping conditions or are at-risk for handicaps (15). Yet substantial barriers still exist to actualizing many of these visions into the practical and accessible service delivery realities that will be needed for the 21st century.

Years of research in early development intervention and related family support have culminated in a strong body of data supporting the effectiveness of early intervention programs for young children with diagnosed handicaps, as well as those who are at biologic or environmental risk for developmental problems. Program effectiveness is increasingly being evaluated along a much wider continuum of dimensions than was historically the case. No longer, for example, are such programs being evaluated solely on the basis of changes in intelligence quotients or similar unitary measures (13).

Rather, much more emphasis is being given today to the acquisition of foundational and developmentally relevant functional life skills, and the maximal utilization of residual abilities and relative strengths toward a balanced and fulfilling life. No developmental assessment of a young child today would be considered complete, for example, without a thorough assessment of relative strengths as well as perceived problems or challenges. Today's early intervention strives to provide the opportunity for each child to achieve his highest developmental potential, and to lead a balanced and happy life in a normalized social context.

Social success and the emotional development of young children with developmental challenges are beginning to be seen as increasingly higher priorities. There is a particular focus on the ability of young children to be socially integrated with their peers, beginning as early as infancy. We believe that such social and developmental integration provides equally rich learning opportunities for young children without handicaps as for those with developmental challenges. Further, integrated learning opportunities for young children with special needs enable parents of these children to remain with their natural peer group as well. There is a newfound awareness of the extent to which segregated educational opportunities for children also segregate their parents from other families in the community.

Our early intervention research has made the milestone leap from a history centered around the question "Is early intervention effective?" to more current questions such as, "For whom and under what conditions is early intervention effective?" (13, 26). It should be noted that our research has taken on a much stronger family support component, as our view of our target population has broadened to include not only the child with developmental challenges but her entire family.

In fact, family support is now recognized as an integral best practice component of an effective early intervention program. The term "family support" is used here instead of the more traditional "parent support" to reflect a very real shift in our thinking in which we have consciously moved from a focus on parents to a focus on the entire family unit as the target for our support. We have also moved from our previous emphasis on the "teaching" or "training" of parents to one of providing support that may include, but is not limited to, didactic activities. Further, we have learned a greater respect for the unique support that families can offer one another, and that may meet certain needs that professional support cannot address.

We have made a conceptual shift from seeing families as untrained entities in need of our didactic expertise to a model in which we now see ourselves as temporary co-parenting partners with them, while acknowledging and supporting their own primary and permanent role with their child, and, respectively, our own secondary and transitory role. A family support model of "enablement and empowerment" has now become a central focus in best practice early intervention programs (9). Under this philosophy, families are gradually supported to a greater realization of their own inherent strengths and resources (including their family and community) to solve problems and to meet challenges, rather than encouraged to rely on external professional support.

We have become more aware of the important role of the early intervention program in helping to develop "marathon skills" for families as foundational preparation for the psychological "pacing" required for the long road ahead in caring for young children with particularly severe handicaps (32). There is more attention today to assuring that parents do not "burn out" in the first three years by being overinvolved in strict regimens and long hours of home therapy. Instead, there is a new emphasis on helping parents to attain a balanced lifestyle not completely centered on the one handicapped family member. Recent research has indicated that, rather than being hurt by the presence of a child with handicaps in the family (as was previously thought), siblings of children with handicaps often benefit in important ways from the experience (33).

FEDERAL LEGISLATION MAKES A DIFFERENCE

In 1986, P.L. 99-457, the most sweeping piece of federal legislation ever to impact on young children with handicaps and their families, was enacted and signed into law. Public Law 99-457 incorporates both a preschool component (Part B) and an infancy component (Part H). The preschool component extended down to age three all the earlier provisions of P.L. 94-142 (the "Right to Education" law), which guaranteed school-aged children with handicaps the right to a free and appropriate public education in the least restrictive environment. Forty states as of this writing have now enacted legislation to extend these rights and protections down to age three, consistent with the federal guidelines. This means that public schools must provide for early intervention programs for three-year-olds with handicaps, and that these programs cannot be socially segregated from normal peers. Many challenges lie ahead in the full implementation of this legislation, and these challenges cannot be met without the full cooperation of the broader early childhood community.

The infancy component of P.L. 99-457 (Part H) now enables states, at their discretion, to provide services from birth for their handicapped infants, with an additional option to include developmentally at-risk infants. To date, over 70 percent of the states have adopted policies for services from birth. Under this landmark legislation, states adopting such policies must meet a number of requirements in order to access related federal funds.

Among these are requirements for written individualized family service plans (IFSPs) to be developed and implemented by interdisciplinary professional teams in home-or center-based (or combination) early intervention models, utilizing a case management approach, and with adherence to specific timelines for initiation of assessment and intervention. If states commit to participation in the Part H program, a comprehensive state system of early intervention must be developed under a state-designated Lead Agency, guided by a governor-appointed state Interagency Coordinating Council (ICC). For families whose newborn has just been diagnosed with a handicapping condition, this means that help may be just around the corner, and that they will not be told that "there is a waiting list" for admission into a program both they and their infant need right away.

The Handicapped Children's Early Education Program (HCEEP), funded by the Office of Special Education, has long been a pioneer and standard-bearer in supporting the development of national model early intervention programs representing accepted best practice components. This exemplary program has provided critical seed money to initiate, establish, and evaluate innovative early intervention program models in local communities throughout the nation. An unusually high percentage of such programs are still in operation subsequent to the termination of federal funding. These model programs have been instrumental in furthering the development of the field over the past 20 years.

THE SOCIAL INTEGRATION MOVEMENT IN EARLY INTERVENTION

There is a strong movement from our history of segregated services for young handicapped children, and a new thrust on the social and educational integration of programs for all young children (29). While most day care, nursery, and kindergarten professionals might not think of their programs as socially or educationally exclusionary, many parents of handicapped or at-risk children still find these doors of opportunity closed to them and to their child from as early as infancy. While the exemplary Head Start program has long been a notable exception, it is not unusual for infant or family day care, nursery school, or kindergarten providers to refuse access to young children who may have developmental differences or who may be medically fragile. While often related to a lack of specialized training or sufficient funding to enable responsible levels of specialized care, nonetheless, such an event is still perceived by many parents as the first of many doors to be closed to them and to their child.

Those of us in the field of early intervention want nothing more than for these early childhood doors to be open, not only because it is the humane and kind thing to do, but because it sends such a powerful early message to families about the way their child is going to be perceived and the level of support they can expect from their community in their efforts to care for their special child at home (17). Parents of children with special needs are not different from any other parents in their desire for their children to have a normal, satisfying, happy, and productive life (33). The early childhood community is the gatekeeper for a normal life in which young children with special needs are allowed to enter programs with other young children to play with, to learn from, and to care for. Of all the types of specialized support such families may require in the nineties, none will ever be as profound as that first open door.

CATEGORIZATION SYSTEMS, ATTITUDE SHIFTS, AND LINGUISTIC MARKERS

One area of increased sensitivity in the field of early intervention projected to impact in the nineties and beyond has to do with the perceived inherent value of diversity in general, and of children with handicaps in particular. As in civil rights movements for minorities and women, our language is frequently our most reliable barometer of underlying attitudes and beliefs about the relative value of people. From this understanding has come an enhanced sensitivity toward the words we use to describe children who have developmental differences or who are faced with developmental challenges.

Parents have reported their acute awareness of the profound difference it makes to them when people see their child first and foremost as a child, and only secondarily as a child with differences in development. It has been suggested that the term "children with handicaps," while carrying an extra syllable, may be preferable to the term "handicapped children," as it places the child ahead of the disability. Similarly, the use of the term "normal" to differentiate and exclude those with handicapping conditions has been challenged. It has been argued that the occasional occurrence of handicaps is a much a "normal" part of our human existence as the occasional occurrence of giftedness. Perhaps it is not typical, but it is normal. While some may initially object to what may appear to be the use of semantic trivia, others feel that to do otherwise is to perpetuate our unfortunate history of judgmental attitudes regarding the value of certain young human lives.

Building on these concepts, it is now recognized that administrative funding formulas of the past have often placed service providers in the dilemma of either labeling young children with their perceived disability or denying them access to services. Further, such funding formulas have been charged with encouraging a segregation and categorization within special education that has never had a basis in research, and has often resulted in exacerbation of many of the larger social dilemmas we are now trying to address. Like other segregation issues in the nineties, however, today's exclusionary tactics are much more subtle than those of the past.

While schools of the past blatantly excluded children with handicaps by advising parents to leave them at home (on the incorrect assumption that such children could not benefit from instruction), too many of today's schools exclude handicapped children by assigning them to separate facilities or programs (on the incorrect assumption that this grouping is necessary in order to allow them to benefit from instruction). Particularly at the preschool level, the rationale has frequently been used

Perspectives on Early Childhood Education

that these children need time in the segregated program to prepare them for later integration. We know of no data to support this notion, but there is data to support that children may learn to function in particular types of environments, with resultant difficulties in transferring to different types of environments.

In fact, young children with developmental challenges rarely have a single, easily categorizable, discrete deficit, affecting only a unitary function. More typically such children experience varying levels of strengths and difficulties in a range of developmental domains. Therefore, P.L. 99-457 no longer requires that children be labeled with a specific disability label in order to qualify for special education and related services.

Service to young children with handicaps in the twenty-first century may be expected to be "cross-categorical" in nature, moving away from categorizations that have historically placed all children with a single disability together in the same special education classroom or special school. We can no more imagine proceeding in this way today than we can imagine assigning blacks, Asians, or women to separate classrooms on the basis of race, ethnicity, or sex. There are far more defensible developmental rationales for grouping children in such a way as to allow for a wide and healthy range of diversity and developmental challenge. These changes have implications for our teacher preparation programs, which have typically promulgated the categorical preparation model, and our state certification programs, which have also traditionally been based on categorical systems. We are rapidly moving away from programs that appear to have been designed for administrative convenience and toward service delivery systems that are more responsive to the diverse needs of young children and their families.

THE HOSPITAL NEONATAL INTENSIVE CARE UNIT: AN EMERGING NEW EARLY INTERVENTION SUBSPECIALTY

One of the newest and most exciting areas emerging in early intervention today is the provision of developmental and family support services for newborn handicapped and at-risk infants in hospital neonatal intensive care units (12). Recent research has documented strong and lasting positive effects of specialized neonatal interventions (1). In modern hospitals today, weekly newborn child-find efforts are well underway, and families begin receiving knowledgeable support from developmental specialists within the first 24 hours of birth (16). Successful medical/developmental collaborations allow for developmental support during the initial hospitalization, which, for many premature and handicapped infants, may involve the first three to six months of life (21). Such programs offer a smooth transition to community infant intervention programs for infants and families, and are rapidly becoming important adjuncts to the traditional hospital health care team.

Advances in medical science have also enabled many more infants with special needs to be diagnosed prenatally, thus enabling parents, in an increasing number of instances, to know prior to the birth that they will be delivering a newborn with handicaps. In some such cases, surgical and medical intervention now occurs prenatally, as does early intervention counseling and the arrangement for developmental services (19). When their child is born, such families may react very differently from families who expected a newborn without handicaps. For example, parents expecting the birth of a child with myelomeningocele (spina bifida) may be told that accompanying hydrocephalus is possible, and may be delighted and relieved at the time of birth to learn that no hydrocephalus is present. Having had months to adjust to the fact of their child's handicap prior to the birth, they may be much farther along in their understanding and acceptance of the handicapping condition by the actual time of birth than parents for whom the handicapping condition may have come as an unexpected shock.

FUTURE CHALLENGES AS WE APPROACH THE 21st CENTURY

The special education community is particularly concerned with the unprecedented rise in recent years of drug-addicted newborns, babies born with AIDS, boarder babies, and medically fragile infants. These are relatively new additions to the early intervention population, and require an intensification of activity not currently supported by additional funding. Recent advances in neonatology have increasingly enabled very young premature infants to survive, beginning at as early as 25 to 26 weeks' gestation, although such children frequently experience ongoing developmental challenges. In an early intervention program I currently direct, we have an infant who was actually stillborn, and successfully resuscitated. Such dramatic additions to traditional early intervention populations will represent important challenges for the field in the coming decade.

Today's economic climate demands that both parents work in most households, thus presenting severe fiscal and child care challenges to a working family with a newborn handicapped child. It is not unusual for families with premature infants to leave today's hospital neonatal intensive care unit with $250,000 in medical bills. Parents of young children with special needs have the same needs as all parents for safe, affordable child care that complements the employment schedule of two working parents. In addition, their needs are often even greater, as many programs available to most families are not accessible to families whose infant may pose special care-giving challenges. Further, it is no longer to be assumed that a stay-at-home parent will be available to care for a child with handicaps in the first few years of life (nor is this seen as necessarily desirable). These factors have important implications for the design of future service delivery systems.

While we are attempting to rise to the challenge of providing specialized services to ever-expanding populations, limited funding resources and restrictive insurance industry policies have continued to be a barrier to full implementation of needed services. It is not unusual for parents of children with special needs to find, for example, that their insurance policy will not cover "preexisting conditions" (such as congenital handicaps) or that it requires that developmental delays be documented by specific instruments that may not be sensitive enough to identify developing problems in very young children. Health insurance policies that pay 80 percent of hospital costs may sound reasonable until families calculate that 20 percent of the $250,000 in hospital bills that they may receive for their newborn is $50,000 . . . and that they may face a lifetime of additional expenses for certain medically fragile children.

As has been the case for many traditionally female professions, the field of early childhood special education is experiencing major current and projected shortfalls in the number of professionals needed to adequately serve this population. This personnel shortfall includes not only early intervention teachers, but also related service providers such as occupational and physical therapists, speech/language pathologists, social workers, and psychologists trained and experienced in best practice service delivery in early intervention (34). Most existing related service providers are trained and experienced in working with school-aged populations, and it is considered highly inappropriate for them to offer services to younger populations without additional and specialized preparation. We are also concerned about the small numbers of racially and ethnically diverse personnel currently in the field, and we are currently examining factors that may attract greater numbers of such individuals to early intervention. The preparation of additional personnel needed to serve our youngest children with special needs is one of the major challenges we will face in the coming years (23).

Despite the wonderful legislative impetus provided by P.L 99-457, the current limited funding allocations for this program continue to threaten its ultimate success. While decades of research have clearly demonstrated the long-term cost effectiveness of early intervention programs, our political system tends to operate around short-term goals that can be achieved within a given individual's term of office. Our future elected officials must have the courage to take humanistic and moral stands that may benefit the children of the nation, or of their state, for generations to come, whether or not the results can be measured in short-term dollar savings.

There is still a tremendous need for public education with respect to early learning for all young children, and for children with special needs in particular. In his 1990 State of the Union address, President Bush put forward the following goal for America: "By the year 2000 every child must start school ready to learn." It would be my recommendation that a somewhat loftier goal may be in order: By the year 2000, every legislature and state will have comprehensive policies and programs in place that are based on our current research, knowledge, and understanding that *every* child (even the most severely mentally retarded or multiply handicapped child) is "ready to learn" from birth, and that, under P.L. 99-457, families whose children have special needs should expect "school" to begin at birth for their children.

The achievement of 21st century early intervention goals for young children and their families can only be met through the united effort of all early childhood professionals, together with the families of all young children, and all citizen advocates who want to be a part of making America a bit kinder, gentler, and less exclusionary for all young children and their families. Today's society presents significant barriers to children with special developmental needs and their families that far outstrip the constellation of problems inherently posed by any handicap ever diagnosed. Such factors are potentially within our control and represent critical social challenges that we can and must meet as we approach the 21st century.

REFERENCES

1. Als, H.; Lawhon, G.; Brown, E.; Gibes, R.; Duffy, F. H.; McAnulty, G.; and Blickman, J. G. "Individualized Behavioral and Environmental Care for the Very Low Birthweight Preterm Infant at High Risk for Bronchopulmonary Dysplasia: Neonatal Intensive Care Unit and Developmental Outcome." *Pediatrics* 78 (1986): 1123-32.
2. Bailey, D. B., Jr. "Case Management in Early Intervention." *Journal of Early Intervention* 13, no. 2 (1989): 120-34.
3. Bailey, D. B., Jr.; Winton, P. J.; Rouse, L.; and Turnbull, A. P. "Family Goals in Infant Intervention." *Journal of Early Intervention* 14, no. 1 (1990): 15-26.
4. Beckman, P. J.; Pokorni, J. L.; Maza, E. A.; and Balzer-Martin, L. "A Longitudinal Study of Stress and Support in Families of Preterm and Full-Term Infants." *Journal of the Division of Early Childhood* 11, no. 1 (1986): 2-9.
5. Bush, G. State of the Union Address, Washington, D.C., 1990.
6. Calhoun, M. L.; Calhoun, L. G.; and Rose, T. L. "Parents of Babies with Severe Handicaps: Concerns about Early Intervention." *Journal of Early Intervention* 13, no. 2 (1989): 146-52.
7. Deal, A. G.; Dunst, C. J.; and Trivette, C. M. "A Flexible and Functional Approach to Developing Individualized Family Support Plans." *Infants and Young Children* 1, no. 4 (1989): 32-43.
8. DeKlyen, M., and Odom, S. L. "Activity Structure and Social Interactions with Peers in Developmentally Integrated Play Groups." *Journal of Early Intervention* 13, no. 4 (1989): 342-52.
9. Dunst, C. J. *Enabling and Empowering Families.* Cambridge, Mass.: Brookline Books, 1988.

10. Flynn, L. L., and McCollum, J. "Support Systems: Strategies and Implications for Hospitalized Newborns and Families." *Journal of Early Intervention* 13, no. 2 (1989): 173-82.

11. Fowler, S. A.; Chandler, L. K.; Johnson, T. E.; and Stella, M. E. "Individualizing Family Involvement in School Transitions: Gathering Information and Choosing the Next Program." *Journal of Division of Early Childhood* 12, no. 3 (1988): 208-16.

12. Gilkerson, L., and Crocker, A. C. *ACCESS to Developmental Services for NICU Graduates.* Boston: Wheelock College and The Children's Hospital, Project ACCESS, 1985.

13. Guralnick, M. J. "Efficacy Research in Early Childhood Intervention Programs." In *Early Intervention for Infants and Young Children with Handicaps: An Empirical Base*, edited by S. Odom and M. Karnes, 75-88. Baltimore: Paul Brookes, 1988.

14. Johnson, L. J., and Beauchamp, K. D. F. "Preschool Assessment Measures: What Are Teachers Using?" *Journal of the Division for Early Childhood* 12, no. 1 (1987): 70-76.

15. Kaiser, C. E. "President's Message." *DEC Communicator* 16, no. 3, 1990.

16. ___. "New Ideas for Supporting Families with Special Care Newborns: Project ECHO is Making a Difference." *National Perinatal Social Workers' Newsletter* 9, no. 4, 1989.

17. ___. Author and Producer. *Young and Special.* In-service training series consisting of 30 documentary television programs, 30 leader guides, and student materials. Baltimore: University Park Press, 1982. International distribution through Open University, England.

18. Kaiser, C. E.; Als, H.; and Gilkerson, L. *Developmental Intervention and Family Support in Hospital Neonatal Intensive Care Units.* National white paper from the Division of Early Childhood of the Council for Exceptional Children. In development.

19. Kaiser, C. E.; Fulbright, G.; Barrett-Zitkus, J.; and Torgerson, K. *Neonatal developmental intervention and family support.* In development.

20. LeFebvre, D., and Strain, P. S. "Effects of Group Contingency on the Frequency of Social Interactions Among Autistic and Nonhandicapped Preschool Children: Making LRE Efficacious." *Journal of Early Intervention* 13, no. 4, (1989): 329-41.

21. Long, T.; Katz, K.; and Pokorni, J. "Developmental Intervention with the Chronically Ill Infant." *Infants and Young Children* 1, no. 4. (1989) 78-88.

22. McCollum, J. A. "Charting Different Types of Social Interaction

Objectives in Parent-Infant Dyads." *Journal of the Division for Early Childhood* 11, no. 1 (1986): 28-45.

23. McCollum, J.; McLean M.; McCarten, K.; and Kaiser, C. E. "Recommendations for Certification of Early Childhood Special Educators." *Journal of Early Intervention* 13, no. 3 (1989): 195-211.

24. McLean, M.; Kaiser, C. E.; and McEvoy, M. *Cross-Categorical Early Intervention Services.* National white paper to be published in the *Journal of Early Intervention.* In development.

25. McLean, M., and Odom, S. "Least Restrictive Environment and Social Integration." National white paper. *Journal of Early Intervention,* 1988.

26. Meisels, S. J. "The Efficacy of Early Intervention: Why Are We Still Asking This Question?" *Topics in Early Childhood Special Education* 5, no. 2 (1984): 1-12.

27. Odom, S. L., and Karnes, M., eds. *Early Intervention for Infants and Young Children with Handicaps: An Empirical Base.* Baltimore: Paul Brookes, 1988.

28. Odom, S., and Warren, S. F. "Early Childhood Special Education in the year 2000." *Journal of the Division for Early Childhood* 12, no. 3 (1988): 263-73.

29. Sainato, D. M.; Strain, P. S.; and Lyon, S. R. "Increasing Academic Responding of Handicapped Preschool Children During Group Instruction." *Journal of the Division for Early Childhood* 12, no. 1 (1987): 23-30.

30. Smith, B. J., and Schakel, J. A. "Noncategorical Identification of Preschool Handicapped Children: Policy Issues and Options." *Journal of the Division for Early Childhood* 11, no. 1 (1986): 78-86.

31. Strain, P. S. " The Evaluation of Early Intervention Research: Separating the Winners from the Losers." *Journal of the Division for Early Childhood* 12, no. 2 (1988): 182-90.

32. Turnbull, A. P. "The Challenge of Providing Comprehensive Support to Families." *Education and Training in Mental Retardation* (December 1988): 261-72.

33. Vincent, L. Invited Keynote Presentation, Annual Special Education Conference, Massachusetts State Department of Education, 1988.

34. Yoder, D. E., and Coleman, P. P. *Allied Health Personnel: Meeting the Demands of Part H, Public Law 99-457.* Chapel Hill: University of North Carolina, Carolina Institute for Child and Family Policy, 1990.

ECS
Education Commission of the States

9. School Readiness and State Action

by **Frank Newman, President,** *Education Commission of the States. ECS is a constituent-based organization representing 49 states, the District of Columbia, American Samoa, Puerto Rico, and the Virgin Islands. ECS headquarters are at 707 17th Street, Suite 2700, Denver, Colorado 80202-3247.*

In February 1990, the president and the nation's governors approved six national performance goals that will guide education in the next decade and in the next century. According to the document the National Governors' Association released, the goals lay the foundation for a strong and responsible democracy and a prosperous and growing economy.

The first goal has to do with school readiness: By the year 2000, all children in America will start school ready to learn. Three objectives—having to do with disadvantaged and disabled children, parents as a child's first teacher, and nutrition and health—spell out how schools will accomplish this goal.

Some obvious questions—for this goal and the others as well—immediately comes to mind for states: What is readiness? Who will pay for children to be ready for school? Does this national goal go far enough? As the cornerstone in the foundation, what is it we want American students to be able to know and do as adult citizens and workers, and how will school readiness get us there? When do we begin—intrauterine, postpartum, first birthday, day care, in preschool, at the first day of kindergarten? What is the role of parents? And what is the role of states and state policy in all of this?

These are a few of the questions that states must ask to arrive at a vision for school readiness and for education as a whole. Without a vision, it is difficult to design effective policy, and the goals and objectives that follow remain illusive.

States and the federal government are already involved in school readiness. There is, however, little agreement within states, among states, or between states and the federal government about what school readiness is or is not. Though some states have early childhood and school readiness policies, elementary, secondary, and postsecondary education policies often are not integrated.

Child readiness currently is determined by various educational, developmental, and psychosocial scales, and by arbitrary age cutoffs. With the federal government's new emphasis on child readiness as expressed in the national goals, education leaders and policymakers have expressed a number of concerns about the fallout. Lorrie Shepard of the University of Colorado and Mary Lee Smith of Arizona State University are concerned about shoehorning children into programs that don't fit them. They suggest "developing a school culture where teachers share a commitment to adapting curriculum to a wide range of individual differences" as a more positive solution (1).

Like Shepard and Smith, a number of school leaders and state policy makers are concerned that readiness in this diverse, multicultural society will be artificially determined in terms of a mythical homogeneous group of children. This then will lead to a rigid system of readiness checkoffs.

This approach fails to address the infinite variety of factors that children bring to school, not the least of which are racial, ethnic, and cultural diversity, and the learning styles that will shape who they are as learners. Preschools and kindergartens should be places where all children can learn and where differences in learning readiness, learning styles, race, and culture are accommodated, valued, and built upon.

Preschools and kindergartens should be places that take children where they are and with whatever they bring. They should foment and pique children's natural penchant to investigate, discover, and create. And day care providers, parents, prekindergarten and kindergarten teachers, and state policymakers should work in concert to bridge the gap between a child's prekindergarten education and experiences and kindergarten.

Quite frankly, every school in America—preschool and kindergarten, elementary, secondary, and postsecondary—should be a place where students learn to investigate, discover, and create. And schools should teach the youngest and the oldest students to think critically, solve problems, analyze, synthesize, reflect, and work collaboratively in ways appropriate to their age. Exploring, wondering, examining, creating, questioning, and investigating are natural dispositions in children—all children—and they should be encouraged and regarded as the building blocks for learning—lifelong learning.

WHAT STATES ARE DOING

The following is a sampler of what states are doing in the area of school readiness. What it demonstrates is that Missouri, for instance, felt its citizens needed a good start to their young lives and said so in a policy. This policy was in turn interpreted by a program. Policies have varying slants—early involvement and parent programs, at-risk youth, transition and continuity and interagency collaboration—but in some fashion they all mean preparing children and their parents for a successful learning experience.

Early Involvement and Parent Programs

Missouri has taken school readiness to heart with its successful Parents as Teachers program (PAT). Begun in 1981, PAT provides a variety of services for parents including information on child development before and after birth, child education, and sensory development screening, home visits, monthly parent meetings, and a Parent Resource Center for learning materials and child care. The program has been replicated in Oregon, Texas, and Ohio; it begins in the third trimester of pregnancy and continues until the child is three-years-old.

Minnesota has a program similar to Missouri's, begun in 1974, called the Early Childhood Family Education program (ECFE). It is based on the premise that parents are the child's first and most important teachers and that the early years are a critical stage in life. The goal of ECFE is to enhance and support the competence of parents guiding their children from birth to kindergarten.

At-Risk Youth

Indiana has targeted $2 million of a $22 million budget for at-risk youth to fund the preschool portion of a broader program that includes full-day kindergarten, remediation, tutoring, parent and community involvement, expanded use of school counselors, individualized programs, and model alternative programs.

South Carolina took its Education Improvement Act of 1984 one step

ECS

further to specifically include at-risk four-year-olds. Target 2000 expands the state's early childhood development program as well as its parent education program. The state also created a task force of principals, teachers, and administrators to improve continuity in early childhood programs. Indiana, Iowa, Ohio, Vermont, and Virginia also have targeted programs to serve children at risk. West Virginia requires local school boards to develop a coordinated interagency service plan for at-risk youth from birth through age five.

Transition and Continuity

In Michigan, the Standards of Quality and Curriculum Guidelines help local agencies assess existing prekindergarten programs and guide in the design of new programs. The guidelines address class size, teacher-pupil ratio, developmentally appropriate curriculum, staff training, and parent and community involvement. The governor also proposed that teams of social workers, health specialists, and other agency representatives relocate within schools.

New Jersey has established a task force of teachers, administrators, day care providers, and parents to address the issue of better continuity between the prekindergarten experience and kindergarten. The department of education focused on effective communication among all the players. The task force believes that both prekindergarten and kindergarten programs for at-risk three- and four-year-olds.

California created a diversified prekindergarten system called the Child Development Programs. These programs are operated at the local level by private agencies, school districts, cities, colleges, and other public agencies. All operate under the same regulations and guidelines. Services are comprehensive and include developmental activities, health and nutrition, parental involvement, staff development, and evaluation. Facilities have extended hours five days a week, year-round. The program also assesses family needs and makes referrals to appropriate agencies that can provide assistance.

Collaboration

North Dakota will initiate a program in January 1991 that will monitor children from birth to age five who are at risk of developmental delays. Interagency collaboration is a key component. Delaware created the position of coordinator of services for young children to facilitate intra-agency and interagency planning and delivery of services. Programs and services for young children and their families will be offered through a network of groups.

The New York Department of Education initiated a project involving 10 demonstration elementary schools in disadvantaged neighborhoods in New York City. The schools will serve as community centers for the provision of a wide range of education, social, and health services. The schools include a preschool and child-care component. Each community school plans to extend its hours to include evenings, weekends, and summer hours.

Alaska, Florida, Missouri, and Nebraska have single agencies that are responsible for the comprehensive needs of children ages 0-5, or formal policies covering comprehensive services.

THE FUNDAMENTAL QUESTION

Necessary as they are, early screenings and parental involvement, programs for at-risk children, transition and continuity between preschool and kindergarten, and interagency collaboration simply are not enough. Just as states must now ask, "Restructuring for what?" so too they must also ask, "Readiness for what?" Preschool children doing kindergarten work is a hollow reform; this is more parent- than child-focused and does not fully consider the developmental needs of children. What is it we want children to know and do? What will prepare children to be citizens in a democracy and workers in an increasingly diverse, global society? Preschool and kindergarten are the foundations upon which the remaining school years must rest, but they are also part of a much bigger vision of what we want in a society. This decade and the next century require a different set of attitudes, skills, and dispositions. School readiness policy must guide the vision.

REFERENCE

1. Shephard, L., and Smith, M. L. "Escalating Academic Demands in Kindergarten: Counterproductive Policies." Special issue. Programs for Four- and Five-Year-Olds. *Elementary School Journal.* Fall 1988.

IRA
International Reading Association

10. Trends and Strategies in Early Literacy Education

by **Lesley Mandel Morrow**, *1990-91 Chairperson, Reading/Language in Early Childhood Committee, IRA; Introduction by* **Dale Johnson, 1989-90 President**, *International Reading Association. IRA has a membership of 90,000, with headquarters at 800 Barksdale Road, Newark, Delaware 19714.*

INTRODUCTION

During the past 20 years, there has been a virtual explosion of information relevant to how young children learn language and literacy. Interest in children's language development and their early reading and writing has received special attention. Contemporary researchers have built upon the work of earlier scholars to create new paradigms for the instruction of young children. The new research has strong implications for changing some deep-rooted practices. Old notions that separated "pre-reading" and "pre-writing" from formal instruction have given way to theories that do not demarcate development.

The early years are no longer viewed merely as a period of readiness for reading and writing. Learning literacy is seen as a continuous process, beginning in infancy with exposure to oral language, written language in books and stories beginning in the home and extending to the school. Although preschoolers and kindergartners may not be literate in the skilled or conventional way that adults read, they have acquired some knowledge about literacy that must be acknowledged and has implications for instructional practice.

The focus on early literacy could not have occurred at a better time. Never before has there been more interest in the education of young children. More and more children are entering early education programs and more public schools have extended the range of their offerings to full-day kindergarten and programs for four-year-olds. Accompanying the growing interest, there is the discussion and concern about what constitutes the best possible programs for these young children. Since literacy remains a top priority at all levels of education, it is not surprising to find that much of the discussion and concern is focused on oral language, reading, and writing development.

The International Reading Association is playing a major role in trying to make known the new research and the implications for instruction to the educational community through its conferences, publications, and a published statement on Literacy Development and Pre-First Grade.

—Dale Johnson

Not too many years ago, if four-year-old Tiffany had run excitedly up to you in your preschool classroom, clutching a paper full of scribbles and drawings she had produced for her grandmother, most professional observers would have considered the incident charming and perhaps even promising in what it said about Tiffany's interests and motivation. Few, however, would have been willing to accept the act as a vital, central accomplishment in literacy development. Tiffany's "drawings" were at best rudimentary, and the "captions" or "text" illegible to the adult, even though seen from a distance the scribbles somewhat resembled letter-like forms.

Today, given the same incident, we can be quite sure that Tiffany is demonstrating rather remarkable literacy development and awareness. Even though her writing is not yet conventional and she cannot read in the traditional sense of reading, she apparently knows the relationship between writing and reading, the difference between print and pictures, and the distinctive nature of all three literary elements. Her scribbles tend to go from left to right. The story she "reads" to you from the paper has something to do with her illustration.

EMERGENT LITERACY

Perspectives widely accepted in theory and documented in research in recent years focus on Tiffany's accomplishments as *emergent literacy behavior*: the demonstration of a young child's knowledge of and skills in literacy, whether or not the immediate evidence appears thoroughly conventional. Tiffany has used several different forms of language to achieve a specific and realistic purpose—communication with her grandmother by paper and ink (or graphite or crayon). She has done so within a social context, and has been actively involved throughout. Such performance is to be rewarded and encouraged.

Over the past decade, emergent literacy has been defined by a number of its characteristics and by certain basic assumptions that support them:

1. Literacy development vastly precedes formal school instruction. Some maintain it begins as early as birth.
2. Children build and bring to school with them early reading and writing experiences based on knowledge they have already acquired.
3. Listening, speaking, reading, and writing are interrelated and overlap during a child's early development.
4. Literacy develops best when it is based on functional, purposeful experiences.
5. Children develop literacy in social settings, especially in interaction with adults and peers.
6. Although emergent literacy can be described in generalized "stages," individual children vary widely in exhibiting its characteristics. There is no universal pattern of development.
7. Adults serve as models for literacy behavior by demonstrating their own use of books and print. (12)

Emergent literacy, first used as a term by Marie Clay (3), should not be confused with older, more conventional concepts often connected with early childhood language development and education. Emergent literacy is *not* tantamount to pre-reading or reading readiness, both of which were traditionally seen as precursors to reading. Indeed, reading readiness implies that children know little about literacy before coming to school. Prescribed "reading readiness" skills are taught in the questionable belief that all children arrive in preschool or kindergarten at similar levels of development. Furthermore, reading readiness skills focus on relatively abstract and isolated activities rather than on the holistic act of reading. Many of those activities thus yield little meaning or function to the child (26).

In contrast, Teale (25) sees emergent literacy developing through a child's active involvement in reading activities that are mediated by "more literate others," social interaction being one significant factor. Such literacy events not only teach a child the conventions and societal function of reading, but also couple reading with enjoyment and satisfaction, increasing the child's motivation toward further literacy activity and development. Vygotsky's (27) more general theory of intellectual development holds that all higher mental functions are internalized social relationships.

In discussion (11) the adult-child reading interactions in homes, where much of the research on emergent literacy began, Holdaway notes:

> The way in which supportive adults are induced by affection and common sense to intervene in the development of their children proves upon close examination to embody the most sound principles of teaching. Rather than provide verbal instructions about how a skill should be carried out, the parent sets up an emulative model of the skill in operation and induces activity in the child which approximates towards use of the skill. The first attempts of the child are to do something that is like the skill he wishes to emulate. This activity is then "shaped" or refined by immediate rewards. . . (p. 22)

Four processes can be seen at work in the young child's literacy development:

- observation—being read to, for example, or seeing adults themselves read and write;
- collaboration—interaction with another person, usually older, who provides encouragement, motivation, and help;
- practice—trying out what has been learned role playing, for instance or using invented spelling—without direction or adult observation;
- performance—sharing what has been learned and seeking approval from adults who are supportive and interested. Others have supported views similar to Holdaway's. (1,2)

IMPLICATIONS FOR PRACTICE

Homes in which emergent literacy seems to develop best generally support literacy involvement, both through activities and atmosphere. They tend to be rich in materials for reading and writing: books, magazines and newspapers, pencils, markers, and writing paper. Adults themselves regularly engage in literacy activities, many of which relate to everyday functions and purposes: e.g., writing grocery lists, reading newspapers, accepting information from school or job, and using recipes for cooking. They draw on environmental print, print that is part of the normal surroundings: cereal boxes. fast-food logos, traffic signs. Literacy experiences are often social activities: adults and children share books they have read, talk to each other, and communicate in writing (2, 6, 18, 24). Much of what we know about those homes can be translated into school practice.

Library Corner. Teachers can dramatically emphasize a rich literacy environment in the classroom by establishing and maintaining a library corner and a writing center, with abundant materials in each for reading, writing, and oral language activities, integrated as much as possible with content area teaching and designed to emulate functional life experiences.

Library corners offer children immediate access to books and increase their participation in literacy activities (16). Involve children in designing and managing the library corner. Let them develop rules for its use and keep it neat and orderly (15). Define the area clearly, making it inviting and comfortable, but also affording privacy. Furnish it with pillows, a rocking chair, a rug, a table and chairs at which children can use headsets to listen to taped stories, and an oversized carton in which children can curl up and enjoy books. Provide story props: a felt board and story characters, roll movies, stuffed animals.

House most books on regular shelves, but feature some on open-face shelves. Stock five to eight books at three or four different grade levels. Include a variety: picture storybooks, fables, fairy tales, informational books, magazines, and poetry. Stock multiple copies of popular books and replace about 25 books very two weeks, either with new books or by recycling favorites.

Code books so that children learn that regular libraries are organized systematically for easy access. Devise an easy checkout system so books can be borrowed for use at home.

Writing Center. A classroom writing center requires a table and chairs, felt markers, crayons, pencils, and unlined paper in a variety of sizes, kinds, and colors, and, if available, a typewriter or word processor and a tape recorder for children's story dictation. Book-making materials are essential. Include a punch, a stapler, and construction paper. Provide a separate writing folder for each child's work. Key blank books to special occasions and welcome children's contributions to them. Position an author's chair from which children can read their work to others. Place mailboxes, stationery, and envelopes for message exchange. Display children's writing on a bulletin board (19).

Play Areas. Involve children in literacy activities in other classroom areas as well. Design the dramatic play or block area, for instance, as a doctor's office. Provide prescription pads, patient record forms, appointment cards, an address and phone book, a telephone, good health posters and pamphlets, and magazines for the waiting room—all materials to encourage literacy activity (23).

Environmental Print. Many preschoolers can already read road signs, food labels, and logos, suggesting how important it can be to provide and use environmental print in classrooms (9). Identify learning centers and each child's cubby with labels. Post daily routines, helper charts, attendance charts, news bulletins about classroom events, new words from units of instruction with illustrations next to them.

Story Reading. Research indicates that reading to children increases their interest in learning to read, enhances background information and sense of story structure, familiarizes them with differences between written and oral language, and helps them recognize that printed words have sounds and that print carries meaning. Listening to well-structured stories develops comprehension and language skills. Children learn how to handle a book, become sensitive to left-to-right and front-to-back directionality, recognize that stories have beginnings, middles, and ends, and develop the concept of authorship (4, 7, 10, 13, 20, 21).

Children's active participation accounts for much of the value in such reading events; adult and children cooperatively construct meaning as they pause to comment and respond during the reading, providing the child direct channels for information (17). The warmth that accompanies storybook reading also lasts beyond the experience as children and teachers mutually develop special relationships with stories. When things are not going well in the classroom, more than one teacher *or* child has said, "I guess we are having a terrible horrible no good very bad day," quoting from Judith Viorst's book with a similar title and refrain.

DLTA. A Directed Listening-Thinking Activity (DLTA) helps children develop an organizational framework that can be internalized through frequent use and transferred when new material is presented. It follows certain steps:

1. Preparation for listening. Provide background information and ask children to predict what might happen. Set a specific goal for listening, such as "Try to remember which parts of the story you like best."
2. Read the story. Use expression, show illustrations, and pause at natural breaks for reactions, comments, or questions.
3. Discuss the story. Focus on the original objective. Let children relate the story to their own experiences. Prompt and reinforce children by modeling or "scaffolding" responses so they will know how to respond next time—for instance, "Those animals weren't very helpful to the little red hen, were they?"

Shared Book Experiences. One way to stimulate the active participation of children in reading is to pause before predictable phrases, letting them fill them in—for instance, "Are you my *MOTHER* ?" from P. D. Eastman's book of that title. A shared book experience with a big book (about 24 x 36 inches in size) is ideal for the purpose. Mount it on an easel and place it so that all the children can see the words and pictures as the story is read. Use a pointer during the reading to reinforce left-to-right progression and the correspondence of spoken and written words.

Repeated Readings. Beyond the pleasure of familiarity, children's responses to repeated stories become more sophisticated as they interpret, predict, and associate events in such stories to real life. Children begin to narrate familiar stories with the teacher's reading and often begin to focus on elements of print, asking names of letters and words, for instance.

Retelling. Retelling stories engages children in holistic comprehension and organization of thought and allows for personalization. With practice, children learn to introduce a story with its setting, recount its theme, outline its plot episodes, and conclude with its resolution. Through retelling, children demonstrate comprehension of story details and sequence, adding inferences and interpretation as well (18). To encourage students in initial retellings, use verbal prompts, felt boards with story characters, roll movies, and puppets (14).

Writing Experiences. Even when young children are still scribble writing, they can develop writing skills by participating in functional, purposeful activities. Pen-pal programs are one example, initiated with another class or with children in another building. Let children participate in writing invitations for parent visitation, thank-you notes to guest speakers and other classroom visitors, and greeting cards for special occasions. Ask them to collect their "Very Own Words" on 3 x 5 index cards, stored in file boxes or coffee cans—words they decide individually that they want, based on home or school experiences. Initiate journal writing for sharing thoughts, even if the earliest journals contain drawings rather than words. Use children's literature to motivate writing. For example, suggest they write their own stories about the central character in such a series as Freeman's *Corduroy* books (18).

HOLISTIC DEVELOPMENT

Generally, ideas offered here in the context of promoting emergent literacy also reflect earlier theories and philosophies that favor child-centered classrooms (See Froebel [8]; Pestalozzi in Rusk and Scotland [22]; Dewey [5]). Research in emergent literacy not only supports those theories, but also targets real promise for programmatic literacy development in early childhood by approaching that development holistically and meaningfully rather than through skill exercises abstracted from the total act.

Instructional strategies described here allow the child to observe the teacher and other children in literacy activities. They encourage collaboration between teacher and children in social contexts where they cooperatively construct meaning about print as they negotiate and mediate their verbal exchanges about stories they have heard and writing they have done. Children can be actively involved in the library corner, writing center, or play areas as they practice skills they have learned. Finally, they perform or share what they have done with others, reading their stories to classmates while sitting in the author's chair, or retelling stories they have heard.

While such practices are not totally new, research has demonstrated that they are not simply frills and rewards. They are very appropriate for developing literacy in the early years.

NOTE

This material was adapted in part from "New Perspectives in Early Literacy," by Lesley Mandel Morrow, published in *The Reading Instruction Journal*, Winter 1989.

REFERENCES

1. Calkins, L. M. *Lessons from a Child: On the Teaching and Learning of Writing*. Portsmouth, N.H.: Heinemann, 1983.
2. Clark, M. M. *Young Fluent Readers*. London: Heinemann, 1976.
3. Clay, M. M. "Emergent Reading Behavior." Ph.D. diss., University of Auckland, New Zealand, 1966.
4. Cohen, D. "The Effects of Literature on Vocabulary and Reading Achievement." *Elementary English* 45 (1968): 209-13, 217.
5. Dewey, J. *Democracy and Education*. New York: Free Press, 1966.
6. Durkin, D. *Children Who Read Early*. New York: Teachers College Press, 1966.
7. Feitelson, D.; Kita, B.; and Goldstein, Z. "Effects of Listening to Series Stories on First Grader's Comprehension and Use of Language." *Research in the Teaching of English* 20 (1986): 339-56.

8. Froebel, F. *The Education of Man.* Clifton, N.J.: Augustus, Kelly, 1974.
9. Goodman, Y. "The Development of Initial Literacy." In *Awakening to Literacy*, edited by H. Goleman, A. Oberg, and F. Smith, 102-9. Portsmouth, N.H.: Heinemann, 1984.
10. Hoffman, S. J. "Preschool Reading Related Behaviors: A Parent Diary." Ph.D. diss., University of Pennsylvania, 1982.
11. Holdaway, D. *The Foundations of Literacy.* Sydney: Ashton Scholastic, 1979.
12. International Reading Association. *Literacy Development and Pre-First Grade.* Newark, Del.: IRA, 1985.
13. Mason, J., and Au, K. *Reading Instruction for Today.* Glenview, Ill.: Scott, Foresman, 1986.
14. Morrow, L. M. *Supertips for Storytelling.* New York: Scholastic, Instructor Books, 1981.
15. _____. *Promoting Voluntary Reading in School and Home.* Bloomington, Ind.: Phi Delta Kappa Educational Foundation, 1985.
16. _____. "Promoting Voluntary Reading: The Effects of an Inner City Program in Summer Day Care Centers." *The Reading Teacher* 41 (1987): 266-74.
17. _____. "Young Children's Responses to One-to-One Story Readings in School Settings." *Reading Research Quarterly* 23, no. 1 (1988): 89-107.
18. _____. *Literacy Development in the Early Years: Helping Children Read and Write.* Englewood Cliffs, N.J.: Prentice Hall, 1989.
19. _____. "Preparing the Physical Design of the Classroom to Promote Literacy." In *Emerging Literacy: Young Children Learn to Read and Write*, edited by D. Strickland and L. M. Morrow. Newark, Del.: International Reading Association, 1989.
20. Ninio, A. "Picture Book Reading in Mother-Infant Dyads Belonging to Two Subgroups in Israel." *Child Development* 51 (1980): 587-90.
21. Pellegrini, A., and Galda, L. "The Effects of Thematic Fantasy Play Training on the Development of Children's Story Comprehension." *American Educational Research Journal* 19 (1982): 443-52.
22. Rusk, R., and Scotland, J. *Doctrines of the Great Educators.* New York: St. Martin's Press, 1979.
23. Schickedanz, J. *More Than ABC's: The Early Stages of Reading and Writing.* Washington, D.C.: National Association for the Education of Young Children, 1986.
24. Teale, W. "Positive Environments for Learning to Read: What Studies of Early Readers Tell Us." *Language Arts* 55 (1978): 922-32.

25. _____. "Toward a Theory of How Children Learn to Read and Write Naturally." *Language Arts* 59 (1982): 555-70.
26. Teale, W., and Sulzby, E. "Emergent Literacy as a Perspective for Looking at How Children Become Writers and Readers." In *Emergent Literacy: Writing and Reading*, edited by W. H. Teale and E. Sulzby, vii-xxv. Norwood, N.J.: Ablex, 1986.
27. Vygotsky, L. S. *Mind in Society.* Cambridge: Harvard University Press, 1978.

NABSE

National Alliance of Black School Educators

11. The Rhetoric of Early Childhood Education Must Be Replaced by Decisive Action

J. Jerome Harris, 1989-91 President, *National Alliance of Black School Educators. NABSE has a membership of 4,000, with headquarters at 2816 Georgia Avenue, N.W., Washington, DC 20001.*

That America's early childhood education deliberations continue, void of any visible and profound resolve to act with sustained commitment and comprehensive determination, strikes me as blind, willful negligence. There has never been a time in the life of the American Public School when we have not known all we needed to know in order to teach all those whom we chose to teach. We know how to successfully educate our children. The fact that we have not done so apparently revolves around some basic questions and fundamental issues. The questions are numerous. The critical issues: it is not the child; performance factors are under the school's control; we cannot blame the family. There are pathways to be taken.

It is absurd that arguments persist against the significance of early childhood education in the educational journey of our children. The plethora of research has repeatedly set forth the merits. Early childhood development works, it is productive, it is lasting and far more economical than childhood incarceration.

Historical chronicles and research findings by noted early childhood respectables have given us cause for confidence and decisiveness. It is right and just to provide early education for this nation's young children. From Piaget (14, 15) to Biber (1, 2); and more recently, from Feeney (9) to Hilliard (10), to Edelman (7), and Comer (4, 5); the list goes on. The tireless work of these and other dedicated advocates for quality early education serves as a warning signal. The health of a community can be measured by its success in educating *all* of its children. The literature continues to call into question our true expressions of concern for our greatest resource, our children. To ignore the data makes dubious our enlightenment, our pedagogical rationalism, our intellectual discernment. Problems with the education of children are an indication of fundamental deficiencies in the adult community.

The educational and legislative constituency of this country has never demonstrated a true understanding nor taken seriously the adult importance and responsibility as the saving factor in shaping and nurturing the lives of young children. The incredible paradox of continued rhetoric about the urgent need and the failure to act, to mobilize resources, and to move unapologetically on behalf of young children is harsh, merciless, shortsighted.

Nowhere is that horrible historical neglect more blatantly visible than with the children of the poor. For this population, deficit conditions worsen, become more acute, and obviously deadly. When the suffering young are of African-American, or Black heritage, and poor, insensitivity and benign mediocrity seem to reign supreme. Unless many more safe, sincere, and beneficial programs such as Head Start and Follow Through are expanded, amelioration and long-term cure will continue to mimic folly and empty oration. The crisis must be addressed.

If downhill indifference continues to consume us, if we do not soon confront and ably manage the issues, this nation will know no peace. We must answer the questions, and mandate solid, purposeful equitable programs or the expensive price of ignorance will devastate any semblance of educational reconciliation. I want now, as president of the National Alliance of Black School Educators, to continue my discourse by posing some basic early childhood education questions, the critical issues, and offering some pathways to national survival.

THE QUESTIONS

Among decision makers, where are those who have the will, the conviction, and the stamina to act? In the absence of action, what will go on happening for this nation's children, especially those of African-American heritage? Shall we continue to doom these minds, these lives, these anxious hearts to the ranks of the already overwhelming statistics of prisoners, street beggars, the homeless, the family-shorn wanderers, or those relegated to contrived invisibility? Shall these lost young souls exist, starkly unequipped to function productively in a universe that is

Perspectives on Early Childhood Education

increasingly complex, technological, competitive, international, and multicultural?

Can we afford to continue to allow young children to teeter on the icy edges of anything less than full intellectual and cultural development? I think not. Young children, poor, Black young children, and yes, all young children, must begin, right now, to be born into a world influenced, shaped, planned, and ordered by caring, knowing, educationally sane adults.

These adults must be accepting of the inalienable rights of young children. These adults must feel and share a developmental and moral imperative to guarantee every young child a public, safe, academic, aesthetically and culturally rich and rewarding educational agenda. In 1959, the United Nations published, for the world to embrace, the *Declaration of the Rights of the Child*. Our children are in need of our recognition and establishment of the rights of every child as requirements, supported by standards.

DECLARATION OF THE RIGHTS OF THE CHILD

I. All children, without any exception whatsoever, shall be entitled to these rights, without distinction or discrimination on account of race, colour, sex, language, religion, political or other opinion, national or social origin, property, birth or other status, whether of himself or herself or of his or her family.

II. The child shall enjoy special protection and shall be given opportunities and facilities, by law and by other means, to enable him or her to develop physically, mentally, morally, spiritually, and socially in a healthy and normal manner and in conditions of freedom and dignity.

III. The child shall be entitled from his or her birth to a name and a nationality.

IV. The child shall enjoy the benefits of social security. He or she shall be entitled to grow and develop in health; to this end, special care and protection shall be provided both to him or her and to his or her mother, including adequate pre-natal and post-natal care. The child shall have the right to adequate nutrition, housing, recreation, and medical services.

V. The child who is physically, mentally, or socially handicapped shall be given the special treatment, education, and care required by his or her particular condition.

VI. He or she shall, wherever possible, grow up in the care and under the responsibility of his or her parents, and in any case in an atmosphere of affection and moral and material security; a child of tender years shall not, save in exceptional circumstances, be separated from his or her mother.

VII. The child is entitled to receive education, which shall be free and compulsory, at least in the elementary stages.

VIII. The child shall in all circumstances be among the first to receive protection and relief.

IX. The child shall be protected against all forms of neglect, cruelty, and exploitation.

X. The child shall be protected from practices which may foster racial, religious, and any other form of discrimination.

(United Nations, 1959)

What kind of a people can go on losing a great percentage of its children? Why do we not recognize that we must invest in our children? The costs are formidable of continuous failure to provide our children with the best possible public education. Can we go on lending truth to the universal belief that America relegates its young children to entrenched, provincialistic educational inadequacies? Do we really have the desire to expand the abilities of our children to compete in world challenges? Strategies for reformation of thought and behaviors must be refocused on those paradigms that will compel us and our children to move toward actions that result in the greatest good for all.

Unless this nation takes up the cause of children, addresses the issues, and finds effective solutions, the talents of millions of children will be unused. Such a nation cannot continue to position itself as world leader. If Nicaragua can hold a democratic election and witness one of the most monumental upsets in world politics; if Russia's president Gorbachev can give the world *glasnost* and *perestroika*; if the Berlin wall can crumble; if East and West Germany can unite; then certainly we in America can design and support an educational system where all children can learn.

CRITICAL ISSUE ONE: IT IS NOT THE CHILD

The Committee for Economic Development (6) reports:

> As a group, children are now the poorest segment of the nation's population. They are nearly seven times as likely to be poor as those over 65. Over 20 percent of all children under 18 currently live in families whose incomes fall below the poverty line, and 25 percent of all children under six are now living in poverty. Although almost two-thirds of all poor children are white, both Blacks and Hispanics are much more likely to be poor; 43 percent of Black and 40 percent of Hispanic children live in poverty. Black children are nearly three times as likely to live in poverty as white children, and the average Black child can expect to spend five of the first 15 years of childhood in an impoverished home.

This tragic condition demands concerted actions by family, school, church, industry, business, the general community. We must hear the message. We can no longer blame the child. It is ours to play a direct role in forging remedies that will cure the erroneous posture that we do not need to concentrate extensive energies and resouces on teaching young children how to learn, how to think critically, how to solve problems, and how to manage themselves and the world's resources.

It is factual. Some of our children most in need of early childhood nurturing see schools as places of fear and danger; places to be put down; places of insecurity; places of heightened self-consciousness, and infertile grounds for total development. These impressions must be eradicated. Short- and long-range goals must be designed and followed for educational quality, excellence, relevancy, and humane but managed instructional experiences.

Persons who work in these learning places must be open-minded, well-prepared, caring, trainable, thinking, global-minded individuals. They should be people who understand the range of human growth and development possibilities. They must enter the field of early childhood development because they have their eyes on the rewards that come with living effective schooling. In such an atmosphere, our young children will grow, flourish, and blossom into realizing the fullest extensions of themselves. In an article entitled "Why They Excel" (3), Asian parents maintain that the reason their children success in school is "hard work," while Americans say, "it's talent."

CRITICAL ISSUE TWO: DIFFERENCES IN PUPIL PERFORMANCE ATTRIBUTED TO FACTORS UNDER THE SCHOOL'S CONTROL

> If we imbue them with knowledge, with love, and a sense of justice, we write on those tablets something that will affect and brighten all humanity.
>
> —Ruth Love (12)

The American public school system continues to function on the belief that children enter our schools with innate abilities to learn. As students enter the public schools, they tend to be placed in one of three categories: red birds, robins, blue jays, etc. But the truth is, once students are placed in the red bird group, they often remain red birds—from kindergarten through graduation. Our schools place students in these categories because the students are perceived to have innate abilities; failure by the child to put those abilities to work spells failure. How often have you heard the declaration, "These children just do not try . . ." This absolves us as educators from having any negative feelings when our students fail. But failure merely confirms the previous assumption. We simply cannot afford the damnation associated with continuing to fail large numbers of our children. Our children do want to learn; they are teachable. Children of African-American heritage bear an extra burden when failure becomes real in their lives.

Failure in early childhood education may relegate the Black child to perpetual family scorn. He or she may become an object of ridicule for "flunking out of kindergarten." The resulting and lasting conditions may be transferred to the child's perception of self as "poor," "worthless," "dumb."

What is needed is a different way to look at our inner-city early childhood students. We need to believe and demonstrate the belief that "All Children Can Learn" and that this learning will most likely take place if we can get our children to make an extra effort. Research shows that students will make an extra effort if their confidence is high. Greater confidence leads to improved learning, the Cycle of Success (see Figure

2). The cycle of success evolves from the Efficacy Model (Figure 1). This model is most clearly explained in the works of Jeff Howard and Associates.

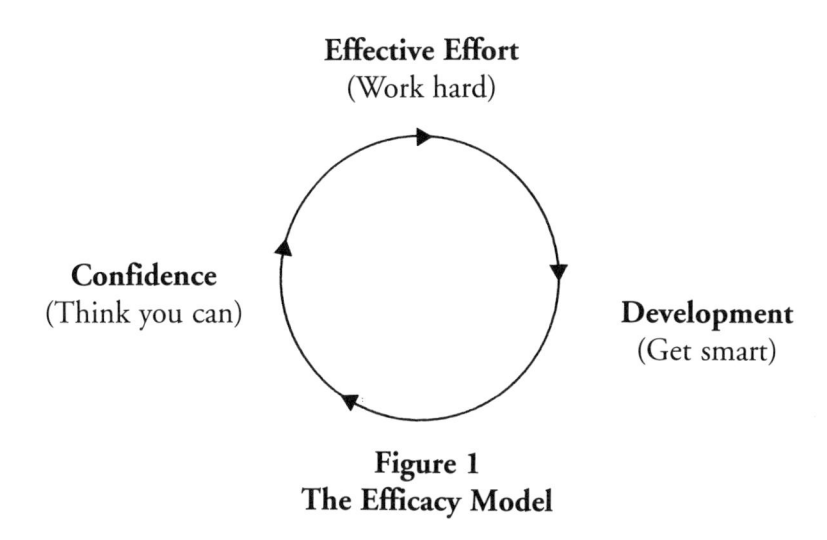

Effective Effort
(Work hard)

Confidence
(Think you can)

Development
(Get smart)

Figure 1
The Efficacy Model

Howard writes, in the *Harvard Educational Review* (13): "Efficacy works to plant an alternative idea in the child's mind: 'If I work hard enough, I can get smart' . . ." The Efficacy Model of intellectual development is based on motivation. It places emphasis on the process of development and returns some measure of control to the child.

Reformation of thinking must move us away from the traditional American model that tends to limit the confidence and extra effort of our children. Howard (11) believes the health of a community can be measured by its success in developing all of its children. He urges us to understand and act upon the belief that the intellectual development of our children is our responsibility; it is the key to rescuing them from the high possibility of certain death. It is the building of confidence, effort, and development. Each is interrelated to the other. Therefore, we must organize to ensure that our public schools are effective and that those effective schools consciously provide for children planned, well-managed experiences that will move them through *"the cycle of success"* (Figure 2) as opposed to the *"cycle of failure"* (Figure 3).

The cycle of success, buoyed, surrounded, and proffered by loving, knowledgeable humane teachers will invite children into realms of high academic achievement and enhanced self-concept.

Howard supports the chorus of voices who proclaim that our children who are in the low performance categories do not want to be there. And, if we believe them, and work on removing children from these lowest levels of achievement, if we know what we are doing, and if we set positive expectations, from kindergarten through high school graduation, our children will get out of the cycle of failure. I believe these conscious efforts must have their genesis in early childhood education.

CRITICAL ISSUE THREE: FAMILY IS THE PRINCIPAL DETERMINANT AS TO WHETHER OR NOT PUPILS WILL DO WELL IN SCHOOL—THUS ABSOLVING EDUCATORS OF THEIR PROFESSIONAL RESPONSIBILITIES TO BE INSTRUCTIONALLY EFFECTIVE

> How many effective schools will you have to see to be persuaded of the educability of all children?
>
> —Ron Edmonds (8)

No one can offer a convincing argument against the significance of the role of the family in contributing to the total well-being of the child. However, differences in types and depth of intellectual experiences that families can offer their young offspring may vary from many to few. Children from different family settings will come to the formal school setting with a kaleidoscope or patchwork of preparation for learning. But that is not the guiding principle. Nor should it be the determiner of planned, sequential programs. Once children enter school, their further enrichment and learning become ours to manage.

No family experience can, or should, be expected to substitute for effectively functioning school life. There should be no dissonance between home and school. One should compliment the other. Every child brings some experiential background into the school setting. As

STUDENTS IN EFFECTIVE SCHOOLS EXPERIENCE

THE CYCLE OF SUCCESS

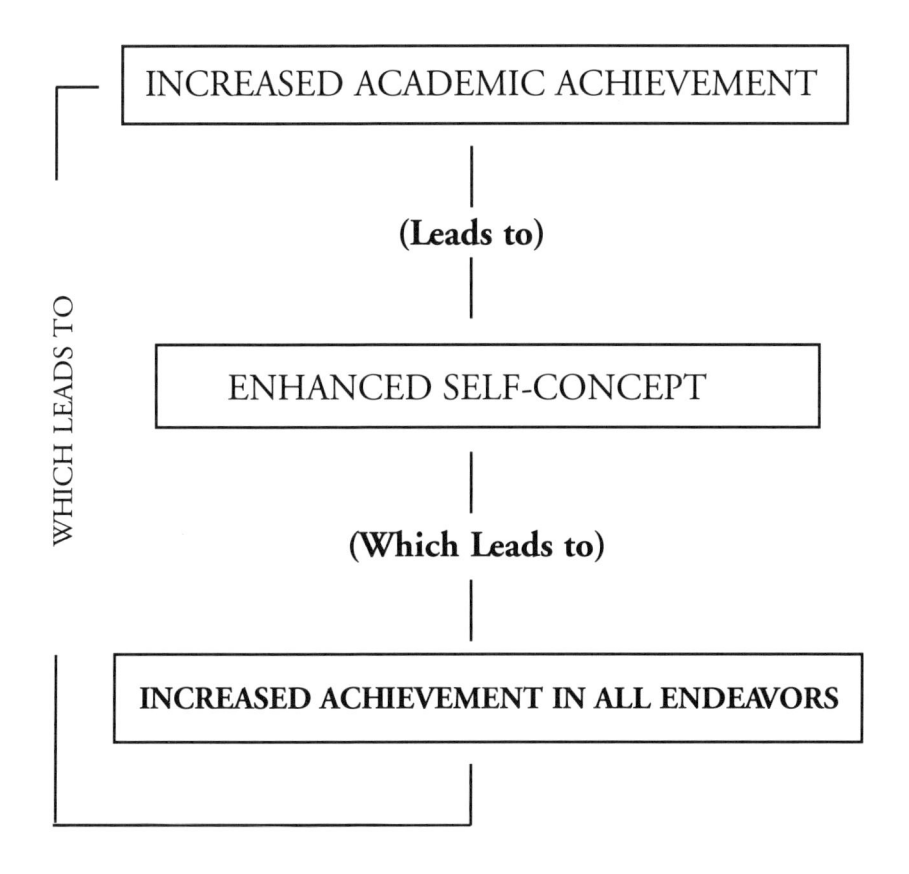

```
            ┌─── INCREASED ACADEMIC ACHIEVEMENT ───┐
            │                    │                 │
            │                (Leads to)            │
   WHICH    │                    │                 │
   LEADS    │         ENHANCED SELF-CONCEPT        │
   TO       │                    │                 │
            │              (Which Leads to)        │
            │                    │                 │
            └─── INCREASED ACHIEVEMENT IN ALL ENDEAVORS ───┘
```

Figure 2
The Cycle of Success

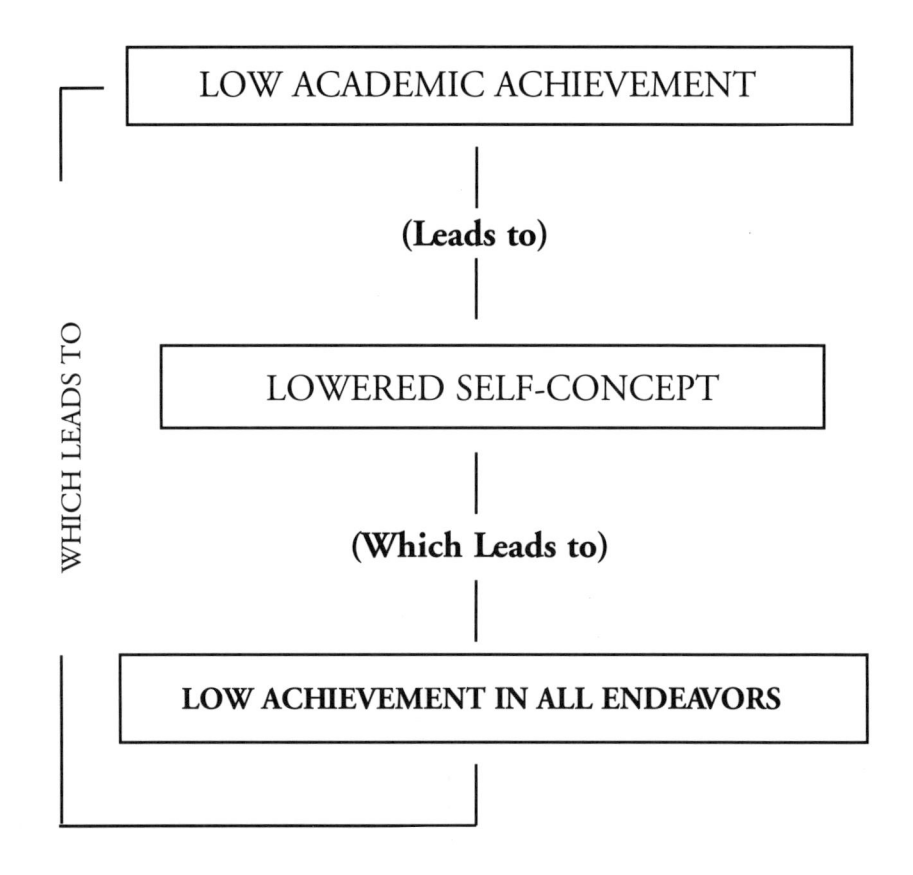

```
            ┌─────────────────────────────────────┐
          ┌─│     LOW ACADEMIC ACHIEVEMENT        │
          │ └─────────────────────────────────────┘
          │                    │
          │               (Leads to)
          │                    │
          │ ┌─────────────────────────────────────┐
  WHICH   │ │       LOWERED SELF-CONCEPT          │
  LEADS   │ └─────────────────────────────────────┘
   TO     │                    │
          │              (Which Leads to)
          │                    │
          │ ┌─────────────────────────────────────┐
          │ │   LOW ACHIEVEMENT IN ALL ENDEAVORS  │
          │ └─────────────────────────────────────┘
          └────────────────────┘
```

Figure 3
The Cycle of Failure

Perspectives on Early Childhood Education

educators of all the children, we ought to build the bridges that will help children tread smoothly across the pathways between home and school.

Successful educators of young children deserve every accolade. If successful, they have shared in and managed the child's instruction, socialization, sometimes character building, and always the stimulation of love for school. These are the admirable educators who have looked the part, felt the part, behaved the part; all of which translates into what is best for children. They are the occupied ones; the ones who strive daily to welcome young children into an environment so compatible with what the young child needs to know and be able to do that they have no time for blaming. They are the ones consumed by professional pride and intrinsic persistence in preparing young children to function in an increasingly complex universe. As educators of this nation's children, we cannot be absolved from this charge.

Every young child who enters any preschool or kindergarten classroom should enter into an arena of learning built upon a foundation where quality, standards, values, high expectations, and demands for excellence in performance and total development can never be questioned.

Asa G. Hilliard, III (10) reminds us that early childhood care is just as important as later schooling and must be supported on both a universal and a high-quality basis. He goes on to tell us that high-quality child care comes from high-quality people. Then, he raises a soul-wrenching question:

> Is there anyone in our profession who really needs more years of research and experience to discover that a high-quality environment for children is one in which—
>
> - children are well nourished,
> - children are healthy,
> - children are safe,
> - children have adequate space,
> - children have ample materials and equipment for learning,
> - staff are trained in child development and teaching methods,
> - there is good planning and organization, and
> - strong links to parents are maintained?

Hilliard continues by restating that talk has gone on for some time, that we cannot wait until children are adults to treat them as human beings.

Talk must be transformed into action. He further indicates that children will never become comfortable with their own feelings and spirituality if they are ignored in their early years. And, I would add, nor will they survive.

The school must become, for young children, the realization of their most exhilarating educational fantasy. The school environment should be clean, beautiful, well-managed—an open invitation to artistic exploration, critical thinking, questioning, communicating, building humane relationships, and exchaning ideas.

It is important that we move rapidly away from the idiom: *Schools teach those they think they must and when they think they needn't, they don't.* Schools exist for children. Children do not have the age or the smarts or the position to access the political process; nor should they have to build their own advocacy. Children, therefore, are dependent upon adults to make their needs visible and heard until they are able to speak for themselves. Children, therefore, are dependent on us to take the pathways not yet taken.

THE PATHWAYS

> Issues of school reform have the potential of bypassing a segment of this nation's children: the poor, and the black and poor. Those of us who have the power to create, monitor, and sustain change must take a stand on behalf of children and their needs.

As the newly elected president of the National Alliance of Black School Educators (NABSE), I am imploring every member of NABSE and all others who consider themselves educators of all children to become more deeply involved in more than advocacy.

While advocacy is a key ingredient in the substance of change, investment of self in saving our children, early on, must become an internalized mandate, a driving force, a creative vision. We must no longer accept, without question and action, watered-down support for early childhood programs that lack the necessary energy, compassion, courage, understanding, and empowerment to move the obstacles. There is a war going on for the minds and bodies of our young children. Organizations such as NABSE and other caring groups must move deeply and swiftly to repel the assault. We must break the logjams. How?

Perspectives on Early Childhood Education

What are some pathways not consistently taken?

- *Leadership:* Educators who are skilled, prepared through study, research, experience, demonstrated caring, and determined advocacy must take substantive leadership in pushing ahead to develop within us unity, purpose, confidence, and the will to act. These are the inspired leaders. These are the ones who must access the political process and fight to destroy inadequacies in legislation, provincialism of thought, evilness of intent, and curriculum that is inappropriate for our young children. The leadership must be persuasive, expansive, professional, with styles replicable for continuity. These leaders must be trustworthy. They will have to be well developed and willing to take responsibility for turning back the clock, for correcting the miseducation of an African-American people. We must challenge the historians. Nowhere is this more crucial than in early childhood education. We must spread the word of our convictions. Our children need the guarantee that never again will African-American children, or any other ethnic group, be denied their self-esteem because they do not know who they are. Curriculum processes must be closely examined and where necessary changed. Monitoring and review must become a given; advisory committees must be commissioned; public relations and community liaisons must be structured. We must produce usable products, become world class consultants. The rest of the story must be told, the deficits must be countered. These maneuvers must be commanded by capable leaders. According to Howard (11), less developed people are unhealthy. We need leaders who are willing to change fundamental assumptions. The world must know the truth: *"All Children Can Learn"*—even the child of African-American heritage.

- *Expanded Voices:* We are living in an era driven mad by every known and unknown threat and danger to a life in which children will grow and thrive. Child abuse through drugs, incest, beatings, and more is choking the natural zest for life from too many children. Most parents want healthy, socially productive, and comfortable lives for their children. Therefore, planning, development, and implementation of programs of advocacy, outreach, inclusion, positive direction, and consequences must branch out into homes, churches, schools, child-serving and medical agencies, professional organizations, and colleges and universities. These groups must become partners, they must be intricately involved in the branching. Each group will have to take an active role to ensure that the most accurate information is steadily fed into revolving plans of action. Once sensible and useful goals and objectives are established, a systematic, regular reexamination and revision of curriculum must take shape and grow.

- *Reshaping the Curriculum:* There should be no debate about what learnings are best for today's young child. From the date of entry, a curriculum should be presented that is global, home-school focused, yet also nationally, regionally, and locally directed. The current world order should influence the curriculum. The youngest toddler entering preschool has most likely watched hours of television, has seen events and circumstances previously unknown. We should not be surprised that many children bring with them language, questions and thoughts about foreign countries, peoples of the universe, cultures, and ethnicity. The planned curriculum ought to provide many opportunities, daily, for interrelating home and school, history and culture. There should be interplay between the language, curiosity, and needs that the child brings to school and the curriculum that trained educators have built. The reshaped curriculum must be predicated upon what we know about how young children develop, grow, and learn. Such a curriculum will most likely cause us to cease and desist the practice of failing alarming numbers of our children—in kindergarten. The curriculum must seek to reach and teach all young children, first about who they are—their history, their culture—and then the broader universe of which each is a vital part.

The National Alliance of Black School Educators is standing on the threshold. We invite all to join us in saving the African-American child and all young children because quality and excellence in education are in the best interest of all children. Things are happening. In the cities of

Jackson, Mississippi, and Atlanta, Georgia; in the states of California, New York, and South Carolina, efforts are underway. NABSE, with its growing membership, can serve as the brain trust to move the nation to action. In our ranks we have classroom teachers, administrators, university professors, business leaders, and parents. Our challenge is to merge and emerge ourselves in seizing of the time.

In summary, our right frame of reference to advocate and build educational movements for young children must focus on taking on the critical issues through vibrant leadership, networking, and a thriving curriculum. The curriculum must say to young children: you are our most important resources; you are capable of brilliance; we will love you and we will teach you to love; we will respect your thoughts; and we will also demand of you academic excellence.

This nation will never know internal peace or sustained international influence until the educational welfare of all its children is given serious resourceful attention.

REFERENCES

1. Biber, B. "A Learning-Teaching Paradigm Integrating Intellectual and Affective Processes." In *Behavioral Sciences Frontiers in Education*, edited by Eli M. Bower and William G. Hollister. New York: John Wiley and Sons, 1967.
2. Biber, B., and Franklin, M. B. "The Relevance of Developmental and Psychodynamic Concepts to the Education of the Preschool Child." *Journal of the American Academy of Child Psychiatry*, January 1967.
3. Butterfield, F. "Why They Excel" *Parade Magazine* (January 21, 1990): 4-6.
4. Comer, J. P. "Education Is the Way Out and Up." *Ebony Magazine* (August 1987): 61-66.
5. ____. *Maggie's American Dream*. New York: New American Library, 1988.
6. Committee for Economic Development. *Investing in Our Children. Business and the Public Schools*. A statement by the Research and Policy Committee of the Committee for Economic Development. New York: CED, 1985.
7. Edelman, M. W. *Children and Congress*. Children's Defense Fund's Nonpartisan Congressional Voting Record of 1988. Washington, D.C.: CDF, 1988.

8. Edmonds, R. "Effective Schools for the Urban Poor." *Educational Leadership* 37 (1979): 15-17.
9. Feeney, S. et al. "Who Am I in the Lives of Children?" *An Introduction to Teaching Young Children*. Columbus, Ohio: Charles E. Merrill Co., 1983.
10. Hilliard, A. G., III. "What Is Quality Child Care?" In *What Is Quality Child Care* by the National Association for the Education of Young Children. Washington, D.C.: NAEYC, 1985.
11. Howard, J. "Advancing Intellectual Development of African-American Students: A Framework for Analysis and Action." Efficacy Institute, Inc. Lexington, Mass., July 12, 1989. Ron Edmonds Summer Academy, Atlanta.
12. Love, R. "Assessment and Effective Schools." In *Effective Schools: Critical Issues in the Education of Black Children*. Washington, D.C.: National Alliance of Black School Educators, Charles D. Moody Research Institute, 1989.
13. Moses, Kamii, Swap, and Howard. "The Algebra Project: Organizing in the Spirit of Ella." *Harvard Educational Review* 59, no. 4 (November 1989): 423-43.
14. Piaget, J. *Judgment and Reasoning in the Child*. M. Worden, trans. London: Routledge and Kegan Paul, 1928.
15. ____. *The Child's Concept of the World*. J. and A. Tomlinson, trans. New York: Harcourt, Brace, 1929.

NAEA
National Art Education Association

12. The Visual Arts in Early Childhood Education

by **David W. Baker, 1989-91 President,** *National Art Education Association. NAEA has a membership of 14,200, with headquarters at 1916 Association Drive, Reston, Virginia 22091.*

The very first contacts children have with the world they inherit are multisensory—through sounds, smells, touches, and sights. Of the senses, the one that is the most critical throughout their life is that of sight. As observations of young children continually suggest, and as years of formal study have confirmed, behaviors that relate to the sense of sight preoccupy them. Sight-related behaviors are at the center of all that they do and become the primary means by which they make emotional and conceptual "sense" out of perceived phenomena. Activities enhancing the sense of sight must then be given very serious attention when adults interact with children, and especially the youngest ones, in school settings.

MARKING AND KNOWING

The very first marks children make are simply accidental. They result from a kinetic impulse whereby children hit a resistant surface with a mark-making object they happen to be holding. At some point, most children recognize that they had something to do with the occurrence of the marks and they then engage in a compulsive process that eventually leads them to a mastery of the abstract, highly conceptual symbol systems that we call pictures, alphabets, and numbers. This remarkable process is essential to the growth and development of all children. It first allows them to act upon their immediate environment and, as their thoughtfulness about the relationship between mark-making acts and the possibilities that reside in assigning meanings to their markings increases, they acquire the power to shape ideas and share them with others. As their mark-making becomes picture-making, children literally create for themselves a way in which they can mediate reality; give meaning to the relationships they perceive in the world and the unique encounters they have with them; and communicate in an abstract manner with what they understand and feel.

From the first strikes very young children make on a surface, to the renderings that everyone makes in later life to reveal what they see, feel, and understand, to the study of artworks that embody the histories and maintain the memories of any given culture, art-like behaviors and the concomitant skills they promote make knowing possible. Picture-making and object-forming activities are increasingly understood to be the primary means with which preschool and primary grade children prepare themselves to master the conceptual sets, beliefs, values, and behaviors that make them functional within their culture. And to the extent that artistic behaviors are encouraged and supported during their early childhood years, their ability to function as knowledgeable adults is enhanced. This being the case, it is imperative that educators emphasize art-like behaviors and the content of the visual arts in the schooling of children. And this art emphasis is especially crucial in educational practices designed for early childhood.

ART EDUCATION AND CHILD ART

Over the past 200 years, educators have reflected on the nature and value of the image- and object-making behaviors of young children. Our understanding of what is commonly called child art is accelerating and as it does, several adjustments to how it is characterized and supported in school settings are called for.

It has long been a given that art-like behavior is pervasive in the human condition; we can readily observe its emergence in children soon after birth. The discernment of forms, colors, and space is among the earliest work of children; this evolves into a search for a way to more fully express what they know and feel. As they do so, they eventually discover how to use their innate image-making capabilities to communicate. In most instances this type of behavior manifests itself in ways that adults see as "artistic."

It must be understood by all who work with young children that they do not make "art" in the adult sense of the term—they do not consciously produce an object with aesthetic intent or according to a set of formalized standards. Young children make pictures and construct objects that have meanings, but these meanings are, with rare exception, very concrete. They are seldom purposefully "expressive." They just represent the attempts of children to translate their knowing of something they see into personal symbols and, eventually, a system of generalized symbols that make sense to others. It is only after they create their symbol system that they manipulate it to communicate abstract ideas about what they see, know, and feel. As children mature, and as they become more proficient at picture-making, their work reflects more and more consciously considered formal properties and unique expressive qualities. It then becomes more consistent with the creative behavior we recognize in adult artists.

Art educators have long demonstrated that art-related and artistically relevant instructional practices give vital nourishment to the natural processes that govern the growth and development of children. Moreover, they are increasingly sensitive to the fact that these practices must be developmentally appropriate—adult notions about art and adult-like behaviors cannot be imposed on young children without serious consequences. Thus, the methodological advances they are advocating emphasize the fact that those in early childhood are not artists by adult definitions of the term; characterizing their behaviors as "artistic" confuses thinking about developmentally sensitive instruction. More to the point, art educators are beginning to argue that they and teachers in general have the responsibility to provide young children with experience, guidance, and information that provide a strong *base* for artistic behavior as they mature.

The maturation process has now become a major issue for educators who are informed and sensitive to the critical need children have for support and guidance in the visual arts. The emphasis in art education is shifting from classical practices that tend to impose adult art forms and adult-like art activities on young children to those that establish a solid foundation from which artistic behaviors develop as they age. Thus, the need to give far greater attention to the way the field practices early childhood education is gaining enlightened responses from art educators who are beginning to offer long-overdue help to those working with preschool and primary grade children.

ARTFUL INSTRUCTION FOR A NEW CENTURY

As *developmentally appropriate practice* has become the catch-phrase for early childhood education, so it is coming to characterize methodologies espoused for this level of instruction by a growing number of art educators. And as it signals ways of thinking about their curricular practices, it is directing a reappraisal of what constitutes proper art instruction for preschoolers and primary grade children. While ideas and practices regarding the visual arts in early childhood education have yet to become fully formalized in theories and curricula, these ideas are accumulating and promise significant change in the way visual arts activities and content are presented to young children. Several significant trends are now obvious.

The importance of tactile/kinetic activity that supports the sense of sight is becoming recognized as a precondition to image-making and a support to cognitive development. Reaching, pushing, pulling, grabbing, stacking, touching, arranging, etc., contribute to very young children's spatial acuity, motor control, dimensional comprehension, and part-to-part relationships. These contributions are essential "knowings" that they exploit as they develop their mark-making skills—and move on to the abstract processes of image-making and, eventually, language and mathematics. Three dimensional activities, whether with clay, cardboard, paper, fabrics, found-materials, cannot be overstressed in the art instruction of young children.

Concurrent with building/forming/arranging activities is the compulsive need children have to explore and master their self-made marks. Drawing thus becomes an essential activity from the first time they repeat marks on purpose to their production of and response to images as mature adults. Since drawing activities and picture-related behaviors permeate all human modes of comprehension, communication, and expression, they simply must be central to all that we do with children in schools. Teachers must make drawing materials readily available, make children aware of how much they value their drawing activity, and make every effort to find ways to integrate picture-making and responding into all parts of the school environment. And this support for two-dimensional visual activities, so critical for the very young, must continue throughout their school life.

The home and school environment is also gaining importance as art educators gain insight into the ways young children grow and develop, especially in visual acuity and skill. Art educators are beginning to attend to the impact school and home environments have in early childhood education—and it is significant. At this level of development, children have a profound need for rich images to contemplate, rich and complex configurations of color, shapes, forms, textures, light, etc., to interact with, and information about how the things in their environment got there and what utility they may have. Reproductions of the painting, prints, and drawings of master artists are far more nourishing to children than are Snoopy-dog posters, Garfield-cat cutouts and cartoon-like images of objects, events, or stories. Likewise, various-sized blocks and containers, great piles of fabrics and garments, ropes/threads/strings/yarns, bins of found-objects and the like—rather than commercially produced games, building kits, or cartoon-character dolls—are invaluable sources of information and motivation. They are the stuff of information, manipulation, and imagination for preschoolers and primary grade children.

Methodologies insisting that young children acquire "proper" art vocabularies and master "correct" sequences of response to art and art-like phenomena are found wanting by a growing number of child-centered art educators. While satisfying to adults, formal processes of looking and talking about artful things intimidate and constrain young children. Thus, teachers who engage them in looking and talking activities that focus on art objects, places, and/or things should take care to ensure that such experiences *enhance* their responses. Rather than manipulating "right" responses with formal discussion schemes, teachers should simply urge children to share artistic encounters in any manner that seems appropriate to them on a regular basis. They should be aware that a pause, shrug, pointed finger, or roll of the eyes is as much a response as is a word stressed—"Its got pretty colors"—when one is six-years-old! The natural struggle to translate one form of experience into another—to go from sight to sound—takes skills that very young children cannot be expected to have. Looking and talking about artful stuff is important for young and old alike and it should occur often and be constantly encouraged—but it should not be forced.

Finally, of all that is known about developmental processes children undergo, there is overwhelming agreement that they learn in a manner that goes from general, holistic experiences to discrete comprehension and specific understandings. Consequently, instructional strategies that isolate subject matter and keep it disconnected from the daily routines and general experiences of very young children must be carefully considered. Arbitrary or poorly integrated art activity is not very productive at any level of instruction and it is most likely to be counterproductive at the preschool or primary level. Integrative experiences and information, then, should characterize the nature of art instruction for young children. Image- or object-making activities serve them best when they are a logical and natural aspect of other activities. Reading, writing, drawing, modeling, looking, and talking simply go together in childhood's world.

PARTNERS IN ART EDUCATION

Historically, schools have treated children as though they were simply unknowing young adults and, unfortunately, they too often continue to do so. If the schooling of young children is to evolve in positive ways, changes in caregivers' and teachers' values, beliefs, and skills must first occur. Consequently, as art and art-like instructional practices gain recognition as critical elements of an early childhood education, the field is looking closely at those who provide the care and instruction children in this age group require for healthy and productive growth. Several important changes are getting underway and the need for others is becoming apparent.

A major trend that is developing is placing more and more responsibility for art instruction on elementary classroom teachers. Art specialists have long argued that caregivers and general classroom teachers should participate more fully in providing art education for children and this notion is beginning to influence early childhood educators. In responding to this responsibility, the latter are calling for more developmentally appropriate pre-service learning experiences, in-service programs, and instructional resources that relate to art instruction.

Art-sensitive educators are also insisting that teacher training programs in early childhood education must increase requirements for appropriate course work in art education; that school administrators must underwrite and promote in-service programs to upgrade art instruction at the primary levels; and that both administrators and general classroom practitioners must be prepared to see the role of art specialists change. Concurrently, those responsible for the art programs in higher education that contribute to the pre-service preparation of teachers are encountering demands that their courses of study be overhauled to meet the needs of the very young.

Elementary art teachers/specialists now essentially provide class coverage when contract-assured preparation periods are scheduled for their classroom colleagues. Their methodology is designed to function in the arbitrary and fragmented ways this employment demands. Their expertise would far better serve students—and in fact, an entire elementary school faculty—if art teachers were properly utilized as master resource teachers and subject matter specialists. Future employment patterns must call for a major redefinition of art teachers' roles on elementary faculties, and particular attention must be given to their impact on early childhood education. At this level, art specialists will be far more effective if they function as teachers who have flexible scheduling options that better suit their subject and the way young children learn; as resource people who teach in tandem with general classroom educators for extended times and/or with in-depth units of integrated study; as experts in a very demanding area of study who can design and develop age-appropriate resource materials and instructional strategies for teaching colleagues; as in-service programmers and curriculum developers; and as school/parent/community resource agents.

Art educators are also recognizing that far too little attention has been given to the kind and quality of the art education very young children receive in their homes. Because of the pervasive nature of art and art-like behaviors in all aspects of their lives, children are more affected by home experiences than has been commonly understood. Future methodologies must become better informed by home experiences and receive stronger parental support than has hitherto been the case. Teachers must find ways to communicate to parents how important drawing and modeling experiences are for their children; they must urge parents to encourage their children to draw, model, and discuss art-like things; they must educate parents about ways they can support home art activities and how they can engage in them with their children; they must better relate school art experiences with children's home experiences; and they must find ways to effectively integrate community resources—i.e., museums, recreational programs, libraries, artists—with school/home support for the art education of young children.

There are overwhelming reasons to carefully integrate the general classroom practices of teachers, the expertise of art specialists, and parental support for the arts in early childhood education. Of them all, the most cogent one centers on the importance of holistic learning and the investment all of the "art partners" have in the art education of very young children—whether they recognize it or not.

CURRENT PRACTICES, A PROMISING FUTURE

In sum, the role of the arts and art educators in early childhood education is just beginning to be defined. Yet for all that is unknown, current practices in art education at this level of instruction and inquiries about them indicate that it will be an exceptionally large and important role. A promising future for the arts in early childhood education is predicted by what art educators now know and believe: art forms and techniques are universal modes of comprehension, communication, and expression; drawing/modeling behaviors and skills ground the ability of children to comprehend, understand, and master cognitive processes related to letters and numbers; art and art-like activities ground children in the forms and processes of their culture; all who work with children have a responsibility to ensure that their innate art-like behaviors are encouraged and educationally nourished; and supportive adult attitudes toward the arts should permeate their home, school, and community experiences. And for all that is now known, art educators are convinced above all else that the young child has a very special need for the kind and quality of learning instruction that the visual arts and art-like activities provide.

NAESP

National Association of Elementary School Principals

13. The Critical Preschool Years

by **Gary D. Salyers, 1989-90 President,** *National Association of Elementary School Principals. NAESP has a membership of 26,000, with headquarters at 1615 Duke Street, Alexandria, Virginia 22314-3483.*

In the last 25 years, the percentage of three- and four-year-olds attending some form of preschool has quadrupled, from slightly less than 10 percent in 1964 to 40 percent today.

From one standpoint, this burgeoning parental interest in pre-schooling is the most heartening, promising development in American education since we began the painful, still unfinished but essential process of dismantling racial segregation in our schools and society. In my opinion, the extension of high-quality early childhood programs throughout the country offers more potential for educational advancement than all the reform reports put together.

As we look forward toward the 21st century, it is appropriate to reflect on the forces that have stimulated this massive increase in preschool enrollment, on how to maximize the potential benefits of the preschool experience, and on the unfinished preschool agenda that remains to be addressed.

In recent decades our attitudes about the value of early childhood education have changed dramatically. Until the 1960s, psychologists and educators generally believed that human intelligence was fixed at birth. It followed that any effort to stimulate cognitive development was pointless. Early childhood programs, it was thought, should limit themselves to grouping youngsters in enjoyable surroundings so they could learn to express themselves and get along with others.

Then, in the early 1960s, a group of researchers emerged—J. McVicker Hunt, Benjamin Bloom, Jerome Bruner, and Burton White, among others—who disproved the doctrine of fixed intelligence and demonstrated that even infants in their cribs had a positive appetite for learning. To their work was joined the provocative developmental theory of Swiss psychologist Jean Piaget, originally published in the 1930s but not translated into English until 1952. The ideas of these researchers, along with a revised interest in those of Maria Montessori, set the stage for the explosion of early childhood programs that forthrightly emphasized cognitive development.

Undoubtedly, the best-known program that reflected these ideas was Head Start, which aimed to expose low-income, culturally deprived preschoolers to the "hidden curriculum of the home" that was assumed to be a given in the homes of middle- and upper-class children. The idea then spread to other parents: if preschooling was good for children of the poor, it should be beneficial for children of the fortunate as well.

The diffusion of the idea that preschool could be beneficial to all children converged with several powerful social trends that add up to what Sam Sava, Executive Director of NAESP, has called the "Family Revolution."

Since 1964, the divorce rate has doubled. At current rates, half of all marriages can be expected to end in divorce. The ratio of children under 18 being raised by single parents has also doubled, from 10 percent to 21 percent, and to more than 50 percent for Black children. And the proportion of married women who work outside the home, and who also have children under six-years-old, has doubled to nearly 50 percent.

Because of the intimate linkage between a child's home environment and the learning process, these social changes have had important implications for the education of our children as well.

Parents are a child's first teachers. Educators have always known this; they have long spoken of the "hidden curriculum of the home," and realized that much of their success with first graders could be traced to the informal preschooling children received before they started school.

University of Michigan researcher Harold Stevenson, in conjunction with Asian colleagues, demonstrated dramatically that what happens to children before they enter school is more likely to cause achievement problems than what happens to them afterward. In 1983, Stevenson and his colleagues published a study of 5,000 carefully matched first and fifth graders in Minneapolis; in Sendai, Japan; and in Taipei, Taiwan. They found that American children lagged behind their Asian counterparts as early as the fifth month of first grade.

Utterly surprised by this finding, Dr. Stevenson and his colleagues concluded that "the trouble lies not only in American schools, but also in American homes." Their finding is reinforced by the fact that children entering kindergarten have "recognition vocabularies," the number of spoken words they understand, ranging from 4,000 words at the low end to 12,000 words at the high end. This three-to-one disparity does not reflect innate intelligence; it simply reflects the amount of spoken language children hear in their homes before entering school. But because reading is nothing more than the process of interpreting the printed symbols that represent spoken words, this difference in the size of recognition vocabulary gives the more articulate children an enormous head start over their classmates.

Preschool enrollment has increased more in response to the needs of working parents for supervised day care than it has from any widespread recognition of the developmental value of early childhood education. Some of the enrollment growth can also be attributed to the spread of the "Superbaby Syndrome," which prompts more parents to enroll children in preschool programs out of fear that without a head start, their progeny will fall hopelessly behind in the race for admission to a topflight college some 14 years hence.

I believe that each child deserves at least three good years at home with a full-time parent. For many children, however, that happy day will never arrive. For now, and probably for the early decades of the 21st century, it is up to educators to take advantage of the increased interest and participate in preschool to give more children a better start, not only on learning, but on life. Both of these possibilities are within the reach of fine preschool programs operated by well-trained teachers.

Even the youngest children have a natural appetite for learning. They take pleasure in it, and their early learning can be stimulated by carefully designed programs that provide them with a rich environment to explore under the guidance of a specialist trained to spot, and respond to, the "cues" that indicate a child's interests. Preschool education, should and does, help children do better in school.

Unfortunately, it is observed, there is still a muddled understanding of what constitutes "learning" for a preschool child; there is a tendency to equate "learning" and "development" with the academically oriented, subject-centered learning and teaching that quite properly characterizes formal schooling.

Manifestations of this confusion include flashing word cards at three-month-olds and Picassos at one-year-olds, playing classical music to influence fetuses still in the womb, and "testing" toddlers before admitting them to prestigious nursery schools.

In the view of many parents, the purpose of early childhood education is to offer preschoolers bite-sized nibbles of the three Rs today so that when they encounter the "real" curriculum tomorrow, they can digest larger chunks of it more rapidly. These adults conclude that most of the activities so visible in preschoolers—seemingly aimless puttering about with sand, water, paints, and thing that go bang—have no payoff in later life; that they're pointless, trivial, time killers, just "kid stuff."

Yet "kid stuff" is precisely what preschoolers should be engaged in at their stage of life. Preschoolers have important lessons to learn about themselves, and their own kinds of skills to develop that have virtually nothing to do with "education" as adults often understand it. What may appear to be "aimless puttering about" helps preschoolers develop control of their bodies, investigate causes and effects, and follow up on the innate human curiosity that is at the root of all high achievement. In summary: Play *IS* learning for preschool children.

These observations should not be taken to mean that any preschool activity related to future scholastic achievement is to be avoided in a preschool program. For example, the single skill that appears to be most critical in intellectual achievement is the fluent understanding and use of language. Some children display an interest in the printed word and in reading when they are as young as three-years-old. Others show no interest until they are six or even older, at which point a teacher must intervene. However, virtually all three- and four-year olds display an interest in stories, and one of the most powerful means of developing their fluency with language is to read aloud to them. In addition to giving them a sense of narrative that will help them express themselves through writing in the upper grades, having interesting stories read to them encourages preschoolers to listen closely, a skill that will be important to their school success in later years.

Research evidence shows that improved student performance in the

Perspectives on Early Childhood Education

primary years and beyond results not from early exposure to reading, writing, and arithmetic (matters in which most three-and four-year-olds have little or no interest), but from exploiting the interests preschoolers already have to develop in them two vital characteristics: first, a sense of pleasure in learning; and second, a growing self-confidence in their ability to accomplish more challenging tasks. These two characteristics, especially if developed early in life, go far toward guaranteeing success in all future learning.

The burgeoning American acceptance of early childhood education is clearly no fad, no trendy innovation that will wither for lack of sustained social and parental interest after a few years of enthusiasm. Constant enrollment increases demonstrate that this interest will continue. Our continuing exploration of methods to encourage the development of our preschoolers' potential in every significant human dimension at a time when learning is still fresh and exciting for them represents one of the most heartening aspects of today.

For the last 15 years American educators have been on the defensive, challenged to explain why our youngsters show up near the bottom in one international competition after another. Our schools' performance, coupled with concern about our future work force, has triggered an avalanche of task-force reports and an outpouring of state mandates intended to correct deficiencies.

Some of these have made sense. Yet we will make no substantial, lasting improvement until we realize that the roots of our students' deficiencies lie in their earliest years, in their family lives, not in our classrooms. But until the day arrives that we see "parent reform," in which children are conceived only when the parents can provide adequate time, support, and nurturing, educators must continue to search for and take steps to ensure that every child who needs it has the opportunity for a positive preschool experience.

We already lag behind most West European nations in providing preschool to all children, regardless of income. In France, for example, 97 percent of children three years and under are enrolled; in the United States preschooling is available to only about 20 percent of three- and four-year-olds from low-income families.

Thus, in addition to striving to educate parents about the substance of a good preschool education, we must move on several fronts to achieve our goal. That means taking the following steps:

1. Adopting a national policy of providing free preschooling for all children beginning at age three, unless parents do not wish to enroll them. There should be no cost to low-income families for enrolling their children; some costs for children of upper- and middle-income families might be partially recovered by taxes on the extra income earned by two-income families.
2. Providing before- and after-school day care and study centers, usually in schools, for children from latchkey homes. Public funds should be made available to enable schools to work with other community agencies in developing and operating such programs.
3. Reducing pupil-teacher ratios for at-risk children to 15:1 for children in kindergarten through third grade. Our best chance of plucking a struggling child from a scholastic rut and putting him or her back on track is with special attention in the *FIRST GRADE*, not in the first year of high school.
4. Mobilizing older children and youth to provide one-on-one tutoring to younger ones.
5. Offering school-sponsored short courses to parents who want to do a better job with their children but simply don't know how.
6. Creating local programs to encourage and train care givers for children from birth to preschool age whose mothers work outside the home. These programs should be based on the recognition that both parents and children will benefit if we assist such care givers to meet health and safety standards and to provide learning experiences for the children, rather than penalizing them for not doing so.

These proposals may sound hopelessly utopian, the pipedream of an educator. Yet the Committee for Economic Development, composed of chief executives of Fortune 500 companies, has called for the investment of $5,000 per year for preschooling for every at-risk three- and four-year-old.

Troubled children are a disaster waiting to happen. Eighty percent of American prison inmates are high school dropouts, and each costs an average of $24,000 a year to incarcerate. If we do not head off school failure today, we will most assuredly pay for it in future years, in the hard coin of welfare benefits, unemployment compensation, prison costs, and another generation of poverty that will produce *more* troubled children.

For most of this decade, educators have been trying to implement reforms prescribed for us by task forces of prominent people. We have also been taken to task by sideline critics, most of whom would not survive three days in a first grade classroom.

But if instead of reacting to the agenda other people write for us, we were to unite as a profession in writing our own prescription for educational health, I believe that educators, speaking in a single voice to school boards, state legislators, and Congress, would command the audience that fundamental, lasting school reform, including excellent preschool education for all children whose parents want it, requires.

NAEYC

14. The Implications of National Education Goals for Early Childhood Education

by **Ellen Galinsky, 1988-90 President,** *National Association for the Education of Young Children. NAEYC has a membership of 70,000, with headquarters at 1834 Connecticut Avenue, N.W., Washington, DC 20009.*

Our imminent passage into the 21st century has prompted a societal interest in stock-taking, assessing where we are as this century ends, and determining where we want to go in the next century. It is impossible to try to define our future as a nation without considering children, for the young children of today will be the adults of the 21st century. A concern about children leads directly to a concern about their education, to asking how well our educational system is preparing children for the kind of future we envision.

It is no accident that we are focusing on education as the number of young people continues to decline ("the baby bust generation" coming of age). Our society can no longer afford for so many young people to be school dropouts, functionally illiterate, teenaged parents, or drug users.

In the following chapter, I will discuss the pitfalls and the promise of this current interest in education, specifically the education of young children. I will use the recently released National Education Goals jointly formulated by the president and the nation's governors as a basis for my discussion because I think these goals illuminate some of the challenges facing us if we are to improve early education.

COMPREHENSIVE GOALS

The president and governors begin their report by stating that "America's educational performance must be second to none in the 21st century. Education is central to our quality of life." They desire that

> Our people must be as knowledgeable, as well trained, as competent, and as inventive as those in any other nation. All of our people, not just a few, must be able to think for a living, adapt to changing environments, and to understand the world around them. They must understand and accept the responsibilities and obligations of citizen-

ship. They must continually learn and develop new skills throughout their lives.

These goals are similar to ones that I frequently hear from the corporate executives with whom I work in my role as a work and family life researcher. These executives deplore the story of AT&T's having to interview 22,000 people to find 3,000 literate enough for entry-level jobs. They point out that our current system of education is predicated on the needs of an industrial society; thus in many classrooms, children are expected to be quiet, sit still, give the correct answer (often framed as a multiple-choice selection), and compete with each other. These may be useful skills for working on assembly lines but not for an information-based economy. The business executives I talk to say that the requisite skills for the twenty-first century are (1) to be a continuous learner, to cope not only with rapidly changing technology but with the 10 to 11 career changes employees of the future are expected to make; (2) to solve new problems, to think divergently, posing many possible solutions to problems before arriving at one to try; and (3) to work in teams, to cope well with the diversity in cultural background, in education and in training that will be commonplace in work groups in the next century.

A RECOGNITION OF THE IMPORTANCE OF THE EARLY YEARS

It is very positive that the president and governors are cognizant that these kinds of goals cannot be achieved without beginning in the earliest years. That understanding has been a long time in coming. The very first objective posed by these national leaders is aimed at preschool children: "By the year 2,000, all children in America will start school ready to learn."

"Ready to learn"—this phrase implies that real learning doesn't begin until school entry. The very word "preschool" further implies that this is a preparatory stage rather than a stage in and of itself. We certainly need better societal understanding and appreciation of this stage in life.

A CALL FOR DEVELOPMENTALLY APPROPRIATE PROGRAMS

And yet this report does reflect an understanding that the content and methods of teaching of young children must be geared to the way they learn best. The president and governors refer to developmentally appropriate programs, specifying that "All disadvantaged and disabled children will have access to high quality and developmentally appropriate preschool programs that help prepare children for school."

This is both a commendable and realizable objective. The early childhood field has reached consensus on the ingredients of high-quality, developmentally appropriate early childhood programs. These characteristics—originally drawn from research findings and extensively field-tested—have been codified into accreditation standards by the National Association for the Education of Young Children (NAEYC). To date, 1,000 early childhood programs have been accredited and over 3,000 are in the process of being accredited.

School systems are likewise beginning to adopt NAEYC's accreditation standards for their classrooms serving young children. For example, the Southern Association of Colleges and Schools (SACS, covering Alabama, Louisiana, Mississippi, North Carolina, South Carolina, Tennessee, Texas, and Virginia)—one of the six regional organizations accrediting public schools—and NAEYC are piloting a joint accreditation for programs serving four- and five-year-old children.

Not only is there a research basis for the standards of high-quality programs, there is also considerable evidence that participation in such programs, especially for children from low-income families, has long-lasting effects on their development. According to numerous studies, children in high-quality early childhood programs fare better than their counterparts without access to such programs. These programs prevent the decline in IQ typical of children in this socioeconomic group, although this IQ boost washes out over time. Such children have fewer placements in special education classrooms and have a better chance of graduating from high school. Some, though not all studies, have also found evidence of reduced juvenile delinquency, lower rates of teen pregnancy, and reduced dependence on welfare.

A CONCERN: SEGREGATING AT-RISK CHILDREN

These studies indicate the greatest benefits of early childhood programs accrue to children from low-income families. Combined with budgeting constraints and the fact that higher-income families already tend to enroll their children in preschool programs, policymakers have increasingly emphasized using public dollars to target early childhood programs for the so-called "at-risk" children. This is clearly the intent of the National Education Goals; they call for programs for "all disadvantaged and disabled children." The consequence of this public policy trend may have an unfortunate consequence—the creation of a whole new stratum of children. I find that even their teachers use the term "the at-risk class." Furthermore, such groups tend to be disproportionately minority. What we are, in fact, doing is tracking and segregating children at younger ages. In addition to the stigma and perhaps self-fulfilling prophecy that these decisions may set into motion, we may also be depriving these children of being around children from families who are engaged in and enthusiastic about learning. We may be depriving them of being around children who are verbally proficient. There is strong evidence that children learn a great deal from each other. For these reasons, NAEYC's guiding principles for early childhood legislation state that

- Programs should be designed to include children from a variety of ethnic and socioeconomic backgrounds.
- Policies that intentionally or unintentionally result in segregation on the basis of ethnicity, socioeconomic status, or special need, including "at-risk" status must be rectified.

NAEYC acknowledges that limited funding should be targeted at the most needy, but warns that "provisions must be made to avoid segregation." We feel that if the states continue in the direction of separating the so-called at-risk children, problems will be created that will only have to be remedied in the future. Why not begin by designing early childhood programs to serve an appropriate mix of children?

Yet the states seem to be moving away from creating programs for a mix of young children. The debate around finding just the right month for kindergarten entry tacitly presupposes that if the right age is found, the children will be more homogeneous, ignoring the reality that in every group of children, no matter the cutoff age, there will be a two-to-three-year developmental span. Regrettably, we seem to be moving in the direction of trying to fit the children to the curriculum rather than fitting the curriculum to the children.

THE USE OF TESTS

A correlate of this trend in the alarming growth in the use of tests as the basis for school placements for young children. As testing becomes more prevalent, teachers report having to teach to the test, having to follow a standardized curriculum ("so that no one else's class will be ahead of mine"). In such an atmosphere, teachers often report less joy in teaching.

NAEYC has developed a strong position statement, deploring the use of testing as the sole or even the major means for making decisions about young children's future. In this regard, the National Education Goals are exemplary. The report states: "Placement decisions for young children should not be made on the basis of standardized tests."

THE UNFORTUNATE SCHISM BETWEEN EDUCATION AND CARE

The biggest problem with the National Education Goals is that they seem to assume that in order for young children to learn in early childhood programs, they must be in schools or school-like settings. The report states that eligible children must have access to "Head Start, Chapter 1, or some other successful preschool program." Why not mention the many child-care programs with developmentally appropriate curriculums? The reason behind the omission is linked to the deep-seated but erroneous assumption that child care is custodial while schools are educational.

In reality, the quality of the program is what makes the difference—not the auspice, not the location of the program, and not the number of hours the program is open. Among NAEYC-accredited programs are those that have part-day and full working-day hours. NAEYC believes that all children need both nurturing and developmentally appropriate educational experiences in order to thrive.

The schism between education and care is increasingly responsible for many of the problems in the early childhood field. As states begin to invest in early childhood programs, some are putting all their resources solely into school-based programs, in effect ignoring the fact that there may be excellent programs in community-based settings. Because school-based programs are typically part-day, they increase the complexity of the child-care arrangements employed parents must make for their children. NAEYC believes that policy decisions should be based on what is best for children. We believe that families need part-day and full working-day choices. Our legislative guidelines state that "efforts must be made to ensure that programs meet family needs for child care so that children are not placed in multiple programs over the course of a day."

Other states and localities—for example, Michigan, Colorado, and Oregon—are creating a system in which early childhood programs are funded in both schools and community-based organizations. Quality standards are the same in these two systems. This flexibility avoids pushing preschool programs on those principals who feel they have enough on their plates right now and don't want to take on increased obligations, and preserves the public investment in many excellent community-based early childhood programs.

THE NEED TO ADDRESS THE CHILD-CARE STAFFING CRISIS

In order to provide a range of high-quality, stable early childhood programs in schools and community-based organizations, we need to address the crisis of low salaries and high turnover in child care. The National Child Care Staffing Study has documented the fact that teachers' salaries have declined by over 20 percent in the past ten years, and that turnover has tripled. NAEYC has been addressing this crisis with its Full Cost of Quality Care Campaign. We are now working to reach consensus within our membership on the criteria for pre-service and in-service training requirements and classroom staffing models. When agreement is reached, communities will be able to compute the full cost of quality programs and then employ a variety of strategies to raise the money to pay these costs, while being mindful of not raising fees beyond what low-income parents can afford to pay.

THE IMPORTANCE OF PARENTAL INVOLVEMENT

A positive feature of the National Education Goals is the emphasis on parental involvement. The report states: "Every parent in America will be a child's first teacher and devote time each day helping his or her preschool child learn; parents will have access to the training and support they need."

The report further specifies all preschool programs must have "strong parental involvement." Such directions build on the research finding that successful early childhood programs do much more than teach children. They affect the family system, helping parents have higher aspirations for their children, value education more, and have a proactive stance toward the problems they face. The president and governors' report acknowledges that parent/school involvement is not a one-way street—parents make significant contributions to the programs by their involvement.

A CONCERN: IGNORING THE NEEDS OF INFANTS AND TODDLERS

The president and governors are to be commended for not focusing rigidly on four-year-olds, although the report does state: "Our policy must be to provide at least one year of preschool for all disadvantaged children." If we as a nation do not find ways to provide developmentally appropriate experiences for the numerous infants and toddlers who are in child care, we will certainly pay the price later on. How can we expect to intervene successfully at four when a sizable number of infants and toddlers have spent three years in poor-quality settings? True prevention efforts must begin at the beginning, with our very youngest children.

THE NEED FOR ONGOING COMPREHENSIVE SERVICES

The report does, thankfully, acknowledge the needs of families for health services. It states: "Children will receive the nutrition and health care needed to arrive at school with healthy minds and bodies, and the number of low birthweight babies will be significantly reduced through an enhanced prenatal health system."

Attention to the health needs of children is critical, but it must be recognized that these health needs may be formidable at this time when one out of every ten children is born chemically addicted. Attention to health needs, however, is not sufficient. Neither is a focus on the child alone. A focus on the period before school entry is also insufficient. Families' needs for service must be attended to. In sum, if the president and governors truly believe their worthy goal, they must be ready to combat the growing poverty of so many children and the resulting ongoing family need for comprehensive service. This is a crucial prerequisite of educational reform.

HOW WILL SCHOOLS PREPARE FOR THE CHILDREN?

A final problem with the report is that it emphasizes preparing the children for schools while neglecting to consider how schools must change in order to prepare for the children. Good quality preschool programs cannot vaccinate a child against later school failure. Unless significant efforts are made to have good quality, developmentally appropriate elementary and secondary schools, the gains of early childhood education will disappear. Experimentation is needed such as suggested by the National Association of State Boards of Education's report: *Right From the Start*. This includes curriculum reform as well as creating early childhood units within schools and encouraging better coordination between the public schools and the early childhood field.

NECESSARY FACTORS TO BRING ABOUT REFORM

Although I have suggested some crucial and necessary ways to improve the National Education Goals from an early childhood perspective, overall their recommendations for young children are to be commended. But are they realizable? What will it take for us to achieve these goals? I think there are four ingredients:

- *Time.* Educational reform will take time. We cannot allow foot-dragging, but neither must we be faddish, trying out these ideas for only a short time, becoming discouraged, and

abandoning them. We want children to be continuous learners, but adults must likewise be lifelong learners if we are to achieve the kind of success we all want.
- *Problem Solving.* As children must learn to problem solve, so must adults if reform is to succeed. We need to encourage creative thinking as well as innovation at a classroom, program, and community level.
- *Team Work.* It will take collaboration between the various sectors of child care and the public schools, between educators and parents, between educational institutions and other institutions of society, such as the business sector, for reform to take seed and flourish. Again, just as we know that children must learn to work together in the 21st century, adults must put aside turf issues and find ways to collaborate to make educational programs better places for children and adults.
- *Resources.* Although throwing money at problems does not ensure their solution, these reforms *cannot* succeed unless we as a nation are willing to commit the resources needed. Without adequate funding, these goals are empty and hollow.

The dwindling number of young people and the shifts in our economy have triggered a renewed interest and commitment to our educational system. The formulation of National Education Goals is a hopeful first step in bringing about needed change. As the report states:

> America can meet this challenge if our society is dedicated to a renaissance in education. . . . We must recognize that every child can learn, regardless of background or disability. We must recognize that education is a lifelong pursuit, not just an endeavor for our children.

REFERENCES

1. Haskins, R. "Beyond Metaphor: The Efficacy of Early Childhood Education." *American Psychologist* 44 no. 2 (February 1989): 274-82.
2. Lally, J. R.; Mangione, P. L.; Honig, A. S. *The Syracuse University Family Development Research Program: Long Range Impact of Early Intervention on Low-Income Children and Their Families.* San Francisco: Center for Child and Family Studies, Far West Laboratory for Educational Research and

Development, September 1987. (Summary appears in *Zero to Three*, April 1988, as "More Pride, Less Delinquency: Findings from the Ten-Year Follow-Up Study of the Syracuse University Family Development Research Program.")

3. McKey, R. H.; Condelli, L.; Ganson, H.; Barrett, B. J.; McConkey, C.; Plantz, M.C. *The Impact of Head Start on Children, Families and Communities.* DHHS Publication No. OHDS 85-31193. Washington, D.C.: U.S. Government Printing Office, 1985.

4. National Association for the Education of Young Children (NAEYC). *Accreditation Criteria and Procedures of the National Academy of Early Childhood Programs*, edited by S. Bredekamp. Washington, D.C.: NAEYC, 1984.

5. ____. *Guiding Principles for the Development and Analysis of Early Childhood Legislation, 1989.* Washington, D.C.: NAEYC, 1989.

6. ____. "NAEYC Position Statement on Standardized Testing of Young Children 3 through 8 Years of Age." *Young Children* 43 no. 3 (March 1988): 42-47.

7. National Associations of State Boards of Education. *Right from the Start.* Report of the NASBE Task Force on Early Childhood Education. Alexandria, Va.: NASBE, 1988.

8. National Governors' Association. "National Education Goals." Adopted February 25, 1990.

9. Whitebook, M.; Howes, C.; Phillips, D. "Who Cares? Child Care Teachers and the Quality of Care in America." *Executive Summary: National Child Care Staffing Study.* Child Care Employee Project, 6536 Telegraph Ave., A201, Oakland, Calif. 94609: Child Care Employee Project, 1989.

NAME

National Association of Migrant Educators

15. America's Migrant Children: Most at Risk

by **Al Wright,** *1990-92 Treasurer, National Association of Migrant Educators. NAME has a membership of 744, with headquarters at P.O. Box 2132, Baton Rouge, Louisiana 70821.*

Of all children at risk, no identifiable group faces greater disadvantages than America's "children of the road," those young people who travel with their parents on seasonal migrations to harvest crops and do other farm-related work. As noted in the comprehensive Charles Stewart Mott Foundation study of youth at risk, they are saddled with a triple burden of poverty, constant mobility, and, for about 75 percent of their number, a native language other than English. An additional burden has now been identified, one that large numbers of migrant children take on before the age of seven and remains with them throughout their school years, threatening the viability and completion of schooling. Migrant children run a 50-50 chance of being one or more years too old for their grade level by the time they enter second grade. Being overage for grade is, of course, a leading indicator of dropout potential. Being one year behind peers increases the risk of a student's later dropping out by 40 to 50 percent, and being two grades behind increases the risk by 90 percent. The chief reason for their low modal grade, according to research findings: a retention rate two to ten times higher than that for nonmigrant students.

For migrant children, possibly more than any other group, the dropout problem begins in kindergarten and first grade. Educators had been aware that the typical migrant child was one or more years below modal grade, but no broad attempt was made to focus on the causes and effects until a research study completed in 1987 spotlighted the remarkably high rate of retention of migrant students in kindergarten and first grade. A migrant child, the study found, is 8 to 10 times more likely to be retained than a nonmigrant child in kindergarten, and about twice as likely to be retained in first grade. After that, there is little difference in the retention rate, but the die has already been cast. Once retained, these children remain a year behind their age-peers as long as they remain in school.

The research, conducted by Bob Levy of the State University of New York at Oneonta, was designed to find out why such a large proportion of migrant children were below modal grade. It was premised on a comparison of modal grade placement for the general school population. Comprehensive data for the latter was available from the Migrant Student Record Transfer System (MSRTS), a national data bank that contains information on more than half a million children identified as eligible for the federally funded Migrant Education Program. The most startling comparisons: 35 percent of migrant kindergarten students are one or more years older than their classmates as compared to only 5 percent in the general population: by second grade, 49 percent of migrant students are below modal grade as compared to 21 percent of the general population. The migrant population includes children defined either as "currently migratory," i.e., who have moved with their families within the past 12 months, or as "formerly migratory," those whose last migratory move was more than one year but less than six years earlier.

Levy surmised that each instance of a child overage for grade could be due to one of four causes: the child simply started school late, the child was kept on in a Head Start or other preschool program for another year, the child was improperly placed, or the child was actually retained. To obtain a manageable sample population on which to collect information about the actual reasons, Levy asked MSRTS to select at random 500 migrant children ages 5 to 8 with current enrollments in New York, and another 500 currently enrolled in Florida, one of the three largest home-base states for migrant farmworkers.

After ascertaining that the proportion of the New York and Florida samples overage for grade was comparable to the national figures, Levy and his staff began the laborious task of compiling a complete profile on all overage students in the group. They went to the districts and looked at the permanent student records; they asked school officials to answer a series of questions about factors that influenced decisions on promotion or retention. For corroboration, they also interviewed parents of about half the children.

Their findings left little doubt that retention was the primary reason for migrant children's being below modal grade, although there were considerable differences between the two states involved. In Florida, where a pupil progression plan mandates 90 percent mastery of minimum basic skills for promotion, 59 percent of the overage children had repeated kindergarten, and 27 percent had repeated first grade. Only 11 percent were below modal grade as a result of entering school late. Another 3 percent were in so-called transition classes. In New York, 31 percent of the overage children had repeated kindergarten, and 12 percent had repeated first grade. A full 25 percent had started school late, and 26 percent were in transition classes.

Of the nearly 500 students in the two states who were below modal grade, 45 percent had repeated kindergarten, 20 percent had repeated first grade, 18 percent had started school late, and 14 percent were in transition classes, which are considered by some to be a form of de facto retention. Extrapolation of the New York and Florida figures to the nationwide migrant student population would be imprecise, at best, but it is safe to conclude that a significant percentage of migrant students are retained in kindergarten and first grade, including at least a quarter and possibly more than a third of all migrant children in kindergarten. The implications of this condition for educators of migrant children are considerable. Throughout the nation they are starting to take second looks at promotion/retention policies and the palpably harmful ways they are applied to migrant children.

Advocates of migrant children agree with Levy that evidence has "consistently shown that retention does not ensure greater achievement and that personal and social maladjustment result." But, as Levy found, sometimes the system makes decisions on promotion or retention that are entirely arbitrary. The adoption of minimum competency standards that accompanied the school reform movement of the eighties frequently took decisions out of the hands of teachers.

"We need an attitude change plus a policy change," claims Levy, a former secondary specialist now firmly convinced that the key to improving graduation rates for migrant students lies in the prevention of unnecessary retention in the first two years of school. "The best alternative to retention," Levy believes, "seems to be grade promotion in combination with individual remediation." Individual remediation is the stock in trade of the Migrant Education Program, a supplemental program originally created in 1966. In 49 states, Puerto Rico, and the District of Columbia, teachers and aides work individually and in small groups with migrant children to remediate deficiencies in language, reading, and mathematics. Most states also conduct extensive summer programs that offer an even wider range of subjects, usually focusing on skills mastery for elementary students and credit makeup for secondary students. But for more than two decades the emphasis has been on alleviation of existing deficiencies, not on alterations in policies that contribute to deficiencies. Now there is an effort to combine the two objectives.

According to Levy, "There's a great deal that can be done on a very practical level," pointing out a New York-Florida arrangement that emerged from the initial shock of the research findings. "There's a kid in Florida who is going to be retained because he doesn't have 90 percent skills mastery. If he could have summer school, he might make it. But he's not going to be in Florida during the summer—his family is coming to New York to pick crops. We put him in a summer program in New York, and we give him some skills. If we don't know what skills he needs, it won't do him any good, and he'll go back to Florida and be retained. But now Florida will notify New York that this child is likely to be retained, and will tell us what skills he needs to work on. We report to Florida on the skills he has mastered, and he can go back home and enter the next grade."

Levy has calculated the value of such an interstate effort in terms of preventive medicine, as in "pay now instead of paying later." A major effort in Migrant Education summer programs is given over to makeup courses for high school students, often in a packaged format such as the Migrant Education-developed Portable Assisted Study Sequence (PASS), through which students who have traveled to Michigan or Washington in the summer can earn credits they need to graduate in Texas or California. "In summer secondary credit programs," Levy notes, "you work all summer to get the student one credit or a half-credit. But a summer program for elementary kids in danger of retention can do the equivalent of *five* PASS programs."

Levy's research, which was funded through a migrant education

Perspectives on Early Childhood Education

interstate coordination grant, and the coordinated New York-Florida response typified the interstate perspective that migrant educators have inculcated in the two decades the federally funded program has been implemented. It is a similar perspective to that of the National Association of Migrant Educators (NAME), the first grass-roots effort to form a nationwide network of advocates for migrant children. Though NAME is a relatively new organization, chartered in 1989, its members include many of the key leaders and innovators in the design and delivery of services for migrant children. Their message to all educators entrusted with the early education of migrant children is simple: "We know that young migrant children typically demonstrate many deficiencies in basic skills mastery—but please, please, let's think twice about retaining them. They don't need another strike against them."

Many NAME members are hopeful that an increased focus on preschool education will ultimately produce a reduction in the incidence of kindergarten and first grade retention. The optimistic can point to two windows of opportunity that were not on the scene at the time of the Oneonta study. First it is the expansion of the age range of children included in the Migrant Education funding formula; second is the implementation of Migrant Even Start projects.

The Hawkins-Stafford reauthorization of the program, which took effect in 1988, included three- and four-year-olds in the funding formula for the first time, and it also included specific language directing provision for preschool education needs of migrant children. The expansion of the age range, however, was not accompanied by a commensurate increase in appropriation. Additionally, preschool services had been authorized anyway, and in many cases preschool migrant children were receiving some services. The compilation of state performance reports for the 1986-87 school year showed that 12 percent of all migrant children receiving services in regular term Migrant Education projects—and 21 percent in summer term—were in prekindergarten and kindergarten. For children in those categories who received services before reaching the age of five, the providing states had to use funds generated by eligible children between the ages of 5 and 17 to support the services.

Now that the funding formula includes three- and four-year-olds, it is likely that more preschoolers will be served. But this will be due more to the mandatory nature of the requirement—at least for currently migratory children—than to the change in the funding structure. Because the Migrant Education Program was funded at only 35.56 percent of its authorized level in fiscal 1990, and because modest yearly increases in funding have not kept pace with the inflationary spiral, services for previously unserved preschool migrant children can be provided only by diverting resources originally designated for school-age children. Migrant educators make every effort to get migrant children placed in other programs, but the mobility of migrant children often presents an insurmountable barrier to placement in a preschool program for a stable population. The Migrant Head Start program, funded by the Department of Health and Human Services, is grievously underfunded.

Funds available under the Even Start program are even more limited. This new program, the creation of Pennsylvania Congressman William Goodling, takes a family approach to early childhood education, placing equal emphasis on parents and children. Even Start not only provides direct developmental and instructional services for children ages one to seven, but it also trains parents to provide learning experiences for children at home and opens doors to educational and training opportunities for the parents. There is a 3 percent set-aside for migrant children and families in Even Start. Only a little over $14 million was appropriated for the first Even Start grants awarded in 1989, of which some $440,000 was available for migrant children. It was divided among Even Start projects in three states—New York, Louisiana, and Washington.

The three Migrant Even Start projects differ greatly from one another. The New York project, which serves primarily intrastate children whose families make frequent moves to work on dairy farms, is based on a home literacy model developed through the state's tutorial outreach format for serving migrant children. As far back as 1977, the state's migrant education leaders initiated a network of tutors whose main function was to assist parents, supporting their role as the primary teacher in the lives of their children. Over 50 such tutors are currently employed. The model was a natural for adaptation to Even Start, with additional emphasis on direct instruction for both children and parents.

In Louisiana, where a small concentration of Hispanic workers from Texas and Mexico arrive each spring to work on the strawberry, cucumber, and bell pepper crops, the progress of the initial group of preschoolers exceeded expectations. Additionally, parents responded enthusiastically for the chance for twice-weekly sessions on helping their children and English language instruction on two other nights. Two months into the program, many were attending every night even after spending hard days working in the fields. "We're trying to get parents to spend more time interacting with their children in Spanish," notes Betty Kraft, education specialist with the Louisiana migrant education bureau. "These people work so hard and such long hours they haven't had much time to interact. They so want their kids to learn English they don't understand the need to speak Spanish. I feel we need to do a lot with the kids in Spanish—we need to provide them with a lot of experiences they haven't had. And of course we need to get parents to understand that being bilingual is a wonderful thing. But the parental component is a great strength of Even Start."

The Washington project is actually a cooperative interstate effort involving the Washington, Texas, and Michigan Migrant Education programs. It is targeted on mobile children home-based in the Texas lower Rio Grande Valley who migrate annually to selected school districts in Washington and Michigan, the two leading destination states for Texas-based migrants. One hundred Texas families conforming to the model were chosen for the project, although only 20 bound for Washington and 20 for Michigan were initially served. Facilitator-instructors in Texas identified individual family needs and prepared information packets for transmittal to the destination states prior to summer migrations. Families were notified about facilitators to contact in Washington or Michigan, who would be prepared to direct families to appropriate services upon their arrival.

Even Start has not been operational long enough to make any suppositions about its potential for improving the success of migrant children in kindergarten. Probably its greatest impact will be as a model, especially for furthering the role of migrant parents in preparing their children for school. It is not likely to be funded at a level whereby any significant proportion of preschoolers will be directly affected. But it promises to demonstrate to all educators that parental involvement closely integrated with a sensible preschool developmental program has great potential for reducing retention of migrant children in kindergarten and first grade.

The National Association of Migrant Educators vigorously supports early educational experiences for migrant children, coupled with sincere efforts to reach out to migrant families to empower them to become important contributing partners in their children's educational growth. NAME members are unrelenting advocates for migrant children, who are deserving of special consideration from all teachers and administrators because their circumstances are indeed different from those of other children. By creating greater sensitivity to the unique needs of migrant children—such as a compelling need to seek alternatives to retention at early grades—NAME members are making progress toward the goals of their organization.

All persons who share in a concern for America's half-million migrant children are welcome to join the Association and share in the effort.

REFERENCES

1. Henderson, A. et al. *A Summary of State Chapter 1 Migrant Education Program Participation and Achievement Information.* Washington, D.C.: Decision Resources Corp., 1989.

2. Levy, B. *Grade Retention and Promotion: Considerations for Dropout Prevention.* Oneonta, N.Y.: State University College, 1989.

3. Marks, E. L. *Case Studies of the Migrant Education Program.* Washington, D.C.: Policy Studies Associates, 1987.

4. Migrant Student Record Transfer System. *MSRTS Management Report 1B: Student Distribution Summary; Report for Nation.* Little Rock, Ark.: MSRTS, October 18, 1989.

5. National Association of Migrant Educators. "Most at Risk." Brochure. Washington, D.C. NAME, 1989.

6. Prewitt-Diaz, J. O., et al. *The Effects of Migration on Children: An Ethnographic Study.* Harrisburg: Pennsylvania Department of Education, 1989.

7. Smith, R. C., and Lincoln, C. A. *America's Shame, America's Hope: Twelve Million Youth at Risk.* Chapel Hill, N.C.: MDC (for the Charles Stewart

Mott Foundation), 1988.

8. Taranto, S. "Reaching and Teaching: New York Project Equips Parents for Role in Children's Educational Development." *MEMO* 5, no. 6 (January 1987): 12-13.

NASBE

National Association of State Boards of Education

16. Early Childhood Education—A Continuum

by **Roseann Bentley,** *1990-91 Immediate Past President, National Association of State Boards of Education. NASBE has a membership of 650, with headquarters at 1012 Cameron Street, Alexandria, Virginia 22314.*

When the National Association of State Boards of Education selected the early years, from ages four to eight, as a priority for a yearlong study in 1988, we knew that we were tackling an enormous, amorphous, and potentially controversial subject. Still, the level of interest among our members was intense and the potential for tremendous effect was great. Certainly the need for structural and conceptual change in how we approach learning in these earliest years in the public schools of our country was apparent. The announcement of a national commission made up of some of the finest minds in the early education field was made; the die was cast. The efforts of the commission, the far-reaching search for the most effective, innovative, exemplary approaches, and the final report of the commission's findings form the substance of this chapter. The results of the commission's work in the year and a half since the report, *Right from the Start* (1), was issued, are also included since the level of interest in the commission's yearlong study continues to astonish us by increasing rather than decreasing.

Early childhood education is definitely not new to public schools. During World War II many schools offered day-care services to children of mothers who were working outside the home for the first time in their lives. Even earlier, during the depression years, the Works Project Administration set up nursery schools within public schools. Now, as we know, there are many more pressing societal issues converging to make the education of young children among the most urgent public policy questions.

NASBE was often asked as we launched our new venture why we didn't focus on the child from birth to eight rather than limiting our study to ages four through eight. The answer was that even though we certainly realize that every month in a child's early existence is of major concern, we wanted to tackle a subject that was more manageable and of more immediate responsibility to public schools. Often during the deliberations and public hearings, our attention was given to the indivisible imperatives of adequate prenatal care and ages birth through three. We did not rule out the possibility of further study of the earliest years at a later time.

Presently, three groups are most readily engaged in some of these early childhood issues: early childhood educators, public school administrators, and state policymakers. The educators are caught up in tangible immediacies, such as materials, housing, staffing, especially poor salaries, and competitiveness between the many different groups offering early childhood programs. Administrators are suddenly facing state-mandated preschool services, federal mandates for preschool children with special needs, and local parents facing unrelenting child-care problems. State policymakers are beginning to wade into the tangle of early childhood offerings; they are trying to make wise choices about the assignment of sponsorship for new early childhood programs and the development of standards and funding systems that can support high-quality services.

The NASBE Task Force brought these three groups together to begin a dialogue around the focal issue for all three: What is best practice for young children? How can their needs best be met?

As a beginning, we set two goals:

- To develop more successful models for teaching in the early years of elementary school, based on our knowledge of child development and the lessons of successful preschool programs.

- To find new ways for public schools to complement and supplement the efforts of other early childhood programs in serving preschool children and their families.

In order to accomplish these goals, the Task Force members drew on the advice of leading experts in the field (many of whom were seated around the Board table), commissioned papers on key issues, spent hours in deliberations and private study. We visited some wonderful classrooms in public schools, Head Start centers, and community-based programs. Also, four public hearings were conducted. Placed strategically around the country to try to offer the widest access for participation, each of

Perspectives on Early Childhood Education

these hearings was a marathon day of testimony that was riveting. From Head Start directors to first-year parents, state legislators, superintendents, teachers, teacher trainers, and even some tiny four-year-olds, the advice we received was cogent, urgent, playful, tragic, hostile, cajoling, teary, and sometimes angry. During it all, the basic messages came through. We are not doing enough for our youngest citizens. Prevention is far preferable to remediation. Education must be restructured to fit the tremendous changes we have seen in our society.

Out of the yearlong study, the report *Right from the Start* emerged (1). Although it parallels other school reform reports in some respects, the focus on the crucial first years of education makes it unique. These years—when children gain the essential skills, knowledge, and dispositions critical to later school success—deserve all the analysis and careful scrutiny that we felt our Task Force committed to them. By broadening and bridging the transitions between other preschool programs and public schools, and by more directly addressing some of the urgent preschool questions, many public policy concerns were answered. *Right from the Start* promotes a vision for early childhood education that combines a restructured approach to schooling for four- to eight-year-olds with a call for new partnerships among schools, parents, and other early childhood programs. At the heart of the report are two recommendations.

1. EARLY CHILDHOOD UNITS SHOULD BE ESTABLISHED IN ELEMENTARY SCHOOLS TO PROVIDE A NEW PEDAGOGY FOR WORKING WITH CHILDREN AGES FOUR TO EIGHT AND A FOCAL POINT FOR ENHANCED SERVICES TO PRESCHOOL CHILDREN AND THEIR PARENTS.

The goals of establishing an early childhood unit are to improve existing programs for children, preschool to third grade, and to plan for new high-quality preschool services. The establishment of these units reflects the Task Force's belief in sound child development principles: that learning occurs best when there is a focus on the whole child; that learning for children and adults is interactive; that young children learn from concrete work and play, much of which is child-initiated; and that young children are profoundly influenced by their families and the surrounding community. Based on these principles, the central characteristics of this new unit as we envisioned it would be:

- developmentally appropriate curriculum
- improved assessment
- responsiveness to cultural and linguistic diversity
- partnerships with parents
- training and support for staff and administrators

> At the heart of every educational process lies the child. No advances in policy, no acquisition of new equipment have their desired effect unless they are in harmony with the nature of the child, unless they are fundamentally acceptable to him. Knowledge of the manner in which children develop, therefore, is of prime importance both in avoiding educational harmful practices and in introducing effective ones. (2)

We did not specify one particular span of grades or organizational structure. We realized that there are many different models that could deliver the essential characteristics of an excellent early childhood unit. Among these models could be a separate facility that would concentrate efforts of the principal, teachers, other staff, and community groups on implementing an approach to school, based on the unique developmental needs of young children. Another model could utilize an early childhood unit director with specialized training in early childhood development, responsible to the school principal and with substantial authority for teacher and program development. A third possibility might be a staffing team with a lead teacher and a focal point of staff development activities for four- to eight-year-olds. By leaving these multiple model decisions at the local level, community differences can be acknowledged and the most suitable model chosen. The focus can thus be placed on appropriate practices for young children, taking into account individual developmental differences and cultural and linguistic diversity.

A repeated concern that emerged during the year of study was the issue of pushing down academic standards and pressures to an ever earlier age. Unacceptable testing practices as well as extended periods of drill and practice, paper-and-pencil exercises totally inappropriate to four-and five-year-olds were heard about repeatedly. The increased use of standardized tests for younger children was linked with greater prevalence of worksheets and workbooks, tracking and retention of children, an increased focus on narrowly defined basic skills, and a segmented and fragmented approach to the teaching of skills and content. These methods are inconsistent with knowledge of how children learn best in their early years of schooling. As Peter Higbee has said so eloquently, "Early learning, if based on exploration, problem-solving, experimentation and creativity, can sow the seeds of a love of learning that carries throughout life" (1).

The importance of parental involvement and family support can perhaps never be adequately expressed. Particularly in the youngest years, we now know, the influence of home and family is absolutely paramount. The envisioned early childhood units must commit to an expansion of parent involvement and family support. Parents are to be valued as the primary influences in their children's lives and as equal and essential partners in their education.

Central to the implementation of the early childhood unit is a well-trained staff supported by knowledgeable and sensitive administrators. There are many decisions to be made concerning staff in early childhood public school programs. Foremost among them are questions of qualifications, training, and compensation. In the best of units, there would be increased in-service training, planning time, and teacher participation in decision making. Teachers in preschool and child care programs sponsored by the school would receive compensation equivalent to that of other school staff with comparable training, experience, and credentials.

2. PUBLIC SCHOOLS SHOULD DEVELOP PARTNERSHIPS WITH OTHER EARLY CHILDHOOD PROGRAMS AND COMMUNITY AGENCIES TO BUILD AND IMPROVE SERVICES FOR YOUNG CHILDREN AND THEIR PARENTS.

A vision of a whole child who is not partitioned or segmented into various parts of his or her existence is necessary. We, as a nation, can no longer afford the consequences of the gaps in service, the fragmentation, the duplication of services, the lack of communication, and the protection of turf that occurs when we look at the needs of a single child. Even highly educated adults get lost in the morass of services, agencies, and programs offered for young children. How can the children themselves possibly make sense out of their fragmented days? We need to create a comprehensive system of early childhood services, including parent education, family support and preservation services, child care, health, social, and mental health services. Public schools could possibly serve as the focal point for information and the logical service delivery arena. Public schools can work with other early childhood programs to build this system through joint planning, advocacy and partnerships in sponsoring services. Just as we work at the other end with businesses and colleges as students graduate, we need to develop similar networks with the early childhood community. "Collaboration is hard for people who are already stretched to their limits in their own programs, but in the long run it is the right way to build a political base of support for early childhood services." (Linnea Lachman, Vermont Department of Education, at the Boston Public Hearing [1])

Our report, *Right from the Start*, seeks to shift the emphasis on development of programs for four-year-olds in the public schools to a much larger arena (1). Public schools can become the models for all that is best in developmentally appropriate practices through the use of an early education *unit*. Public school leaders can serve as the catalysts for building cooperative partnerships between public schools and existing community programs and agencies. Public school leaders and policymakers can plan and develop new services, in cooperation with other agencies, based on community needs and the capabilities of different providers. As Barbara Bowman from the Erikson Institute put it during her presentation about the report to the Chief State School Officers, "It is only when and if schools can change their tradition of working alone that young children at risk will be prepared for school success" (1).

It seems in many ways that the issue of early education has finally reached the public consciousness. Certainly, President Bush's announcement that he is recommending a substantial increase in Head Start funding affirms this belief. We are at a critical juncture in the provision of developmentally appropriate services to our early school entrants. NASBE's report is the most widely circulated publication in our association's history. The keen interest, evidenced by the many requests for speakers about the recommendations within the report as well as for the report itself, tells us that the yearlong effort was not only timely but right on the mark. Our commitment now is to promote the two major recommendations whenever and wherever we can.

> It is a reality that public schools will receive the vast majority of "graduates" from every form of early childhood program. It is clear that high-quality program experiences pave the way for children to succeed in school and in life. Similarly, children from poor-quality or unsupervised preschool settings begin school at a disadvantage and pose additional challenges for the schools. (1)

Our yearlong study and the ensuing report reaffirmed the Task Force's strong commitment to excellent beginnings. We are convinced "that childhood shows the man, as morning shows the day" (John Milton, *Paradise Regained* IV). To assure that the morning of a child's education is bright, that every beginning in formalized education is positive, is the aim of *Right from the Start*.

REFERENCES

1. NASBE Task Force on Early Childhood Education. *Right from the Start.* 1st ed. Alexandria, Va.: NASBE, October 1988.

2. Plowden, B. *Children and Their Primary Schools: A Report of the Central Advisory Council for Education.* London: Her Majesty's Stationery Office, 1966.

3. Schultz, T., and Lombardi, J. "Right from the Start: A Report on the NASBE Task Force on Early Childhood Education." *Young Children* (January 1989): 6-10.

NASN

National Association of School Nurses, Inc.

17. Health Perspectives on Early Childhood Education

by **Shirley Carstens, 1989-90 President,** *National Association of School Nurses, Inc. NASN has a membership of 5,700, with headquarters at P. O. Box 1300, Scarborough, Maine 04074.*

School nurses bring a broader perspective to early childhood education than primary elementary school; it is one that begins with the child's birth. Factors influencing the child's development and education may begin prior to conception, during the mother's pregnancy, or they may be related to the birth.

Public Laws 94-142 and 99-457 have significantly impacted the education system. The latter will continue to cause greater change within the education and health systems, as early intervention programs for children beginning at birth are implemented. School systems are expected to meet the health and education needs of an increasing number of medically fragile children. Only 3 percent of newborns have major birth defects; however, new technology is enabling nearly 2.5 percent of the infants to survive. This percentage does not reflect the increasing number of children arriving at our doors who are the result of their parents' high-risk behaviors, such as fetal alcohol syndrome, "crack" babies, HIV/AIDS, congenital syphilis, and a wide array of psychosocial problems. Educators are required by law to meet the needs of all these children.

To accomplish this, many early intervention education models are being implemented and others are in planning and developmental stages. Knowledge of growth and development, family dynamics, nursing and medical knowledge, and ability to facilitate change often places the school nurse as a key figure in early intervention/early childhood programs.

Healthy children learn better; therefore, health promotion and prevention of illness and injury are concerns for the generally healthy young child in the early elementary years. Often problems in this age group are subtle enough to have been undetected until children enter the school environment, where they are faced with increased mental and physical demands. The school nurse, in collaboration with the parents and educators, monitors the young child's development and health status to maintain an optimal level of wellness and educational success.

To provide the reader with the health trends of this broad age range, from birth through age eight, this chapter includes the perspectives of school nurses participating in a variety of early childhood education settings. Approaches range from (1) a home-based program for infants that progresses to a center-based model and serves many infants whose mothers were addicted to drugs; (2) teaching the parents to teach the child; (3) the "normal child" in a preschool program; (4) the preschool child with mild developmental delays; (5) the needs of the early elementary child; and (6) a perspective on health service delivery models.

A HOME-BASED INFANT PROGRAM
Bonnie Bear, R.N., B.S.N.
San Diego City Schools, San Diego, CA

Medical technology is saving an increasing number of premature babies as well as babies with formerly fatal anomalies. These infants may have cardiac and respiratory problems, immature immune systems, neurological deficits, etc. These conditions necessitate specialized early intervention programs, as defined in PL 99-457, where medical and educational services are blended to focus on the total child rather than on an isolated aspect of development.

Health care for these special needs children must be family-centered, with parents and professionals sharing their experience and knowledge. Family needs and priorities must be validated in designing the Individualized Family Service Plan (IFSP). The transdisciplinary team, with the nurse as health care specialist, must integrate health considerations into the IFSP and make necessary adaptations in home activities and in the classroom environment. Preservice and in-service staff training by the nurse assists the team in understanding the medical/health considerations that influence the child's ability to learn.

Very young infants and medically fragile children from birth to age three are well served with a nurse as a case manager when their health needs supersede their education needs. However, the overwhelmingly complex needs of these children must not eclipse the need for routine pediatric care and vision/hearing assessments, which are essential to ensure health and to determine if their sensory systems are intact. Multiple agencies are involved with these children; the nurse serves as liaison to avoid gaps or duplication of services.

An emerging population of babies with prenatal drug exposure (PDE) are impacting early intervention programs. According to a recent report, 375,000 newborns are affected annually, and this is probably a very low estimate. It is known that the number of neonates affected is reaching epidemic proportions. Los Angeles County has reported a doubling every year since 1983 of the number of infants born with illicit drugs in their urine (8).

Babies with PDE may be premature, have strokes, seizures, reduced brain growth, and/or multiple anomalies. They are also at risk for HIV, herpes, and chronic health problems. Infants with PDE may have poor body-state regulation, poor visual orientation, chronic irritability, and poor interactional skills, which impede bonding. Symptoms that emerge later include inability to concentrate, poor abstract reasoning and memory, poor judgment, a wide variety of behavior disorders, and violent acting-out. In addition to their biological vulnerabilities, these children often go through a series of foster homes or may be reunited with mothers who face health or emotional problems of their own and are thus unable to respond to the child's needs.

Thus, these children experience double jeopardy and need early, family-centered transagency intervention so they will not be caught in the same socioenvironmental bondage that contributed to their mother's drug abuse. Unfortunately, our current assessment tools are not sensitive enough to establish eligibility for an educational program for many of these children. We need more appropriate instruments for evaluation or we need to evaluate the eligibility criteria.

When these children do enter the school system, at birth or later, the educational delivery system must be flexible enough to accommodate the wide spectrum of deficiencies they may manifest and at the same time affirm the parent/child interaction, thereby strengthening the family support systems.

The health care plan for all children in early intervention programs should enhance the maturational readiness of the child as well as remediate or provide compensatory aid for health impairments. It must be a family-focused plan that anticipates and responds to fluctuating child/family needs.

PARENTS AS TEACHERS
June Heckle, R.N., B.S., Head Nurse
Normandy School District, St. Louis, MO

Missouri's internationally known Parents as Teachers program is a home-school partnership designed to give children the best possible start in life and to support parents in their role as the child's first teacher. Parents as Teachers is a primary prevention program designed to maximize children's overall development during the first three years of life, thus laying the foundation for school success and minimizing problems that might interfere with learning. Involving the parents in their child's learning is the key to success. Parents want to be effective parents and welcome the support that empowers them to enhance their children's intellectual, language, physical, and social development. Parents as Teachers is a voluntary program for all parents, but it must be offered by all districts in the state.

In addition to parent education, the program provides periodic screening for the purpose of giving parents information about the developmental progress of their child. The screening also identifies weak areas that need to be strengthened or possible problems to be further evaluated. The earlier a problem is identified, the better the chance for remediation and prevention of more serious conditions. The annual screening includes the areas of language, problem solving, motor and social interaction. Vision, hearing, and general health status are evaluated annually by the nurse, an important member of the multidisciplinary team, who has the knowledge to interpret and assess the health status of each child. The young child's development is related to his/her physical and emotional health and especially to the manner in which the parent applies parenting skills.

The parent may view and relate differently to the nurse and parent educator. Therefore, one or the other may obtain important data that was not previously shared. The multidisciplinary team approach is most effective in meeting the family's needs. As improved medical technology is now saving babies who are more fragile in their early years, these babies are presenting education with greater numbers of children with medical problems, and the need for a multidisciplinary team is great. Providing parents with the appropriate developmental milestones reduces their inappropriate expectations of behavior or skill. Appropriate expectations can reduce the incidence of child abuse, for example. The nurse provides in-service to the educational team regarding the significance of physical and medical problems for the growth and development of the child. The nurse is also responsible for parent education relative to health and safety.

Prevention is much more cost-effective than remediation; therefore, it should be the fiscal focus in all of education. Prevention programs such as Parents as Teachers will enable us to produce more healthy, happy, successful students, who will become productive citizens.

THE THREE- TO FIVE-YEAR-OLD PRESCHOOL CHILD
Sylvia Stivers, B.S.N., R.M., C.H.N.
Bates Home and Family Life, Tacoma, WA

The preschool years are a time when children are growing rapidly and assimilating a great deal. A primary goal of early childhood education needs to be to provide a healthy, safe, and developmentally appropriate environment in which each child's growth in all areas of development can be nurtured. Two key words summarize the focus necessary for health care with this age group—promotion and prevention.

What better time to promote wellness in children than in the preschool years as they are developing lifelong habits and attitudes. Stressing good handwashing practices will help reduce risk of exposure to infectious diseases. Helping them learn to make healthy food choices, value physical exercise, and learn to reduce stress are increasingly important as we learn more about cardiovascular disease and other chronic illnesses that begin in childhood. Encouraging children to feel capable and positive about themselves, express feelings appropriately, and learn problem-solving skills are vital in promoting mental health. These are essential building blocks for successful drug abuse prevention curricula.

Some of the best learning occurs when adults model healthy practices and attitudes and incorporate these into daily classroom routines. It is essential to involve parents in their child's learning in the early years and lay the foundation for continued involvement in later years. Immunizations prevent many of the illnesses that were once so prevalent in this age group. Some of the most common health concerns seen in preschools are visual problems, such as amblyopia ("lazy" eye), hearing loss from fluid in the middle ear, and anemia. Delays in development become more evident. Early identification is important to prevent further delay and promote optimal growth. Valuable tools in identifying potential problems are a staff knowledgeable about growth and development, classroom observations, and health screenings.

Expansion of early childhood education programs, particularly for high-risk children and families, emphasizes the need to focus on prevention and on promotion of wellness to help children succeed in later years.

DEVELOPMENTAL DELAYS IN THE THREE- TO FIVE-YEAR-OLD CHILD
Carol Holman, R.N., M.S.N., C.S.N.
JUST 4 Developmental Laboratory, Mobile, AL

The teacher observing a group of children from three to five years of age would find the most common characteristic to be a cough or "runny nose"; there may also be complaints about a stomachache or vomiting with or without diarrhea. The tendency might be to take care of the child with vomiting and diarrhea, and not think too much about the "runny nose," cough, or stomachache unless there were other symptoms such as fever.

All these signs and symptoms can be associated with middle ear effusion (swelling of middle ear tissue), which is the most common ear problem in preschool children. A hearing test can be given to determine the child's ability to respond to sounds; however, tympanometry (measurement of ear drum movement) can detect middle ear disorders without any response from the child. The otoscopic examination provides visual data about the ear canal and the tympanic membrane as well as some information about the middle ear. When these three tools are used to assess the child with these symptoms, chronic or intermittent ear infections can be identified, successfully treated, and followed in the school setting.

A significant number of these children have delayed speech and language skills or articulation deficits. The child may be inattentive to sounds, such as story time, quiet music, or verbal directions. These signs alert the educator to the child's need for assessment and referral. Another observation that may alert teachers to a speech and language problem is the child who continually breathes through the mouth. The mouth is usually open and the tongue may protrude at times. Teachers may further note this child snores at rest time or her/his breathing is unusually loud. This could be caused by enlarged adenoids or tonsils. Evaluation and treatment can prevent further speech and language delays, while possibly preventing future orthodontia problems.

Communication skills are vital in every aspect of life. Early identification and intervention can prevent permanent communication disorders that would impact the child's education.

THE PRIMARY ELEMENTARY CHILD
Barbara J. Ward, M.S., R.N., C.S.N.
Bow Memorial School, Bow, NH

Educators interacting with the young elementary child must have extensive knowledge of normal growth and development in order to identify those deviations that could impact the child's healthy development and learning. Elementary school children have few serious illnesses, although minor childhood diseases and acute illnesses continue to occur. Routine vision and hearing screening will identify any new defects, but hearing difficulties related to fluid and middle ear infections may persist even with treatment and require classroom modifications.

Although a characteristic of this age group is continued testing of permissible behavior, the possibility that a medical reason can be the cause of behavior problems must not be overlooked. Suspicion that a behavior problem may be related to hearing loss can result in prompt detection and treatment. Allergies or asthma, and drugs used to treat these and other medical conditions, can have undesirable side effects that interfere with alertness, attention span, and ability to learn. Childhood asthma affects 5 to 10 percent of children and causes more school absences than any other chronic disease of childhood. However, recent developments have made asthma a more manageable condition, responsive to school nurse intervention with the family and school staff.

The school nurse can contribute valuable information about the health and medical status of the child and about the family. Changing family patterns have created stresses in young children's lives, with the estimate that one-half of the children born now in the United States will spend part of their lives in a single-parent home. Because the development of self-esteem is essential in these early school years, it is important that all professionals in the school cooperate to achieve this goal. Teacher affection and approval are especially important for achievement, appropriate peer interaction, and positive self-concept.

Attention deficit disorder with or without hyperactivity can affect 3 to 5 percent of the school-age population. Attention deficit disorder is three times more frequent in boys than in girls. The educator who knows that attention span should show dramatic lengthening by age seven will (1) more accurately recognize the signs of this disorder, (2) involve the school nurse and parents, and (3) facilitate early diagnosis and management, which should have a positive effect on learning and emotional development.

School phobia and other adjustment problems of childhood may surface as the child works on the developmental task of separating from parents and establishing the ability to function independently and form peer relationships. Child abuse and neglect may also significantly impact a child's health, emotionally and physically. Educators need to be alert to the many indicators of abuse and involve the school nurse at the earliest suspicion.

Because injuries are still the primary cause of death in elementary school children, comprehensive health education needs to begin early. It should emphasize respect for self and others and responsibility for making decisions conducive to a safe and healthy lifestyle. Communication and cooperation between educators and school nurses can assure that health barriers to education will be eliminated or minimized for all school children.

HEALTH SERVICES DELIVERY IN EARLY CHILDHOOD PROGRAMS
Susan Lordi, R.N., M.S., P.N.P.
Los Angeles County Office of Education, Downey, CA

Health services delivery to children, birth to seven years are categorized by the legislative and regulatory initiatives that govern and finance the needed services. All the initiatives recognize the necessity for speedy provision of services to children who are growing and developing rapidly, particularly through the period of infancy and toddlerhood.

PL 99-457, Part H, established a comprehensive, coordinated interdisciplinary program of early intervention services for handicapped infants and toddlers and their families. The essential construct of this program is that services be family centered and interdisciplinary. Thus the school nurse may provide direct services to these children in the home, or assist the parents to identify and utilize the services provided by educators and community providers. Parents face a bewildering array of providers with different requirements for services. In some cases, services are simply not available. The school nurse in PL 99-457 programs has a unique opportunity to act as a child advocate in forming a bridge between the school, parent, and community in an effort to find comprehensive, unduplicated care for children with special needs.

Children age three to five receive services from multiple categorical programs, among them Head Start, State Preschool, Migrant and Special Education Programs. The school nurse is an integral part of these programs in the public sector. Services range from developmental assessment, provision of physical assessment, screening and immunization programs, case management services, provision and/or supervision of specialized physical health care procedures, consultation to staff and parents, and health promotion activities. Parent education is a component of all early childhood programs and one in which the school nurse has and will continue to play a significant role.

For the child whose first entry in the educational system occurred in early intervention or preschool programs, the school nurse is responsible for assisting in transition to the K-12 system. The welcome afforded parents and children with special needs to the elementary school is critical to a successful education experience. For those children with special health needs, the school nurse is the key player in planning for the provision of appropriate health services at school and for preparation of staff to receive the child with understanding and acceptance.

Health services to children in elementary schools are more traditional in that the school nurse continues to be the primary provider. The school nurse does not serve students in a vacuum but relies on interdisciplinary collaboration to enhance program management; delivery of services to individual students; health promotion activities; and advocacy in obtaining needed remediation, restoration and rehabilitative services in the community.

School health services delivery remains a partnership between educators, parents, community services providers, and the primary provider, the school nurse. For some students, the school nurse is the only health provider they ever see. For other students with increasingly technologically sophisticated health needs, the presence of the school nurse ensures their access to an educational program in the least restrictive environment. For still other students, the school nurse serves as a provider of screening services, a health instructor or resource to their teacher, a role model for health promotion, and a safe harbor when coping with a bad day.

Students will continue to require and receive health services in school. The continuum will range from consultative services to direct primary care. The point of entry to school health services will not be based on age, but on need. The escalating cost of providing health care compels all of us to endorse the delivery of cost-effective prevention and rehabilitative services to children at the earliest possible age. The school nurse will continue to provide those services.

REFERENCES

1. American Academy of Pediatrics. *School Health: A Guide for Health Professionals.* Elk Grove Village, Ill.: AAP, 1987.
2. Head Start Programs. *Series on Mainstreaming Preschoolers.* Washington, D.C.: U.S. Department of Health and Human Services, 1978.
3. Institute for Child Study. *ASCD: Developmental Characteristics of Children and Youth.* College Park, Md.: University of Maryland, 1975.
4. Johnson, D. H.; McGonigel, M. U.; and Kaufmann, R. K., eds. *Guidelines and Recommended Practices for the Individualized Family Service Plan.* Washington, D.C.: National Early Childhood Technical Assistance Systems, 1989.
5. Kendrick, A. S.; Kaufmann, R.; and Messenger, K., eds. *Healthy Young Children: A Manual for Programs.* Washington, D.C.: National Association for the Education of Young Children, 1988.
6. Lewis, K. D., and Thomson, H. B. *Manual of School Health.* Menlo Park, Calif.: Addison-Wesley Publishing Co., 1986.
7. Meisles, S. J., and Provence, S. *Screening and Assessment: Guidelines for Identifying Young Disabled and Developmentally Vulnerable Children and Their Families.* Washington, D.C.: National Center for Clinical Infant Programs, 1989.
8. National Association for Perinatal Addiction Research and Education. "Innocent Addicts: High Rate of Prenatal Drug Abuse Found." *ADAMHA News* (October 1988): 2.
9. National Center for Clinical Infant Programs. *Intent and Spirit of 99-457.* Washington, D.C.: NCCIP, 1989.
10. Plaut, T. F. *Children with Asthma,* 2d ed. Amherst, Mass.: Pedipress, 1988.
11. Staff. *Chadder.* Plantation, Fla.: Children with Attention Deficit Disorder, 1989.
12. U.S. Department of Education and U.S. Department of Health and Human Services. *Report to the Congress: Meeting the Needs of Infants and Toddlers with Handicaps.* Washington, D.C.: Government Printing Office, 1989.

NASP

National Association of School Psychologists

18. Toward Improved Early Childhood Education in the 21st Century

by **Margaret Dawson, 1990-91 President,** *National Association of School Psychologists; and* **Howard M. Knoff, 1989-90 President,** *NASP. NASP has a membership of 15,000, with headquarters at Suite 1000, 8455 Colesville Road, Silver Spring, Maryland 20910.*

While American education has many challenges to confront as it heads into the 21st century, early childhood education surely is one of the most critical. Changing lifestyles and changing family patterns mean that the vast majority of children in this country no longer live in homes with a breadwinner father and a housewife mother. In fact, only 7 percent of American households fit this pattern—a pattern that was the norm only a generation ago. With increased numbers of children from single-parent families, from two-working-parent families, from blended families, and from families living below the poverty line, children no longer begin school with a common core of experience. When children walk through the schoolhouse door for the first time, the challenge for early childhood educators will be to recognize that they all bring unique combinations of needs, backgrounds, and experiences and to create learning environments that accommodate those disparate characteristics. An equal challenge will be to develop a core set of learning experiences that will enable American schools to meet the mandate of equal educational opportunities for all children.

This challenge will require changing the way early childhood education programs are configured. To do this, we will need to understand how societal influences external to schools impact on the job schools have to do. We will need to take what is unique about growing up in the late 20th century and combine it with what we know is immutable about children's patterns of development and learning. We cannot ask schools to solve society's problems. But, we must acknowledge that children bring certain realities to school with them that may make more traditional classroom structures ineffective, and then we must design classrooms that educationally adapt and respond to their needs. If schools are to do this successfully, they will need to draw on all the resources they have to assist with this process. One important resource that most schools have available to them is the school psychologist.

SCHOOL PSYCHOLOGY AND EARLY CHILDHOOD EDUCATION

The training standards of the National Association of School Psychologists (NASP) require that school psychologists receive three full years of graduate training in psychological and educational theory and foundations (e.g., child development, learning theory, educational psychology), school psychological practice (assessment, consultation, and interventions), and research and statistical methods. This training involves as least 60 graduate credit hours and the conferral of a master's degree, and it includes a full-year supervised internship in a school setting. Because of this comprehensive training and their expertise in school and curricular processes, school psychologists understand the individual child in the context of the schooling process. Thus, when a child is experiencing learning or behavioral problems in school, teachers, parents, and administrators often turn to the school psychologist for assistance.

At present, the school psychologist's most visible role in the schools is to work with unsuccessful or troubled children. Typically, this work involves a problem-solving process that assesses three interdependent facets of the school environment: the teacher or instructional process, the curriculum, and the child. Thus, the child is always evaluated in the context of the school's academic and social expectations, and typically, there are multiple explanations and solutions to any problems of concern.

Given this comprehensive problem-solving process, the assistance that the school psychologist offers can take many forms. The school psychologist might (a) observe in the classroom and make suggestions for modifying instructional methods or designing behavioral interventions; (b) meet with the child's parent and focus on ways to foster home-school collaboration and problem solving; (c) provide counseling support for the child and his/her specific concerns. Yet, because of their organizational and systems experience, school psychologists might be in a position to take on an even broader perspective and role, In addition to being specialists on children's learning and behavioral disorders and treatment, school psychologists have training in organizational and group process consultation and in systemic assessment, intervention, and problem solving. With this training, school psychologists can help school systems make the organizational and programmatic adaptations necessary to more effectively address our children's early childhood needs—both presently and preventively. Thus, school psychologists are in a unique position to help schools make the transformations necessary at both the *child and system* levels to meet the complex needs of the children of the 21st century.

THE NATIONAL ASSOCIATION OF SCHOOL PSYCHOLOGISTS AND EARLY CHILDHOOD EDUCATION

The National Association of School Psychologists (NASP) represents more than 15,000 school psychologists throughout the United States. The mission of NASP is twofold: (a) to promote the educational and mental health needs of all children and youth, and (b) to advance the profession of school psychology. With respect to early childhood education, NASP is committed to work for change at two levels, a policy level and a practice level. At a policy level, NASP develops and promotes policies and positions that address critical issues and problems faced by today's schools and children. At a practice level, NASP keeps its members informed and provides training opportunities that enable school psychologists to provide the most effective services they can within the schools in which they work.

In recent years, NASP has issued a broad set of policy statements addressing a variety of critical issues facing the profession of school psychology and education in general. These policy statements, when taken as a whole, represent a vision for early childhood education—a set of reforms that, if implemented, will restructure schools to recognize individual differences and the need for schools to accommodate to children rather than requiring children to accommodate to schools. These policy statements call for—

1. *Quality early child care.* The availability of quality early child care programs increases the likelihood that children will come to school ready to learn and with a common set of learning experiences behind them. Participation in quality child care programs increases prosocial behavior in children and decreases the likelihood of school retention and/or placement in special education.

2. *The availability of appropriate educational services for all children within the regular classroom.* All children have unique learning needs, and some children require specialized services. To the maximum extent possible, these services should be provided within the regular classroom, eliminating the need to classify children as handicapped in order to receive these services.

3. *The use of prereferral screening and prevention/intervention services.* These services ameliorate educational difficulties without the necessity of submitting to costly special educational assessment procedures involving multiple educational professionals and other specialists. Using a group problem-solving format, children's needs can be addressed immediately and directly by providing support directly to classroom teachers to solve learning and behavior problems in the classroom.

4. *The development of alternatives to the use of retention.* Holding students back in school as young as kindergarten and first grade is widely practiced, yet the research shows that, over the long run, retention is likely to have deleterious effects on achievement, self-concept, attitudes toward school, and school dropout rates. Other methods of accommodating students with a range of abilities and skills, such as systematic problem-solving and curricular/behavioral adaptation, are recommended.

5. *The comprehensive restructuring of schools.* Today's schools and traditional models of schooling are failing too many of today's students. Successful schools recognize that children learn in different ways and incorporate experiential and participative learning strategies into instruction. Such schools emphasize heterogeneous classes, cooperative learning, peer-assisted learning, and other adaptive education strategies that meet individual

learning needs in diverse group settings.

At a national level, NASP has shared this vision with other education groups to promote a dialogue and a collaborative effort toward positive change (see the References for a listing of these statements and relevant NASP publications). The primary policy statements underlying our push toward improved early childhood education are briefly reviewed in the following pages.

Advocacy for Appropriate Educational Services for All Children and *Rights Without Labels.* In 1985, NASP and the National Coalition of Advocates for Students (NCAS) passed and published a position statement on *Advocacy for Appropriate Educational Services for All Children.* Recognizing the increasing numbers of at-risk, poor, and culturally diverse children entering our schools, and the disproportionately large percent of these children who are referred and placed into special education, this statement notes that

> On the one hand, access to special education must be assured for all significantly handicapped children who need and can benefit from it . . . Conversely, children are being inappropriately diagnosed as handicapped and placed in special education because of: (a) a lack of regular education options designed to meet the needs of children with diverse learning styles, (b) a lack of understanding, at times, of diverse cultural and linguistic backgrounds, and (c) inadequate measurement technologies which focus on labels for placement rather than providing information for program development.
>
> It is not a benign action to label as "handicapped" children who are low achievers but are not, in fact, handicapped, even when this is done in order to provide them with services unavailable in general education . . . problems originating in th[is] classification system include:
>
> - Labels that are often irrelevant to instructional needs.
> - Categories, based on deficit labels, that are rather arbitrarily defined, particularly for mildly handicapped and low-achieving students, but which come to be accepted as "real" and may prevent more meaningful understanding of the child's psychoeducational needs.
> - Reduced expectations for children who are placed in special needs programs.

- Assessment processes aimed at determining eligibility which often deflect limited resources from the determination of functional educational needs and the development of effective psychoeducational programs.
- A decreased willingness on the part of regular education, at times bordering on abdication of responsibility, to modify curricula and programs in order to better meet the diverse needs of all children.

This position paper went on to state (a) that all children can learn and that schools have the responsibility to teach *all* children in the least restrictive setting and in a positive social environment; (b) that instructional options, based on the individual psychoeducational needs of each child, must be provided *with necessary support services* in the regular classroom; (c) that children's psychoeducational needs should be determined through multidimensional, nonbiased assessment processes; and (d) that children at risk for school failure should receive organized and impactful services as early as possible so that a later need for special education might be prevented. Finally, this paper challenged educators to develop and pilot such alternative service delivery models, systems, programs, and procedures that the dependence on unnecessary special education services can be broken.

As an expansion of the *Advocacy for Appropriate Educational Services for All Children* statement, NASP, NCAS, and the National Association of Social Workers passed a position statement on *Rights Without Labels*. This statement asserts that schools should, as much as possible, serve children who have special needs without labels and without removing them from regular education programs. To accomplish this, it is suggested that regular school personnel should investigate any child's presumed educational or social-emotional difficulty with the support of the school psychologist and other pupil personnel specialists *before* making a formal referral for possible special education services. From a special education perspective, this position statement asserts that, "[o]ur goal is to broaden the classroom situation within which special education resources can be used and to reverse the practice of moving handicapped students to special education situations outside regular classes and schools." But, in general, this statement expresses the hope that children's problems can be identified, confirmed, and addressed in the regular classroom throughout their educational careers so that they can maintain their educational progress, their self-efficacy, and their potential to succeed, graduate from high school, and ultimately enter the work force.

From an early childhood perspective, the *Rights Without Labels* statement recommends that, for children having learning and/or behavioral difficulties, school systems use (a) prereferral screening and intervention procedures and evaluations that include curriculum-based measures, (b) effective teaching and learning methods, (c) curricula that focus on basic skills (e.g., reading, language, self-dependence, mathematics, social skills behavior), and procedures that identify and serve those who need modifications in their instructional program. *Every* child has the right to these services *without* the requirement that they be labeled handicapped or anything else. Clearly, at the early childhood level, one's educational label is irrelevant; the functional and pragmatic issue is whether a student is receiving the instruction necessary to make educational progress.

Significantly, the primary message in both position statements has been heard. This is evident given the growing educational reform movement, the development of a number of regular educational programs that serve at-risk children (1, 2), and the demonstration that many effective interventions are available that can facilitate children's progress in the regular classroom (4). School psychology is at the cutting edge of this movement, these services, and these technological advances. A special education placement *is not* an intervention. A special education placement is simply the optimal environment in which the educational and/or behavioral programs and interventions needed by a specific child are best delivered. Further, a special education placement should be considered only when regular classroom interventions have been shown to be empirically ineffective, and only when evaluations of the special education program have documented sufficient educational and/or behavioral progress. For at-risk children, the same principles and procedures apply. With so many young children at risk for educational and social failure, the National Association of School Psychologists feels that these children have the right to receive appropriate educational services in the regular classroom without the added burden of biased or damaging labels. For us, the bottom line is *service delivery*—a process that involves creativity, training, problem solving, advocacy, and daily consultation and collaboration.

Early Intervention Services and *Early Childhood Care and Education.* As briefly noted above, NASP believes that we must listen to the research that has shown that early intervention with handicapped and at-risk infants, toddlers, and preschool children is effective in terms of benefits to children, their families, the educational process, and society. For example, the Children's Defense Fund in 1988 (3) noted that for every $1 spent immunizing our young children or providing nutritional supplements to low-income pregnant women, we save $10 and $3, respectively, in later health costs. And, for every $1 spent in quality early childhood programs like Head Start for poor preschool children, we save $4.75 in later educational, community, and other costs.

In order to publicize and respond to the implications of these facts and conditions, NASP passed a position paper in 1987 on *Early Intervention Services* that encouraged school psychologists to take part in national, state, and local efforts to—

1. Assure that programs for young children are built on recognition of the needs and developmental characteristics of typical, handicapped, and at-risk children.
2. Work with school administrators, teachers, and parents to develop programs that attend to all important aspects of the development of young children, including cognitive, motor, self-help, social-emotional, and communication development.
3. Promote programs which provide reliable and valid means of screening young children for possible handicapping and at-risk conditions as early as possible.
4. Encourage the use of flexible team assessment approaches which take into account the unique attributes and variability of young children and the influence of home and family factors on their development.
5. Support the provision of necessary individualized services without attempting to assign labels for specific handicapping conditions.
6. Work toward establishing programs which provide a broad spectrum of options for intervention, opportunities for parents to receive

support and assistance, and mainstreaming opportunities wherever possible.

7. Encourage university programs, professional associations, public schools and other continuing education providers to provide opportunities for practitioners to receive professional development experiences that adequately prepare them to serve the needs of young children and their families.

8. Help establish networks of communication and collaboration among the many agencies that provide service to infants, toddlers, and preschool children.

9. Advocate for the provision of state and federal funding to assure that appropriate programs for infants, toddlers, and preschoolers are provided.

As a followup, NASP passed its position paper on *Early Childhood Care and Education* in 1989. This statement, based on the current research, stated that there is (a) a need for affordable, quality early childhood education and care; and (b) that high-quality early childhood care and education can especially benefit economically disadvantaged children and families. The paper ended with NASP resolving to support more federal and state programs that provide equal access to affordable, high-quality early childhood care and education for all children and their families; standards to ensure child care quality; research that continues to investigate factors related to quality early child care; and more home-school-agency partnerships that make accessible and comprehensive early childhood services available to all families who need them.

CONCLUSIONS AND FUTURE DIRECTIONS

Schools and providers of early childhood education must adapt and respond to the way that children are entering the schoolhouse door. In order to do that, many schools may need to restructure their processes toward greater excellence. Combining what we know about the cognitive and social development of children, the social and economic factors that affect the American family, and the most effective educational policies and practices, we can draw a picture of early childhood education in the 21st century. This vision would include the following:

1. Appropriate services, as needed, will be available prenatally to at-risk mothers and postnatally at-risk children.

2. All children will have access to quality day care and early childhood education programs at a reasonable cost to their parents.

3. Appropriate services will be provided to children without the need for stigmatizing labels or evaluations that are completed solely to determine eligibility for services.

4. Service providers will work collaboratively with each other and with parents to ensure that children are served in an integrated and comprehensive fashion.

5. Parent involvement will be a critical component of all early childhood programs. Parents will be encouraged to actively participate in all facets of their children's education.

6. To the maximum extent possible, the needs of handicapped and at-risk children will be addressed within mainstream preschool programs. This will provide these children with positive role models and will enable all children to develop an understanding of and appreciation for individual differences.

7. Early childhood education programs will be designed to educate the *whole* child. Programs will systematically integrate their curricula and activities toward maximum social, emotional, cognitive, and physical development.

8. Early childhood programs will recognize that "typical" development involves a broad range of milestones and behaviors, and that each child's social and educational progress is unique. For this reason, programs will be flexible and individualized, accommodating each child's individual differences with a wide range of ideas, materials, and activities.

9. Early childhood programs will acknowledge that young children learn through play, discovery, and active interactions in diverse environments and with other children. Thus, these programs will guide children's learning using developmentally appropriate strategies, and they will resist external pressures to use the

academically oriented strategies associated with elementary school education.

The early childhood programs of the 21st century will hopefully have greater access to school psychologists who will function in a far more comprehensive role than at present. These school psychologists will bring a wide range of skills and a broad knowledge base to preschool and early elementary school programs, and they will work primarily as collaborative problem solvers with educators and parents to address a wide assortment of educational, social, and behavioral problems. With their understanding of child development, normal and abnormal behavior, behavior management, and curriculum and instruction, school psychologists will be an important resource for teachers as they plan for and work with the children in their classrooms. Similarly, when the need arises, they will work with parents to solve problems that exist at home yet significantly affect school adjustment and performance.

For the profession of school psychology, comprehensive service delivery to schools, school personnel, children, and families will be the key to quality early childhood education. School psychologists will have to use every facet of their extensive training, and integrate their assessment, consultation, and intervention skills to directly impact their primary clients. To do this, consultation will likely become the greatest common denominator of school psychological services. This is the role the U.S. Office of Special Education and Rehabilitative Services has proposed (5), noting that among the empirical and demonstrated outcomes of consultation services are—

1. More assistance available to help students in regular classrooms;
2. More support to classroom teachers, and more teacher satisfaction for the services provided;
3. Improved academic and behavioral performance of students; and
4. A more positive impact on improving classroom teachers' understanding, skills, and confidence when intervening with difficult-to-teach students.

Critically, this is the role preferred by school psychologists working in the field.

The National Association of School Psychologists is working collaboratively with students, parents, teachers, administrators, and other state and national associations to ensure that we will all be ready to educate the children of the 21st century. For us, the watchwords are prevention, appropriate services for all children, excellence, early intervention, advocacy, and rights without labels. We invite our colleagues to join with us, to debate the issues, to forge consensuses, and to face the challenges ahead. Socially and educationally, our students and school systems have lost ground during the 1980s. Hopefully, we can rebound during the 1990s so that our next generation has an equal opportunity for accomplishment and success in the years ahead.

REFERENCES

1. Canter, A., and Dawson, P. *Directory of Alternative Service Models.* 2d ed. Washington, D.C.: National Association of School Psychologists, 1989.
2. Canter, A.; Dawson, P.; Silverstein, J.; Hale, L.; and Zins, J. *NASP Directory of Alternative Service Models.* Washington, D.C.: National Association of School Psychologists, 1987.
3. Children's Defense Fund. *A Call for Action to Make Our Nation Safe for Children: A Briefing Book on the Status of American Children in 1988.* Washington, D.C.: CDF, 1988.
4. Graden, J. L.; Zins, J. E.; and Curtis, M. J. *Alternative Educational Delivery Systems: Enhancing Educational Options for All Students.* Washington, D.C.: National Association of School Psychologists, 1988.
5. Will, M. *The Role of School Psychology in Providing Services to All Children.* Washington, D.C.: Office of Special Education and Rehabilitative Services, U.S. Department of Health and Human Services, 1989.

POSITION PAPERS AVAILABLE FROM THE NATIONAL ASSOCIATION OF SCHOOL PSYCHOLOGISTS

AIDS

Advocacy for Appropriate Educational Services for All Children

At-Risk Students and Excellence in Education: The Need for Educational Restructuring

Corporal Punishment
Early Childhood Care and Education
Early Intervention Services
Minority Recruitment
Rights Without Labels
Student Grade Retention
Three-Year Evaluations for Handicapped Students

STANDARDS DOCUMENTS AVAILABLE FROM THE NATIONAL ASSOCIATION OF SCHOOL PSYCHOLOGISTS

Standards for Training and Field Placement Programs in School Psychology
Standards for the Credentialing of School Psychologists
Principles for Professional Ethics
Standards for the Provision of School Psychological Services

NBCDI

National Black Child Development Institute

19. Public School-Based Child Care and the Black Child: Building Bridges Toward Self-Sufficiency in the 21st Century

by **Evelyn K. Moore,** *Executive Director, National Black Child Development Institute. NBCDI has a membership of nearly 3,000, with headquarters at 1463 Rhode Island Avenue, N.W., Washington, DC 20005.*

As America prepares to enter the 21st century, our nation, in general, and the Black community, in particular, must strive to bridge the gaps that continue to allow many of our children to fail. The future depends upon the creation of solutions that enable our young people to successfully move from one stage of life to the next; that empower children to think critically, meet new challenges, and adapt to new environments. Because several research projects have demonstrated that developmentally appropriate early childhood education programs provide children with the skills that they need to enjoy later success in school and in life, early childhood education programs must become a national priority. Toward this goal, advocacy organizations have kept this issue in the arena of public policy development and Congress has deliberated over the merits of numerous bills calling for the public support of comprehensive, quality child care programming.

In response to the rising concern over the realization of this national goal, the National Black Child Development Institute (NBCDI) has taken the initiative of developing *Safeguards*, a series of guidelines to further the establishment of culturally and developmentally appropriate programming in the public schools for preschool-age children. Using *Safeguards* as a foundation, our schools can begin constructing the first bridge toward self-sufficiency that our children will have to cross.

The placement of preschool-age children in the public schools has always been a controversial issue (1). Supporters of the initiative, such as Edward Zigler, a professor of psychology at Yale University, argue that the unification of the child care system within the nation's institutions of public schooling provides all children with access to dependable and steady child care arrangements regardless of parental income.

Critics of public school programming for preschoolers, however, contend that the problems associated with the initiative far outweigh the benefits of increased accessibility and affordability. They argue that existing public school programming is too rigid to accommodate the developmental needs of three- and four-year-old children in such cases where curricula primarily transfer information out of context and lesson plans rely on passive learning, following instructions, and maintaining order. In contrast, children of this age group naturally absorb information through action: their learning methods can resemble a lack of structure, planning, and control to people unfamiliar with the rudimentary tenets of early childhood development. A recent study of child care in the public schools seems to support the skeptics' fears about the ineffective and developmentally inappropriate content of programs that the public schools offer preschoolers (2).

To further complicate this matter, in a 1984 report entitled "Child Care in the Public Schools: Incubator for Inequality?" NBCDI noted that many public school-based child care programs tend to overemphasize the history, culture, and values of white middle-class society (3). Programs of this type, which do not adequately explore the social contributions or mores of minority peoples, can alienate minority children, and therefore fail to reinforce the children's social and emotional development.

The National Black Child Development Institute takes particular interest in this child care controversy because public school-based programs attract large numbers of Black children. There are four reasons for their high levels of participation. First, many of the programs are designed to serve "at-risk" children; racial and ethnic minorities compose a disproportionately large percentage of the children who are eligible for these services. Second, 58 percent of Black mothers of children under six years of age participate in the labor force (4). Thus, among these women, there is a constant demand for reliable day care arrangements. Third, many Black parents believe that school-based child care programs offer the best means of preparing their children for the academic demands of elementary school. Therefore, when given a choice of child care settings,

Black parents often prefer public schools. Fourth, and finally, for economic reasons, low-income Black parents will choose to place their children in the public school programs where services tend to be free.

For these reasons, using public school settings for the placement of free or low-cost child care programs appeals to Black child advocates. Yet, we support this trend with caution. Our ambivalence stems from our observation that most urban public school systems presently serving Black children are already overburdened. These schools are often being asked to provide more services for children than is currently possible within existing stringent budgetary limits. Thus, many school systems are unable to meet our young people's needs, as evidenced by increasing numbers of children lingering in a chasm of academic failure.

Rather than simply finding fault with the public school system for our children's declining school record, NBCDI is committed to excellence in public school education and to the solution of existing problems in ways that benefit Black children. In fact, we praise and support the individuals who struggle daily to maintain high-quality programming for our children. We also commend those who are receptive to the suggestions and aid of outside organizations to create a national imperative that will lead our children to academic success.

NBCDI believes that public schools can successfully merge child care into existing educational programming by allocating adequate resources and by designing programs based upon sound principles of good early childhood practices. For example, the French-American Foundation recently sponsored a study panel to examine the French system of early childhood education (5). In France, free public preschools serve nearly 90 percent of children three- to five-years of age. The programs in France incorporate trained, dedicated teachers, safe and healthy environments, and activities that promote growth and learning.

The Ministry of National Education staffs and establishes policy and curriculum for the preschools. All preschool teachers in France have the equivalent of master's degrees in early childhood and elementary education. Systematic linkages with the health care system ensure that every child in preschool care receives regular preventative health care. The French system offers one model from which the United States can

NBCDI

learn as the public school system is restructured to incorporate proper early childhood development approaches.

While the United States can look to France for initial guidance on this issue, we must develop national early childhood standards and programs that address the size and varying cultural backgrounds of the American people. The ten *Safeguards* listed below represent a compilation of NBCDI's experience in constructive programming for preschool-age children and offer clear and direct suggestions for ways of ensuring that early childhood education programs in the public schools create a learning environment for Black children that is productive and effective (6). The *Safeguards* include the following:

1. Public school-based programs for Black, preschool-age children should incorporate an effective parent education program.
2. Public school-based early childhood programs should involve parents in the decisions about the curriculum and policy.
3. The staff of early childhood education programs should include teachers who come from the community served by the program and who are racially and ethnically representative of the children served.
4. Teachers in public school-based programs should be required to have specific training in preschool education and/or ongoing, in-service training by qualified staff.
5. Curriculum for preschool-age children in the public schools should be culturally sensitive and appropriate to the child's age and level of development.
6. Public schools which house programs for very young children should meet the same health and safety standards which apply to independent preschools and center-based child care programs.
7. Public school-based early childhood programs should participate in federal and state programs which guarantee adequate nutrition to children.
8. Administrators of public school-based programs for preschoolers should ensure that children entering the programs have access to appropriate health care.
9. In addressing children of preschool age, the administrators of public school-based early childhood programs should not limit

their assessment to, or base their program planning solely on, standardized tests.
10. Public school-based early childhood programs should be subject to regular, external review by community members and early childhood development experts.

NBCDI's *Safeguards* are designed to address the Black preschool child's needs in a holistic manner. Instead of dealing with the child as an isolated being, they encourage public school officials to develop programs that address every factor that could possibly affect the child's school experience. To promote positive experiences in early childhood development programs and to ensure that children are adequately prepared for elementary school, the parents must be involved; the teachers must be trained and qualified; the curriculum must be appropriate to the child's age level and cultural background; the children must be kept healthy, safe, and well nourished; the determination of the child's ability to advance to elementary school must not be based solely on standardized tests; and, finally, the programs must be monitored to ensure that high degrees of quality and safety are maintained. Without all these components, the level of child care in many of our nation's public schools will remain dangerously low. Furthermore, the degree of a child's preparation for elementary school will depend largely on family income as developmentally appropriate child care programming becomes a scarce, expensive commodity. Our nation must correct this deficiency and develop an outstanding and equitable child care system.

The fulfillment of so many different objectives may seem taxing and unnecessary. However, the importance of each *Safeguard* to our children's well-being cannot be overemphasized.

Parental involvement, the objective of the first two *Safeguards*, is important for two reasons: first, the child's need for continuity, and second, a parent's function as his or her child's first role model and primary teacher. Continuity between home and school has been proven to enhance children's development and to maximize children's learning experiences. Parents, many of whom do not really know what developmentally appropriate practices for preschoolers entail, are children's first and most important teachers. Therefore, if we are to prevent the children from experiencing later academic failure, it is imperative that we first reach the parents. School systems must teach parents the elements of developmentally appropriate practices. With this accomplished, teachers and parents will be more accepting of each other's demands and both parties will work more effectively for other children's benefits. More importantly, when teachers and parents reward similar behaviors and maintain similar expectations, children will enjoy continuity between home and school. This consistency provides children with a solid foundation of understanding and self-awareness that facilitates the expansion of knowledge and the ability to face new challenges.

To facilitate the process of parent education and involvement in public school-based early childhood education programs, school systems can implement several strategies. Specially trained parent educators can be hired to organize family-centered activities and to operate districtwide parent education centers, featuring toy and book lending libraries, resource guides, and educational materials. Furthermore, parents will become more of an asset to early childhood education programs if educators enable them to become involved on more than just a superficial level. After all, parents are most familiar with their children's needs. Therefore, parents should be welcomed at child care facilities and their input on curricula and policy should be seriously considered.

The first and fourth *Safeguards* deal with the *staffing of public school-based child care programs.* Young Black children view their teachers as very powerful, important people. Teachers are essential role models for children and it is often through these role models that children's aspirations and goals are set for life. Children need to see people of their own race in positions of power so that they will realize that Black people can function effectively in mainstream society. Furthermore, Black parents often feel more comfortable with child care programs if the staff and administrators reflect the racial and ethnic diversity of the children being served.

The need for teacher training is also very important. The 1989 Child Care Staffing Study restated the fact that teachers are the key determinants of the quality of child care programs (7). Their skills, knowledge, and enthusiasm are the most instrumental factors in deciding how and what the children will learn. Given the burden of this responsibility, schools should employ highly trained individuals and should make additional training available to all employees—i.e., teachers, in addition to teaching assistants, bus drivers, nurses, and community outreach personnel. The study also stresses that the quality of child care that is offered depends upon how teachers are treated. To maximize the benefits of child care services, in addition to formal training opportunities, early childhood education teachers must receive wages and employee benefits comparable to those of other teachers; they must be valued within the school system; and they must be afforded the best of working conditions—i.e., programs must adhere to low student-to-teacher ratios, small group size, and all state regulations.

The fifth *Safeguard* emphasizes the *importance of developmentally appropriate and culturally connected curricula*. NBCDI maintains that programs for preschool children in public schools should not be diluted versions of those offered in the first grade. Educators must bolster preschool children's energy, enthusiasm, and creativity (8). Rigid, academic routines will cause children of this age to miss important information and will dampen their interest in learning.

Culturally connected curricula are also mandatory for retaining a child's interest in his or her preschool program. Because preschool is usually a child's first social experience outside the home, programs must be sensitive to the child's background. Children learn best in familiar surroundings and, therefore, an appropriate child care setting will emphasize the child's family's positive mores and will also demonstrate respect for the child's cultural heritage.

The sixth, seventh, and eighth *Safeguards* deal with *maintaining the health and safety of the children in the public school-based programs*. Children learn best when they are healthy, well nourished, and protected from injury and disease. Therefore, the programs must ensure that children are given wholesome, well-balanced meals, and receive adequate health care. Extra precautions must also be taken to protect children from the spread of disease. All staff and children should be screened to check general health and immunization records. Furthermore, public school settings may require adjustments to ensure that preschoolers can play and learn in areas of maximum safety.

The ninth *Safeguard* addresses the issue of *assessing the performance of young children.* Traditional assessments are often valuable for creating a learning environment, but should not be used to determine entry or promotion. Educators should never depend solely on standardized tests to evaluate the performances of three- and four-year-old children, because, for one of many reasons, at this age, children have not developed a standard way of processing information. Rather than being helpful in determining what a child learns, these conventional tools often lead to tracking and stereotypical classifications. Instead of relying on tests, teachers should chart children's progress and make careful observations of children's styles of learning and play.

The need for *objective assessment of preschool programs* summarizes the focus of the tenth *Safeguard*. External review teams provide teachers and directors with information on how the programs are perceived and with ideas for improving existing policies and procedures. Inviting local business people, child advocates, parents, and concerned citizens to serve on this Review Committee will also benefit the public schools by giving programs access to additional human and financial resources. Child care staff can receive input for making improvements and can probably also encourage those who are suggesting the changes to play an active role in realizing them.

Child care in public schools can be successful if effective, comprehensive early childhood education programs are developed. The *Safeguards* are designed to protect all children from unproductive, spirit-dampening early childhood education experiences. If public school officials incorporate the *Safeguards* as they plan and implement child care programs, children served by these programs will receive benefits equal to those offered more frequently in private sector and community-based arrangements; low- and middle-income children, whom the public school-based programs tend to serve, will be more prepared to deal with the demands of elementary school, and all our nation's children will begin to be more successful in school. The accomplishment of these objectives will bridge the first gap in our education system and will begin to allow our children, regardless of class, ethnic, or racial background, to competently lead our nation in the next century.

NOTES

1. William Tobin, "Will Schools Monopolize Child Care?" *Center Management* 1, no. 3 (1990): 43-44.

2. Anne Mitchell, Fern Marx, and Michelle Seligson, *Public School Early Childhood Study* (New York: Bank Street College of Education, 1988).

3. "Child Care in the Public Schools: Incubator for Inequality?" (Washington, D.C.: National Black Child Development Institute, 1985).

4. "Women in the Work Force," Fact Sheet (Washington, D.C.: National Commission on Working Women and Wider Opportunities for Women, 1990).

5. *A Welcome for Every Child--How France Achieves Quality in Child Care: Practical Ideas for the United States* (New York: French-American Foundation, 1989).

6. *Safeguards: Guidelines for Establishing Programs for Four-Year-Olds in the Public Schools* (Washington, D.C.: National Black Child Development Institute, 1987).

7. M. Whitehead, C. Howes, and D. Phillips, *Who Cares? Child Care Teachers and the Quality of Care in America* (Oakland, Calif.: National Child Care Staffing Study, Child Care Employee Project, 1989).

8. James L. Hymes, "Public Schools for Four-Year-Olds," *Notes and Comments* (Fall 1986).

NCSS
National Council for the Social Studies

20. Social Studies During the Early Childhood and Primary Years

by **C. Frederick Risinger, 1990-91 President,** *National Council for the Social Studies. NCSS has a membership of 26,380, with headquarters at 3501 Newark Street, N.W., Washington, DC 20016.*

One of the most well-respected and prolific specialists in early childhood education, Carol Seefeldt, claims that "[the] social studies include everything that better enables children to understand their world and their place in it" (11, p. 6). In one of the most recently published books in the field, Barbara Day says that "Social studies is the single curriculum area that deals with human experiences entirely" (3, p. 437). Increased attention to the role of social studies during the years just prior to formal schooling and throughout the primary grades has been a consistent factor in educational literature for the past decade. The concept of citizenship, long regarded as the primary focus of social studies education, has been rediscovered by non-social studies educators and public policymakers as an overarching construct of the K-12 curriculum. Research clearly indicates that young children are learning citizenship behavior certainly from their second year. Early in life, children begin to develop knowledge of the "right" and "wrongs" of their society (12, p. 271). Properly implemented, an early childhood/primary social studies program will prepare this nation's young citizens for their role in a rapidly changing, multicultural, technologically rich society. However, all too many teachers, administrators, and school boards view social studies (along with science and the aesthetic arts) as a "frill" or "something to do when we've finished reading and mathematics." The pressure of standardized achievement tests and parental expectations can force teachers and decision makers to overlook laudable long-term goals for short-term results.

Another impediment to effective social studies planning and instruction at the early childhood/primary level is the discomfort that some teachers may feel with the breadth of content usually associated with the social studies. As the Task Force Report on Early Childhood/Elementary Education from the National Council for the Social Studies states, "The social studies are the study of political, economic cultural, and environmental aspects of societies in the past, present, and future" (10). Many teachers of young children may be intimidated by what appears to be an overwhelming amount of content. Marker (8, p. 149) found that secondary social studies teachers reported higher levels of stress than other core teachers and hypothesized that this might be due to the complexity, breadth, and ambiguity of the content of social studies. Still other teachers may recall their own experiences with social studies as filled with memorization, unimaginative textbooks, and less-than-inspiring teachers.

As a result, some teachers, with the tacit approval of administrators, school boards, and parents, relegate social studies to a rear seat in their classroom. These very teachers may contend that they teach social studies every day because "everything is social studies, isn't it?" and point to holiday bulletin boards and a field trip to a local dairy as examples of social studies instruction. Among social studies educators, this is referred to as the "Pilgrims in November and Presidents in February Curriculum."

Yet, social studies could be—should be—the most exciting part of the overall curriculum to teach and learn. This is particularly true of the early childhood years, when the energy, curiosity, and imagination of young children is most pronounced. These active, curious children need, want, and are able to learn skills, knowledge, and values about the fascinating world around them and their relationships with peers, parents, teachers, and others. Social studies can enable children to participate effectively in the groups to which they now belong and prepare for the more complex relationships of puberty, adolescence, and adulthood.

It is this latter focus that should be a compelling reason for teachers of young children to give more emphasis to the social studies. Existing research suggests that prosocial behavior—defined as "social behavior carried out solely to achieve positive outcomes for another person with no additional anticipation of benefit for the self"—can be fostered in young children through activities generally associated with social studies.

These include classroom cooperative activities, role playing, modeling—of teachers and peers, and through stories of other children and adults—and the feeling of esteem that derives from knowledge of one's place in the family, school, and society (7, p. 27). In her excellent book identifying creative learning activities in all curriculum areas for early childhood education, Day lists 27 objectives for the social studies. The first nine are

1. To begin to learn how to solve problems and make decisions at the appropriate level of development.
2. To become aware of, accept, and value unique qualities of the self and others.
3. To develop a positive self-concept.
4. To become more independent and responsible for one's own actions.
5. To learn to recognize and accept one's own feelings and the feelings of others.
6. To learn to make value judgments.
7. To learn to express one's own feelings in acceptable ways.
8. To develop social interaction skills.
9. To understand one's role within the family. (3, pp. 444–45)

Certainly, these goals represent much of what teachers of young children want all their students to acquire as part of their total experience. These objectives cannot be achieved through rote memorization, filling in blanks on a teacher-prepared study guide, or similar strategies. They call for imaginative instructional techniques, cooperative learning, a great deal of social interaction, multiple learning resources, and opportunities to build upon the positive, inquisitive attitudes toward knowledge acquisition that young children have.

As with other core areas, the social studies curriculum has been under rigorous scrutiny for the past several years. Research findings, practical experience, and societal imperatives have combined to bring about some significant changes in the way the social studies experiences of young children are developed and taught. These changes are just beginning to have an impact on state and local curriculum guides, textbook publishers, and local curriculum decision makers. Taken as a whole, these changes should reinforce those teachers who have been actively involved in planning and teaching social studies within a framework of knowledge, skills, and values. They should also encourage teachers who have been hesitant or unable to devote time and energy to a systematic program to include more content and activities from the social studies in their plans.

Perhaps the most significant change now affecting the structure and instructional strategies of the social studies is the movement away from complete reliance on the "expanding environments" or the "near to far" curriculum approach. Long regarded as solid as the pledge of allegiance in the morning, this long-time pattern of having young children first study themselves, then the family, the community, and the state is being questioned. Akenson (1, pp. 33-52) examines the shortcomings of the expanding environments structure and suggests that freeing the curriculum from the developmental theory associated with it would foster a variety of more effective organizational patterns throughout the early school years. By the time they enter kindergarten, most children have a sense of "near," "pretty close," and "far away." For them, the world is not a confusing place, with their house and neighborhood all jumbled up with houses and cities from faraway lands. The case for moving away from the rigid expanding environments structure is made especially well in the thought-provoking volume, *Historical Literacy: The Case for History in American Education*, published by the Bradley Commission on History in the Schools. In a chapter written by Charlotte Crabtree, director of the UCLA/NEH National Center for History in the Schools, Bruno Bettelheim, the distinguished psychoanalyst and educator, says:

> The presently taught curriculum in the social sciences in the early grades is a disservice to the students and a shame for the educational system. Children of this age are sufficiently surrounded by the realities of their lives. . . . What children of this age need is rich food for their imagination or a sense of history, how the present situation came about. . . . What formed the culture of the past, such as myths, is of interest and value to them, because these myths reflect how people tried to make sense of the world. (4, p. 176)

While most state and local curricula, and the textbooks designed to meet their goals, are still structured around the expanding environments approach, teachers should not feel compelled to restrict the activities of young children to these artificial boundaries. Crabtree was a major force in the development of the *History-Social Science Framework for California Public Schools, Kindergarten through Grade 12.* This state curriculum guide deliberately moves away from the expanding environments curriculum with this statement: "This framework introduces a new curricular approach for the early grades (kindergarten through grade three)." Instead of the self-family-community-region progression, the course titles for the primary grades are

Kindergarten—Learning and Working Now and Long Ago
Grade One—A Child's Place in Time and Space
Grade Two—People Who Make a Difference
Grade Three—Continuity and Change (2, pp. 5, 32).

For some time, curriculum planners have followed traditional wisdom about the ability of young children to understand and manipulate concepts of time and space—translated into social studies, that means history and geography. Recent research indicates that preschool and primary children can readily understand the differences between such concepts as yesterday and long ago or tomorrow and next summer. Lanegran, Snowfield, and Laurent (5) found that cardinal directions can be effectively taught in kindergarten and the Center for History, funded by the National Endowment for the Humanities, has learned that time lines, once thought to be too difficult to understand until age 9 or 10, can be understood by children in kindergarten and first grade.

The methodology of teaching history to young children is of paramount importance. One of the most noticeable changes in recent social studies curriculum guides and textbooks for the primary grades is the inclusion of biography and historical fiction to make history more personal, meaningful, and interesting. Levstik (6) found that young children who encountered historical data in the form of biography and historical fiction exhibited more interest and enthusiasm for history and for further investigation in more traditional sources. The California Framework builds upon this and similar research as the foundation of its primary curriculum. In the description of these years, the Framework states:

> In recognition of the shrinkage of time allotted to history-social science instruction in these grades [kindergarten through three], and the need for deeper content to hold the interest of children, this framework proposes enrichment of the curriculum for these grades. While the neighborhood and the region provide the field for exploratory activities related to geography, economics, and local history, the students will read, hear, and discuss biographies, myths, fairy tales, and historical tales to fire their imagination and to whet their appetite for understanding how the world came to be as it is. (2, p. 5)

One outstanding instructional aid is available, at low cost through the ERIC system. In 1987, Rosemary Mease, a Pennsylvania graduate student developed *A Handbook for Teaching United States History to Elementary School Children Using Trade Books* (9). Dividing U.S. history into several chronological units (such as Colonial Life or the Westward Movement), Mease provides synopses of approximately 15-18 fiction and nonfiction trade books for each unit. Additionally, she includes suggested classroom activities designed for use with each unit and a section discussing how to use trade books in the classroom.

In one important area, all the researchers and theorists agree with classroom teachers and administrators. The most effective instructional strategies involve active, hands-on learning. Whether focusing on acquiring knowledge, working with values and attitudes, or developing social skills, young children need to be taught through a developmental approach that emphasizes the total child. It should be an active program in which students participate in "experiencing and exploring their social and physical world through observing, predicting, and communicating" (3, p. 437).

The National Council for the Social Studies has taken an active role in conducting research and developing guidelines for early childhood educators. In June 1988, the NCSS Board of Directors approved a Position Statement entitled "Social Studies for Early Childhood and Elementary School Children: Preparing for the 21st Century" (10). This report examines the most recent research and current practices associated with eight basic questions:

1. What problems do young children encounter as they enter school?
2. What should be the definition of and rationale for social studies for early childhood/elementary children?
3. What are the goals for early childhood/elementary social studies that no other subject in the elementary curriculum can achieve?
4. What are the developmental characteristics of children that should be considered in planning a social studies program?
5. What is the research base for elementary school social studies?
6. What is the current status of social studies in the elementary school?
7. How should we prepare teachers of early childhood and elementary social studies?
8. What type of continued professional development is needed for early childhood/elementary social studies teachers?

After answering these questions, the Position Statement concludes:

If the young people of this nation are to become effective participants in a democratic society, then social studies must be an essential part of the curriculum in the early childhood/elementary years. In a world that demands independent and cooperative problem solving to address complex social, economic, ethical, and personal concerns, the social studies are a basic for survival as reading, writing, and computing. Knowledge, skills, and attitudes necessary for informed and thoughtful participation in society require a systematically developed program focused on concepts from history and the social sciences. (10)

REFERENCES

1. Akenson, J. "The Expanding Environments and Elementary Education: A Critical Perspective." *Theory and Research in Social Education* 27 (1989): 33-52.
2. California State Board of Education. *History-Social Science Framework for California Public Schools: Kindergarten Through Grade 12.* Sacramento: the Board, 1987.

3. Day, B. *Early Childhood Education: Creative Learning Activities.* New York: Macmillan, 1988.

4. Gagnon, P., ed. *Historical Literacy: The Case for History in American Education.* New York: Macmillan, 1989.

5. Lanegran, D.; Snowfield, J.; and Laurent, A. "Retarded Children and the Concepts of Distance and Direction." *Journal of Geography* 69 (1970): 157-60.

6. Levstik, L. "The Relationship Between Historical Response and Narrative in a Sixth Grade Classroom." *Theory and Research in Social Education* 41 (1986): 1-15.

7. Marantz, M. "Fostering Prosocial Behavior in the Early Childhood Classroom: Review of the Research." *Journal of Moral Education* 17 (1988): 27-39.

8. Marker, P. "An Analysis of Occupational Stress Between Social Studies Teachers and Other Core Subject Area Teachers in Two Indiana School Corporations." Ph.D. diss., Indiana University, 1986.

9. Mease, R. *A Handbook for Teaching United States History to Elementary School Children Using Trade Books.* ED 289 776, Education Document Reproduction Service, 1987.

10. NCSS Task Force on Early Childhood/Elementary Education. "Social Studies for Early Childhood and Elementary School Children: Preparing for the 21st Century." *Social Education* 53 (1989): 14-21.

11. Seefeldt, C. *Social Studies for the Preschool-Primary Child.* Columbus: Charles E. Merrill, 1984.

12. ____. *A Curriculum for Preschools.* Columbus: Charles E. Merrill, 1980.

NCTM

National Council of Teachers of Mathematics

21. Engaging Young Minds in Learning Mathematics

by **Shirley M. Frye, 1988-90 President,** *National Council of Teachers of Mathematics; and* **Raymond J. Brie,** *Associate Professor of Elementary Mathematics and Computer Education, California State University, Bakersfield. NCTM has a membership of 78,000, with headquarters at 1906 Association Drive, Reston, Virginia 22091.*

Virtually all young children like mathematics. Children do mathematics naturally, discovering patterns and making conjectures based on observations and active learning. Natural curiosity is a powerful teacher, especially for mathematics. Unfortunately, children and teachers tend to view mathematics as a rigid system of rules that are governed by accuracy, speed, and memory (10). The National Council of Teachers of Mathematics (NCTM) supports the need to offer young children developmentally appropriate mathematics content and learning environments.

A DEVELOPMENTAL APPROACH

This paradigm shift (8) is directed and outlined by the NCTM in the *Curriculum and Evaluation Standards for School Mathematics*. The *Standards* presents a coherent viewpoint about mathematics, children, and the learning of mathematics by children. Learning mathematics is developmental. What is appropriate for young children, in terms of both mathematics pedagogy and content, is very different from what may be appropriate for older children (2, 3). As we strive to provide young "mathematicians" with a developmental approach to their early learning, three important facets to be considered are curriculum, the teacher's role and assessment.

Curriculum

An appropriate curriculum for young children that reflects the overall goals of the *Standards* must do the following:

- Address the relationship between young children and mathematics. It is clear that children's intellectual, social, and emotional development should guide the kind of mathematical experiences they should have in light of the overall goals for learning mathematics. A developmentally appropriate curriculum incorporates real-world contexts, children's experiences, and children's language in developing ideas. Curriculum programs that provide limited developmental work, that emphasize symbolic manipulation and computational rules, and that rely heavily on paper-and-pencil worksheets do not fit the natural learning patterns of children.

- Recognize the importance of the qualitative dimensions of children's learning. The mathematical ideas that children acquire in grades K-4 form the basis for all further study of mathematics. How well children come to understand mathematical ideas is far more important than how many skills they acquire.

- Build beliefs about what mathematics is, about what it means to know and *do mathematics*, and about children's view of themselves as mathematics learners. The beliefs formed by young children influence not only their thinking and performance during this time but also their attitude and decisions about studying mathematics in later years.

Several basic assumptions governed the selection and shaping of the specific K-4 Standards, which are statements about what is valued as outcomes for children. Among them are the following:

- The K-4 curriculum should be conceptually oriented. A conceptual approach enables children to acquire clear and stable concepts by constructing meanings in the context of physical situations and allows mathematical abstractions to emerge from empirical experience.

- The K-4 curriculum should actively involve children in doing mathematics. Learning mathematics involves exploring, discussing, questioning, and constructing mathematical ideas. Children need to be engaged in talking, writing, speaking, listening to, and doing mathematics.

- The K-4 curriculum should emphasize the development of children's mathematical thinking and reasoning abilities. The curriculum must take seriously the goal of instilling in children a sense of confidence in their ability to think and communicate mathematically, to solve problems, to detect patterns, and to analyze data.
- The K-4 curriculum should emphasize the applications of mathematics. Solving real-world problems should be the focus of mathematics instruction, and connecting mathematics to other subjects should be an integral part of all learning activities.
- The K-4 curriculum should include a broad range of content. The curriculum must go beyond computation and arithmetic and include such areas as measurement, estimation, geometry and spatial sense, gathering and organizing data, patterns and relationships, number sense and numeration, and useful applications.
- The K-4 curriculum should make appropriate and ongoing use of calculators and computers. The thoughtful and creative use of technology can greatly improve both the quality of the curriculum and the quality of children's learning.

Classroom instruction should provide intellectually and physically engaging experiences for children (1). Descriptions of two scenarios follow.

1. Young children need a variety of experiences forming groups and looking for patterns and relationships. The ideas underlying number sense and numeration are quite complex. A hands-on foundation for developing these concepts should be done in the early years. A brief example of a teacher's dialogue within a small-group lesson is summarized: "Here is a group of counters. How can you sort them in some way so that your friends can tell

how many there are without counting by ones? Is there another way? Another way? . . ."

2. Young children are best able to work with three-dimensional objects while developing their notion of geometry and spatial sense. By manipulating, examining, and talking about these objects, young children become aware of their attributes. A brief example of a teacher's dialogue within a small-group lesson is summarized: "Reach inside this bag and without looking, describe what you notice about the objects in the bag. Are the objects round, square, flat, solid, etc.? Reach inside the other bags and see if you can find any objects that seem the same. What makes them the same? . . ."

Both lessons encourage children to talk about the mathematics they are doing. Either the teacher or the children could record observations made by the children about the objects. Young children can build on these experiences as a means of constructing meaning for themselves.

The Teacher's Role

Teachers of young children must consider the appropriateness of a given task. Decisions about instruction should be made on the basis of what children already know and can do, what children need to work on, and how much children seem ready to grow intellectually (3).

Children must talk about mathematics, with each other as well as with the teacher. When the teacher does all the talking, children usually receive mathematical ideas without engaging themselves physically in learning. Children should work in a classroom environment that fosters sharing ideas among themselves. Constructing learning in a meaningful context can be done with physical models, through language, and with symbols. The teacher's role is to promote mathematics talk with other children and use the discussion to foster mathematics learning.

Teachers must decide when children should work and talk about mathematics in small or large groups. Talk should focus on making sense out of mathematics based on hands-on experiences. Teachers should engage all children in the instructional activities and talk of the class. Communicating is instinctive and spontaneous at this level.

Teachers need to create an environment that encourages children to explore, develop, test, discuss, and apply ideas. They need to listen carefully to children and to guide the development of the children's ideas and thinking.

Assessment

If children are to be actively engaged in learning mathematics through a developmentally appropriate curriculum, teachers will need to assess formally and informally a child's mathematical knowledge on a daily basis. Teachers in grades K-4 need to collect information in a variety of ways. Observing children participating in a small-group discussion may contribute insights into a child's thinking. Teachers should also interview individual children to complement data collected in small or large groups.

As teachers assess a child's understanding of mathematics, they should ask themselves questions about how a child's conceptual and procedural knowledge relates to the learning environment. Teachers then need to consider what such insights suggest about how the learning environment could be enhanced, revised, or adapted in order to help children learn mathematics (2).

Evaluating the amount and quality of children's growth, development, and achievement is a multifaced and ongoing process. The various assessment procedures must be an integral part of instruction and include diagnosing, recording, and reporting each child's progress. Teachers must be prepared to use a variety of assessment strategies with young children. These strategies should make young children feel comfortable with evaluation as a natural part of learning.

Engaging Young Children. Success in making sense of mathematics in the early years enables young children to build a sound base for mathematics learning throughout their lives. The potential for learning and developing mathematical ideas is unmatched at any other level. Certainly NCTM's vision of *all* students becoming confident in their ability to do mathematics is captured in grades K-4 as teachers engage young minds in learning mathematics.

REFERENCES

1. California State Department of Education. *Mathematics Model Curriculum Guide: Kindergarten Through Grade Eight.* Sacramento: California State Department of Education, 1987.
2. Commission on Standards for School Mathematics. *Curriculum and Evaluation Standards for School Mathematics.* Reston, Va.: National Council of Teachers of Mathematics, 1989.
3. Commission on Teaching Standards for School Mathematics. *Professional Standards for Teaching Mathematics* (Working Draft). Reston, Va.: National Council of Teachers of Mathematics, 1989.
4. Cruikshank, D.; Fitzgerald, D.; and Jensen, L. *Young Children Learning Mathematics.* Boston: Allyn and Bacon, 1980.
5. Elkind, D. "Developmentally Appropriate Practice: Philosophical and Practical Implications." *Phi Delta Kappan* (October 1989): 113-17.
6. EQUALS and the California Mathematics Council Campaign for Mathematics. *Assessment Alternatives in Mathematics.* Berkeley: Regents of the University of California, 1989.
7. Grouws, D., and Cooney, T., eds. *Perspectives on Research on Effective Mathematics Teaching.* Reston, Va.: National Council of Teachers of Mathematics, 1988.
8. Kuhn, T. *The Structure of Scientific Revolutions.* Chicago: University of Chicago Press, 1970.
9. National Association for the Education of Young Children. "Position Statement on Developmentally Appropriate Practice in Programs for Four- and Five-Year-Olds." *Young Children* (September 1986): 20-29.
10. National Research Council. *Everybody Counts: A Report to the Nation on the Future of Mathematics Education.* Washington, D.C.: National Academy Press, 1989.
11. Trafton, P., and Shulte, A., eds. *New Directions for Elementary School Mathematics (1989 Yearbook).* Reston, Va.: National Council of Teachers of Mathematics, 1989.
12. Williams, C., and Kamii, C. "How Do Children Learn by Handling Objects?" *Young Children* (November 1986): 23-26.

NEA
National Education Association

22. Early Childhood Education and the Public Schools

by **Keith Geiger, 1989-91 President,** *National Education Association. NEA has a membership of over 2,000,000, with headquarters at 1201 16th Street, N.W., Washington, DC 20036.*

"By the year 2000," President George Bush vowed in his 1990 State of the Union address, "all children in America will start school ready to learn."

No goal, I believe, ought to have a higher priority for our nation. America's public schools simply cannot succeed for all children as long as some children begin their elementary school careers developmentally ill prepared.

Is the President's readiness goal achievable? I think so—but only if we as a nation get serious about meeting children's developmental needs *before* they enter kindergarten. The United States can no longer afford to pay lip service to the importance of early childhood education.

At the least, we as a nation must stop pretending that the current crazy quilt of early childhood education services offer us an appropriate game plan for the future. What's needed is basic: a thorough-going rethinking of the entire structure of early childhood education.

In the fall of 1989, the National Education Association began an effort to move this rethinking along. Our NEA Board of Directors directed the NEA Standing Committee on Instruction and Professional Development (IPD) to "develop and recommend for adoption" principles and policy positions that could "guide the development of effective public school programs in early childhood education."

After deliberations that included probing discussions with early childhood education experts both inside and outside NEA, the Instruction and Professional Development Committee completed its study in May 1990.

The study's recommendations will now serve as the basic foundation

NEA

for NEA's efforts to help forge a more effective approach to early childhood education.

No real progress in early childhood education, this NEA report makes clear, will ever come unless early childhood advocates collaborate at every policymaking level. We hope our report, which follows, will speed this collaboration.

THE EARLY CHILDHOOD ARENA

Well-known social, demographic, and economic trends identify a tremendous challenge for the United States in providing education and care for young children. These trends are captured in four interconnected phenomena:

1. Changes in family structure and in the roles and relationships of family members.
2. Changes in the makeup of the labor force.
3. Changes in the demography of poverty.
4. Increases in the preschool population and changes in its ethnic composition.

Selected data demonstrate the magnitude of the challenge:

- Between 1960 and 1985, the percentage of traditional households—father, mother, two school-age children—decreased from 60 percent to 7 percent (5).
- More than 3.2 million mothers work outside the home, and 200,000 more mothers join the labor force yearly (8). The U.S. Census Bureau predicts that 80 percent of all children under age six will have mothers working outside the home by 1995 (6).
- In 1980, the number of children under age six was 19.6 million (20). In 1990, the number is expected to reach 23 million, a 17 percent increase (26). Also in 1990, an estimated 5.8 million children under age six will live in poverty (27)—and poverty is the most valid predictor of school failure (23).

- Minority children are disproportionately represented in poverty statistics. The proportion of Black children living in poor families was 51.1 percent between 1983 and 1984 (18). Two out of five Hispanic children under the age of six are living in poverty (23).

The need for education and care programs for young children is not being met. Demand far outstrips supply, and demand for particular types of programs exacerbates the crisis.[1] Moreover, the field of providers is complex, variable, and changing—and implicit in that variability are deficiencies and competition.

Lawrence J. Schweinhart (25), director of the High/Scope Educational Research Foundation, estimates that "today's early childhood programs—day care homes, day care centers, and nursery schools—serve 30 percent of the nation's 16.1 million children under age 5." Nursery schools, which include most Head Start and public school programs, serve only 6 percent of these children.[2]

While the number of states which fund prekindergarten programs more than trebled from 1984 to 1989 (10), the number of available programs still is inadequate to the challenge.[3] Sixty percent of them are part-day programs for at-risk four-year-olds (3). Another 25 percent are programs that may run as long as a full school day (10). Programs in only five states serve children for the length of a work day (3). The public schools also frequently sponsor a range of other programs for children under age five, including Chapter I prekindergartens, preschool special education, locally funded prekindergartens, Head Start, and various forms of child care (9).

There are many other forms of sponsorship of early childhood programs, including employers or industries, churches, United Way organizations, parent cooperatives, private proprietary firms (e.g., KinderCare, Huntington Learning Centers), and Montessori schools. But here enter the issues of access, quality, purpose, stability, and cost. Some of these programs are operated for profit, others are not; some are registered with or licensed by states, others are not; some have working relationships with various social service or community agencies, others do not. The standards for these types of programs and the personnel they employ vary widely.

Quality is key to effective early childhood programming. For as early childhood experts note, "unless program quality is carefully defined and maintained, an early childhood classroom is just another place for a child to be" (24). The components of high-quality programs for young children are rooted in well-established research about the developmental levels of children and about developmentally appropriate education. In addition, newer longitudinal research studies are demonstrating the long-term benefits of higher-quality preschool programs.

The National Association for the Education of Young Children (NAEYC) (11) defines the concept of developmental appropriateness as having "two dimensions: age appropriateness and individual appropriateness." Human development research "indicates that there are universal, predictable sequences of growth and change that occur in children during the first nine years of life." These changes occur in all development domains. At the same time, "each child is a unique person with an individual pattern and timing of growth, as well as [an] individual personality, learning style, and family background."

Developmentally appropriate curriculum and practice thus are based upon teachers' knowledge of the typical development of children within particular age spans and also are responsive to children's individual differences. NAEYC also identifies four developmental age groups—birth to age three, three-year-olds, four- and five-year-olds, and five through eight-year-olds in the primary grades—each requiring differing, appropriate forms of practice. These distinctions derive from the work of such well-known researchers and child development theorists as Piaget, Montessori, Erikson, and others[4].

These distinctions also define *effective, high-quality* programs for young children. NAEYC (15) identifies six critical program characteristics:

1. The curriculum must be developmentally appropriate. It must encourage a child's development through appropriate child-initiated learning activities.
2. Small group size and favorable staff-child ratios are necessary. The recommended class size is two adults to every 16-20 three- to five-year-olds.
3. Teachers and administrators must be well trained in early

childhood education and child development. Schweinhart et al. (24) report that the "one teacher characteristic [which] predicts program quality and effectiveness [is] the amount of job-related training in early childhood education that a teacher has received."

4. Ancillary services—e.g., in-service training, curriculum supervision, evaluation and assessment—must be complementary to and support the child development curriculum.
5. Parents must be actively and integrally involved as partners with teachers in fostering a child's development.
6. Programs must be sensitive to and meet children's health and nutritional needs as well as families' needs for child care and other social services.

Research of the last 20 years indicates that children who participate in high-quality, preschool programs gain distinct, quantifiable advantages in future school performance, in later employment, and in their social and emotional adjustment. Studies of the well-known High/Scope Perry Pre-school Project[5] showed that the children involved (a) maintained IQ gains for up to four years after the program ended, (b) were assigned less frequently to special education classes, (c) were retained in grade less frequently, and (d) were more likely to graduate from high school and pursue post secondary education or training than other children (2).

Family and societal benefits also have been documented by the Perry Preschool studies. Mothers who were involved in the project increased their earning power due to expanded training and subsequent employment opportunities. Programs of this sort were shown to reduce costs for special education and welfare, reduce demands on the criminal justice system, result in higher employment rates among teens, and produce a large return on taxpayer investment (2). A good one-year preschool program for disadvantaged children returns $6 for every taxpayer dollar invested, according to High/Scope (24).

Research of another sort underscores the funding, staffing, and standards dilemmas common to many early childhood programs. The current "staffing crisis" in early childhood programs, according to Granger (7)—

... is not in programs in the public schools. Rather, it is in child-care programs and in such early education programs as Head Start. We can see the problem in the number of teaching positions that are filled by temporary replacements and in a 40 percent annual turnover rate ... [as well as] annual salaries [which] average about $12,000 in Head Start programs and about $11,000 in child-care programs.

PUBLIC SCHOOL EARLY CHILDHOOD PROGRAMS: PRINCIPLES AND STANDARDS

Public schools are the predominant provider of services to five- to eight-year-olds enrolled in kindergarten and in the primary grades. Early childhood advocates generally accede this range of responsibility to the public schools. But debate continues about whether and how the public schools should be a primary provider of services to *preschoolers*. The authors of a 1988 resource guide (1) summarized trends in state involvement in public preschool programs in two words: "growth and uncertainty." They went on to assert that "[u]ltimately, we should be aiming for a continuous ungraded curriculum flow from preschool through 3rd grade. Such a structure would push success upward rather than pushing failure downward."

High/Scope Director Schweinhart (25) identifies three strengths of the public schools: "professionalism, accountability, and universality." He also has made it clear that the "public schools will have to be transformed before they will be able to meet the diverse needs of young children and their families." And, he says, Yale University's Edward Zigler—known as the father of Head Start—recently reversed a position of long standing and "proposed that the public schools become the hub of a universal child care system."

The Public School Early Childhood Study (completed in 1987) examined public school programs for children younger than five over a three-year period (10). While the results were mixed, researchers concluded that the public schools "are likely to become a more common source [of early childhood education] for three- and four-year-olds in the future." They also noted that the "vast majority of [current] public school prekindergarten programs are aimed at certain children—usually poor or otherwise disadvantaged four-year-olds" (9).

The IPD Committee believes that the public schools are and should be a primary provider of early childhood services for preschool, kindergarten, and primary school children.

The committee identified seven key reasons for this position:

1. Programs offered by the public schools are universal, in the sense that all children should have equal access. They are low cost or no cost to the child and his/her family, and they must accommodate all children equitably.

2. Programs offered by the public schools are regularly and publicly accountable—to parents, to taxpayers, to local school boards, to state agencies, to the state legislature, to the Congress and the nation.

3. Participation in programs offered by the public schools enables children to benefit from full and appropriate articulation between the various developmental, educational, and institutional levels comprising the schooling process.

4. Public schools serve as an acknowledged socializing agent, enabling children from all walks of life to interact with and learn from each other in the interests of building a strong, educated, and able citizenry for this democracy.

5. Public school systems are singular and established infrastructures enabling funds to be easily channeled and economies or efficiencies of scale to be realized. Bus routes, school health programs, cafeteria services, and building utilization policies are examples of public school administrative and program structures which enable many services to be provided in an economical or efficient fashion.

6. The public school work force is the most stable and highly credentialed work force in pre-K-12 education.

7. The public schools are and will continue to be engaged in systemic restructuring efforts which necessarily will require consensus building and broad community involvement.

In identifying a set of principles for Association advocacy in the field of early childhood education today, the committee began with the premise that *all* education is developmental in nature—and that education spans an individual's lifetime, from birth to death.[6] These concepts are integral to the NEA's 1984 *Open Letter to America on Schools, Students, and Tomorrow* and its Nine Principles of Educational Excellence. *Developmentally appropriate practice* was noted elsewhere in this report as a tenet of high-quality early childhood programming. It is also a central concept in extant NEA policy about public school prekindergarten and kindergarten programs (Resolution C-3).

To effectuate Association advocacy of the public schools as a primary provider of high-quality early childhood programs in the nineties and beyond, the committee recommends adoption of the following policy position and set of program standards.[7]

Position

The Association believes that the public schools should be a primary provider of high-quality early childhood education programs designed to serve students ages three to eight. The Association urges states to *mandate the availability* of early childhood education programs in the public schools for all three- and four-year-olds. States also should encourage and support efforts by community agencies to identify and place in such programs children who can most benefit from the services provided.

Standards
- Early childhood education programs in the public schools must address the needs of *both* parents and child. Community needs must determine the program model(s) to be employed, and full-day programs must be available.
- High-quality programming should properly integrate day care and education components and be supported by the resources and staff necessary to accomplish the delivery of both kinds of services.
- Both teachers and administrators associated with public school early childhood programs should complete a *distinguishable* preparation program and should hold a *distinguishable* state-issued license to practice.
- Teaching and administrative staff of current public school pre-K-3 programs which are adopting a developmentally appropriate curriculum should be provided training in early childhood

- development at district expense.
- School districts also should offer at their expense appropriate courses of training for educational support staff working in early childhood education programs.
- Assessment methods used in early childhood programs should be appropriate to a child's developmental levels. The use of norm-referenced, standardized testing instruments in early childhood education programs is inappropriate. In addition, such practices as retention in grade and ability grouping are inapplicable to developmentally appropriate programs for young children.[8]
- Teaching, administrative, and support staff working in early childhood education should be compensated in the same manner and according to the same standards established for other, similarly situated district personnel.
- Parents must be actively involved in a partnership with teachers and support staff in the design, delivery, and evaluation of all early childhood services provided by the public schools.
- Funding for new or expanded early childhood programs in the public schools should come from new funding sources and be a shared responsibility of national, state, and local governments.
- The public schools increasingly should serve as coordinating agencies for all community services which need to be brought to bear in the service of parents and young children. This coordinating responsibility can include a variety of diagnostic, training, and networking functions. In time public schools should become the linchpin of community activity aimed at meeting the needs of young children.

ASSOCIATION ACTION: NATIONAL, STATE, AND LOCAL

Efforts to restructure the public schools are the threshold for more serious and far-reaching public school involvement in early childhood education. Those who consistently argue against public school early childhood programs tend to cite public school "traditions" (e.g., high teacher/student ratios) which are inimical to high-quality programs for young children. It is the committee's firm belief, however, that these very "traditions" (and many others) will be evaluated and significantly modified as school staffs restructure the organization, content, and delivery of educational services to students.

It is in this context that the Association can assume a major leadership role in the early childhood field, and that the public schools are likely to become ever more significant providers of services to three- and four-year-olds. As several commentators have noted, "the public schools have a vested interest in early childhood programs, because these programs give children better preparation for K-12 schooling" (24).

Key assets the Association can bring to bear at the national, state, and local levels *in support of and in collaboration with* other early childhood advocates include—

- A track record of activity in support of high-quality early childhood programs.
- The power of the voice of the *organized* profession, together with human, organizational, and financial resources.
- The understanding of and the ability to represent the interests of the wide range of school personnel who deliver services to young children.
- Well-established and effective advocacy of excellence *and* equity in education, as well as a strong commitment to multicultural education.
- A commitment to high standards in practice, undergirded by continuing efforts to strengthen state licensure standards, eliminate substandard credentials, achieve appropriate compensation levels for all education personnel, and proscribe detrimental district employment practices.
- Experience in using the tool of collective bargaining to determine and improve the conditions for teaching and learning.
- Organized efforts to work more effectively with parents and to encourage greater parental involvement in education decisions.
- Access to networks and a well-honed ability to work in coalition with others.

- Political organizing, lobbying, and law-making skills.
- An unabashed commitment to a public school system in the United States which can and will work to develop the full potential of every student.

The IPD Committee believes it is time for Association members to assume a more active, *external* leadership role in the early childhood arena. The committee strongly recommends that this role be *collaborative*—that the Association at the national, state, and local levels work to forge coalitions or join forces with other interests with similar objectives. The early childhood field is heavily populated by diverse but identifiable and established interests with great expertise. The Association can be influential in facilitating collaborative efforts to achieve common ends. Suggested Association activities at the national, state, and local levels follow.

At the National Level:
- Actively pursue NEA's extensive congressional agenda of child care and development issues.
- Seek support for establishment of a national database on early childhood care and education programs.
- Engage in coalition-building with other early childhood advocacy groups.
- Provide Association representation to other advocacy groups.
- Provide membership forums for discussing early childhood education issues and interacting with major figures in the field.
- Disseminate information and suggested action plans on early childhood education issues and trends to affiliates. This should include information about early childhood systems or programs in other countries (e.g., Sweden, France).
- Expand the number of professional publications about early childhood available to members.
- Support experimental or innovative early childhood programs.

At the State Level:

- Encourage or support efforts to engage in significant longitudinal research on intervention and preschool programs.
- Initiate or join pursuit of a state-level early childhood education agenda which echoes (as appropriate) the NEA's national legislative agenda.
- Seek new state funding for the initiation or expansion of public school early childhood programs.
- Establish productive working relationships with established early childhood advocacy groups.
- Pursue strengthened standards for teacher licensure, as well as professional control of state licensure bodies. Determine whether state licensing practices need to be altered to provide for identifiable credentials in early childhood development.
- Examine the need to develop high-quality nontraditional routes to licensure (consistent with recommended NEA guidelines) which will encourage and enable qualified support staff or professionals from other fields to become licensed to work in early childhood programs.[9]
- Become an agent for bringing attention to and building understanding of a state's interest in ensuring that young children's developmental and care needs are met.
- Encourage and enable the development of model public school early childhood programs, potentially focusing on such diverse "markets" as dense urban districts and sparse rural districts.
- Examine opportunities for the creation of incentives to business to collaborate with the public schools in making care and education services for young children available to workers.

At the Local Level:

- Define, as appropriate, the state of or the need for high-quality early childhood programming in local public schools.
- Encourage and enable dialogue among affected Association members and local early childhood advocates about the nature,

sufficiency, and directions of early childhood programming in local public schools. Pursue such discussions with district administrators and the school board as appropriate.

- Organize school staff and informed parents or representatives of local social service agencies to provide information to interested community groups about high-quality early childhood programs. Develop a community education program complete with speakers bureau.
- Build the base of understanding and support within the teaching and support staff ranks in local schools. Establish an inside outreach program designed to persuade current school staff to invest time, interest, and energy in the pursuit of high-quality early childhood programming.
- Determine the local Association's willingness and capability to represent the interests of early childhood educators and support staff in bargaining, or through other advocacy mechanisms.
- Develop and engage in thorough assessment of model early childhood programs in public schools.
- Accelerate or expand efforts at all levels of local schooling to more fully and continuously engage parents in responsibility for and decisionmaking about their children's education.

NOTES

1. For example, while some 95 percent of all five-year-olds are enrolled in public school kindergartens (20), most of these kindergartens are half-day programs which may not meet the needs of working parents.
2. Schweinhart defines day care centers as facilities children attend for full workdays while their parents are otherwise occupied, while nursery schools are center-based, half-day programs.
3. A survey by the National Conference of State Legislatures (19) reported that 41 states identified early childhood education as one of the top five issue areas that should be addressed.
4. Work by these researchers indicates that a child's most productive and influential learning years occur before the age of five. Experts generally agree that 50 percent of intelligence is formed by age four. The greatest

portion of languages is mastered by age three. This growth in learning, together with the development of curiosity and social skills, lays the foundation for all future learning. A child's failure in the early years to develop adequately in these areas has been shown to lead directly to underachievement in the elementary grades and beyond.

5. This ongoing, small, but significant study is tracing the effects of preschool education on the lives of 123 Black youths who were three- and four-year-olds when the study began in 1962.
6. The committee explicitly recognized that present federal law provides incentives to states to provide certain public school services for individuals with specific handicapping conditions from birth to age 21.
7. The committee notes that adoption of this policy recommendation will require review and appropriate revision of extant Association policy by the responsible governance body. In addition, adoption of this policy recommendation will have distinct implications for the work of the NEA Special Committee on Organizational Streamlining.
8. NEA policy on developmentally appropriate programs for young children and on student assessment is lodged in Resolutions C-3, C-6, and E-7. Other resources on assessment and appropriate practice issues include the NAEYC publications named in the list of references appended to this report.
9. See the 1989-90 IPD Committee report entitled "Ensuring High Standards in Nontraditional Routes to Licensure."

REFERENCES

1. Association for Supervision and Curriculum Development. *A Resource Guide to Public School Early Childhood Programs.* C. Warger, ed. Alexandria, Va.: ASCD, 1988.
2. Berrueta-Clement, J.R.; Schweinhart, L.J.; Barnett, W.S.; Epstein, A.S.; and Weikart, D.P. Monographs of the High/Scope Educational Research Foundation, No. 8 *Changed Lives: The Effects of the Perry Preschool Program on Youths Through Age 19.* Ypsilanti, Mich., 1984.
3. *Congressional Quarterly Editorial Research Reports.* "Preschool: Too Much Too Soon?" 1, no. 5, (February, 1988).
4. Feeney, S., and Kipnis, K. "A New Code of Ethics for Early Childhood Educators!" *Young Children.* (November, 1989): 24-29.
5. Futrell, M.H. "Public Schools and Four-Year-Olds: A Teacher's View." *American Psychologist* 42, no. 3 (1987): 251-53.
6. Bridgman, A. *Early Childhood Education and Childcare.* Arlington, Va.:

American Association of School Administrators, 1989.

7. Granger, R.C. "The Staffing Crisis in Early Childhood Education." *Phi Delta Kappan* 71, no. 2 (1989): 130-34.

8. McCormick, K. "If Early Education Isn't on Your Agenda Now: It Could Be and Soon." *American School Board Journal* 172, no. 6 (1986): 30-34.

9. Mitchell, A., and Modigliani, K. "Young Children in Public Schools? The 'Only Ifs' Reconsidered." *Young Children,* (September 1989).

10. Mitchell, A.; Seligson, M.; and Marx, F. *Early Childhood Programs and the Public Schools: Between Promise and Practice.* New York. Bank Street College of Education, 1989.

11. National Association for the Education of Young Children. *Developmentally Appropriate Practice in Early Childhood Programs Serving Children from Birth Through Age 8.* Expanded ed. Sue Bredekamp, ed. Washington, D.C.: NAEYC, 1987.

12. ——. *Testing of Young Children: Concerns and Cautions.* Washington, D.C.: NAEYC, 1988.

13. ——. *Appropriate Education in the Primary Grades.* Washington, D.C.: NAEYC, 1989.

14. ——. *Don't Shortchange America's Future. The Full Cost of Quality Must Be Paid.* Draft. Washington, D.C.: NAEYC, 1989.

15. ——. *Guiding Principles.* Pamphlet. Washington, D.C.: NAEYC, 1989.

16. ——. *Model of Early Childhood Professional Development.* Draft. Washington, D.C.: NAEYC, 1989.

17. National Association of State Boards of Education. *Right from the Start. The Report of the NASBE Task Force on Early Childhood Education.* Alexandria, Va.: NASBE, 1988.

18. National Black Child Development Institute, Inc. *Childcare in the Public Schools: Incubator for Inequality?* Washington, D.C.: NBCDI, 1985.

19. National Conference of State Legislatures. *State Issues for State Legislatures.* Denver, Colo.: NCSL, January 1990.

20. Papageorgiou, M.R. *The National Preschool Data Base.* Position paper prepared for the National Preschool Data Base Planning Conference. Special Surveys and Analysis Branch, Elementary-Secondary Education Statistics Division, Center for Statistics, U.S. Department of Education. Washington, D.C., 1986.

21. Sava, S.G. "Development, Not Academics." *Young Children* 42, no. 5 (1987): 15.

22. Schweinhart, L.J., and Weikart, D.P. "Evidence That Good Early Childhood Programs Work." *Phi Delta Kappan* 66, no. 8 (1985): 524-28.

23. Schweinhart, L.J., and Koshel, J.J., *Policy Options for Preschool Programs.* High/Scope Early Childhood Policy Papers, No. 5. 1986.
24. Schweinhart, L.J.; Koshel, J.J.; and Bridgman, A. "Policy Options for Preschool." *Phi Delta Kappan* 68, no. 7 (1987): 524-29.
25. Schweinhart, L.J. *Looking at the Big Picture: Early Childhood Programs in the U.S. Today.* High/Scope Press, High Scope Resources, 1989.
26. U.S. House of Representatives, Select Committee on Children, Youth, and Families. *Demographic and Social Trends: Implications for Federal Support of Dependent-Care Services for Children and the Elderly.* Washington, D.C.: Government Printing Office, 1984.
27. —. *Child Care Opportunities for Families Act. A Fact Sheet.* Washington, D.C.: Government Printing Office, 1986.

NSTA
National Science Teachers Association

23. Getting Started with Science—Science Inquiry for Early Childhood Education

by **Bonnie J. Brunkhorst, 1990-91 President,** *National Science Teachers Association. NSTA has a membership of 50,000, with headquarters at 1742 Connecticut Avenue, N.W., Washington, DC 20009.*

INTRODUCTION

Science for young children? How can they possibly learn about atoms, photosynthesis, chemical equations, plate tectonics, Newton's laws of motion? What is science for young children anyway? As one child put it: "Science? That's something I can't do because I can't read." Another child: "Science is what we never get to." Many adults have a fear of science. How can we expect four-year-olds to learn science when we had trouble with it? Teaching science to children is often thought of as making them take their medicine. It's good for them but we hate to make them suffer as we did.

Richard Feynman, Nobel prizewinning physicist, described his visit to Brazil's schools to observe their science education programs some years ago. The Brazilian officials were proud of their science emphasis and anticipated his praise. He saw elementary school children in bookstores buying physics books, yet he relates, "It's amazing you don't find many physicists in Brazil—why is that? So many kids are working so hard, and nothing comes of it. I finally figured out that the students had memorized everything; but they didn't know what anything meant." When asked to speak on the science education system he had been observing, he started out by defining science as an understanding of the behavior of nature.

> Then I asked, "What is a good reason for teaching science?"—Then I talked about the utility of science and its contribution to the improvement of the human condition, and all that. . . . Then I said, "The main purpose of my talk is to demonstrate to you that *no* science is being taught in Brazil." . . . Finally, I said that I couldn't see how anyone

could be educated by this self-propagating system in which people pass exams, and teach others to pass exams, but nobody knows anything. (6, pp. 191-98)

The officials were not pleased!

Feynman's observations point out the differences in understanding about what science is all about. Science is not a compilation of facts and equations to be memorized and used by the white-coated, intellectual elite. Science is more a verb—a way of knowing—than a noun—a compendium of increasingly difficult items compiled in the past to be repeated on exams for entrance into a special fraternity. Science should not be a filter to sort out all but the academically worthy, but a pump to enable each person to have the best interactions with her or his natural world. Science should enable the best possible quality of life for every person. The enabling function of science is what science for our children is all about.

WHAT SCIENCE IS

Science is a way of knowing about our world. Science is a human endeavor. Science nurtures our curiosity and values our imagination. With science skills, our children are invited to take charge of their own lives, to ask their own questions, to seek out their own answers using all the available evidence to make their own informed judgments. Science is for all citizens. It encourages an open mind and the willingness to embrace new ideas. Science helps us look at the universe we live in, understand how our bodies work, anticipate change as natural, and see the interdependence of the parts of our world.

We know natural curiosity awakens with the first awareness of infants. The desire to explore their environment is part of our children's human inheritance. Watching an active baby examine everything in its grasp is a ready reminder of the natural wonder humans possess for their world.

WE KNOW HOW TO TEACH SCIENCE

So why does any child find science boring? Leon Lederman, Nobel Laureate from the University of Chicago, reminds us that schools take "naturally curious, natural scientists and manage to beat the curiosity right out of them" (2). Good teaching encourages and guides children's curiosity; it facilitates their inquiry. We know how to teach science. We know using lectures, textbooks, and memorization to give children understanding does not work. Why do we continue to do it? The reasons are complex, but we know we must address the problems if we want our children and our nation to flourish. To *learn* science children must *do* science.

The problems can be reduced to two: (1) what we teach and (2) how we teach. The main goals for science education in early elementary years are to sustain curiosity, allow exploration, improve children's explanations of their world, and contribute to their abilities to make informed choices in their personal and social lives (3). The overarching goal is to reinforce their sense of "I can do it. My questions and answers are important to me and others, and exploring my world is a joy, a wonder." Keeping science a joy involves keeping the natural inquiry intact. Get rid of vocabulary lists. Memorizing words without meaning is contrary to science itself. Children should be able to ask their own questions: What happens to caterpillars in the school yard? They can observe, measure, collect, classify, record, interpret their data, compare data with others. They can test their thinking by "checking it out" with experiments they devise themselves. Teachers can guide by asking them questions: "How can you see if that's true?" If their results surprise them: "How can you check again?" "How can you check your new idea?" Such inquiry takes more time than reading about caterpillars in the textbook, but we have to value depth of inquiry over breadth of coverage. That's really an easy choice since learning something lasting and useful is better than learning nothing lasting or useful. Breadth of coverage is only of satisfaction to the "coverer." The "coveree" will not remember much of anything except perhaps a negative attitude. We're deluding ourselves if we think "covering" is of much value. Inquiry in depth (watching that caterpillar over time, exploring the questions that arise) will give the experience of wonder, respect, and self-confidence for use with the next questions that arise. Inquiry in depth teaches the skills children need now and can use in the future. Developing enabling skills for now and the future is, in

NSTA

large measure, what education is all about.

RECOMMENDATIONS

What and How

The National Science Teachers Association (NSTA) provides guidance on the role of science in early childhood education in the position paper for Preschool and Elementary Science (9):

> Science and Technology influence children's lives daily. Science should be an integral and essential component of every child's preschool and elementary school experience. Science and technology instruction should be integrated with other curricular areas to enhance and reinforce the development of concepts. In preparing students for the future, science instruction should mirror society: science should be a dynamic, interdisciplinary quest that enables students to make meaning out of their school experiences and daily living. The focus of an elementary science program should be on fostering an understanding of, an interest in, and an appreciation for the world in which students live. Elementary science should provide opportunities for nurturing children's natural curiosity and should not be viewed merely as preparation for the next grade level. Children should be able to investigate their world with readily available materials using a hands-on approach. A carefully planned and articulated elementary science program should provide developmentally appropriate learning experiences that will aid students in the acquisition of positive attitudes toward science, process and inquiry skill, and science content. A weekly minimum of 100 minutes in prekindergarten through second grade and 150 minutes in third and fourth grade.

The early childhood science program should include science for

1. *Personal Use:* Children learn a variety of skills that facilitate gathering of knowledge for personal use, including the ability to relate values to rational decisions and to access the consequences of these decisions. What do caterpillars do? Do they cause harm to their environment? What do they contribute to their environment? How should I treat them?

2. *Societal Use:* Students should use information and judgments to infer the impact of certain events on other events in their community, including the understanding that the solution to one problem may create new problems. They need to know that science and the way

we use it (technology) have an impact, for better or worse, on our lives. They need to develop a sense of responsibility for the uses of science and technology. Some people fear caterpillars. People sometimes try to kill them with insecticides or by stepping on them. What's helpful about that? What's harmful about that? Is there a best answer? How do we go about deciding if some of us disagree? Can we know "for sure"? What's *our* best answer right now? What happens if we act out our decision?

3. *Academic Preparation:* There is no set of topics that is "best" for early elementary science. What is best is direct, concrete, explorations of a variety of natural world topics that can help begin a foundation upon which interconnections and increasingly generalizable or abstract understandings can be developed as children move through their school years. Skills with exploration and positive concrete experiences with questions related to the earth, life, and physical sciences are appropriate instructional goals for early childhood science. If caterpillars are not the "creature" that catches the children's attention in their real world, find one that does. The caterpillars are not the important topic; the inquiry about life and systems in the environment is the valued experience. Inquiry skills, curiosity, experience with the pervasive themes of the natural world, in this case in the life science area, and development of the child's self-confidence are the important curriculum goals. The skills, knowledge, and confidence are basic to academic success.

4. *Career Awareness:* Children should develop an appreciation of how science skills and knowledge are used in scientific, technical, and nonscientific jobs. Truck drivers, beauticians, business managers, coaches, pharmacists, dentists, pilots, homemakers, city managers, park rangers, senators, and U.S. presidents all use (or misuse!) science in various ways. The more they understand science and its uses, the better they are at their jobs. (8)

Teachers

NSTA recommends that elementary teachers should have a broad introductory science content background of laboratory or field-oriented biology, chemistry, physics, and geology. They need instructional skills that encourage science inquiry of young children. They need to be able to focus on instructional goals for children to acquire process skills, science concepts, and positive attitudes toward themselves and toward science. They need to be able to use hands-on, minds-on activities to facilitate their children's own inquiry. They need to be able to encourage students to ask their own questions and build their own concepts. Teachers need a variety of strategies for the continuing assessment of their students' growth in science inquiry (8).

As professional educators, teachers of young children need to be active in professional decision making in their classrooms and in curriculum development, professional growth, and policymaking outside the classroom. Teachers should be supported and valued as the key to the science education of our young children (4).

Facilities and Support Systems

The classroom environment should invite and support curiosity and investigation in a variety of interactive modes (8). Flexible seating, water, ventilation, materials, adequate storage, and time to manage planning and materials are requisite support for early childhood science experiences. Administrators' roles are critical at this point. Without the external expectation for an active classroom that encourages a lot of "messing around" (focused inquiry), teachers cannot be expected to teach science well. Young children need to spend time with water, sand, bubbles, cans, boats, blocks, rocks, magnets, caterpillars, fish, crayfish, flowers, bean seeds. They need to be encouraged to mix things together (dirt in water, soft drink powder in water); to separate things (sand sinks in water, iron filings jump out of sand to a magnet, salt is left behind from evaporating ocean water): to build things (a special gerbil-powered pinwheel, a telegraph, a popsicle-stick bridge); to devise schemes to accomplish things (How can we bring a beam of light through the building, down the hall, onto our chalkboard? How can we find out how much styrofoam we're using in the cafeteria? How can we find out how sound travels best? How can we take good care of the fish in the aquarium? How can we use the computer to solve a problem? Why are we supposed to wash our hands so much?). An active classroom requires the flexibility of facilities, availability of materials, and the support of administrators (10).

General Guidelines

Much work has been done in the 1980s to set the stage for science education reform including early childhood science: NSTA's support and advocacy for science education policy development, science teaching advocacy, and science education reform (NSTA's Scope, Sequence and Coordination Project); the American Association for the Advancement of Science Project 2061 (1) for examining the realities of science literacy for all citizens and developing long-range implementation plans; the National Science Foundation's (NSF) increasing ability to encourage research, curriculum development, and teacher enhancement. Outstanding early childhood science projects from coast to coast include projects at the Lawrence Hall of Science in California, the Biological Science Curriculum Studies project in Colorado, the National Center for Improving Science Education in Washington and Massachusetts, and many others. Hundreds of national reports cite the needs for improving access to science education for all our students, especially addressing girls and children from historically underrepresented groups, children for whom English is a second language, and disadvantaged children. Many states have begun to define a quality science curriculum for children with science as an inquiry-oriented, enabling experience (5).

The summary recommendations for reform in early childhood science education have been synthesized well in the National Center for Improving Science Education report on Elementary School Science (7). The *curriculum* should consist of major science and technology themes and concepts chosen so the topics and experiences relate directly to the young child's world. Only a few concepts should be studied in depth. The 1990 California Framework suggests using the themes from AAAS Project 2061: Energy, Evolution, Patterns of Change, Stability, Systems and Interactions Scale and Structure (5). Certainly the children do not learn these as vocabulary. They do not even recognize the terms, but they are having a lot of direct experiences that adults will recognize as belonging to these themes. They are making connections and developing a sense of interest and self-confidence.

Science should be taught in the context of the entire curriculum ("across the curriculum"), using observation, recording, writing, reading, cooperating, speaking, mathematics, art, literature. The *instructional framework* uses the constructivist approach, which means children gradually "construct' their own concepts and skills from their own past and present concrete experiences. Teachers are facilitators for the process. They are "guides on the side." Teachers model inquiry and constantly work to shift the leadership for learning to their students, empowering them to do their own thinking.

Assessment of children's learning should constantly look at what they are doing. Assessment should value foremost children's attitudes and skills with thinking and applying their experiences to new questions. Any evaluation should be related to the curriculum goals.

Support and involvement in the science inquiry of young children should come from the child's entire world—teacher, classmates, principal, science supervisors, parents, community (businesses, organizations, universities, hospitals, adults, political leaders). Children can explore what happens when the water sprinkler runs for a long time. What happens to the water? Where does it come from? Where does it go? Why does it get cold at night? Where does electricity come from? What makes the best rubber-band-powered toy car? Why does the ground shake? How do people change as they grow up? What configuration of batteries and wires makes the brightest shining light bulb? What will work for the wires? How do chickens get out of their eggs? Why won't the grass grow on the lawn where we walk? Why do some things, like the school building, never seem to change? What does a caterpillar look like with a hand lens? What combination of detergent and water makes the best bubbles? How can I make a big bubble? How can I make a bubble inside a bubble? Where does sugar go when it gets mixed into the lemonade? Why did the dog die? What happens to the jack-o-lantern after Halloween? How does the cake mix change in the oven? What happens to popcorn kernels when we heat them? Why don't some of them pop? What makes the best paper airplanes? How can I find out? How can I find out with my friends? Are my questions important? Am I important? Can I do it? *Who am I?*

The best goals for early childhood science learning are to enable our young children to continue to be curious and to gain the confidence that they can ask questions and find some answers. Their *need to know* should be empowered with a *way to know* about their world.

REFERENCES

1. American Association for the Advancement of Science (AAAS). *Science for All Americans.* Project 2061. Washington, D.C.: AAAS, 1989.

2. Begley, Sharon, et al. "RX for Learning: There's No Secret About How to Teach Science." *Newsweek*, April 9, 1990, p. 55.

3. Biological Science Curriculum Study (BSCS). *Biological Science Curriculum Study and IBM New Designs for Elementary School Science and Health.* Dubuque, Iowa: Kendall/Hunt Publishing Co., 1989, p. 1.

4. Brunkhorst, Bonnie J. "A Science Teacher's Mind Is a Terrible Thing to Waste." *NSTA Reports!* National Science Teachers Association, November/December 1989.

5. California State Department of Education. *California Science Framework.* Sacramento: State Department of Education, 1990.

6. Feynman, Richard P. *Surely You're Joking, Mr. Feynman!* New York: Bantam, 1986, p. 195.

7. National Center for Improving Science Education. *Getting Started in Science Education.* Andover, Mass.: The Network, 1989.

8. National Science Teachers Association. *Position Statement: Preschool and Elementary Level Science Education.* Washington, D.C.: NSTA, 1986.

9. ____. *Position Paper, Preschool/Elementary Science.* Washington, D.C.: NSTA, 1990.

10. ____. *Position Paper on Laboratory Science, Preschool/Elementary.* Washington, D.C.: NSTA, 1990.

PTA
Parent Teacher Association

24. Early Childhood Education: The Parents' Perspective

by **Ann Lynch, 1989-91 President,** *National PTA. PTA has a membership of 6,800,000, with headquarters at 700 North Rush Street, Chicago, Illinois 60611*

The 1980s will be remembered as the decade when educators and government officials rediscovered the importance of parents' role in education. I hope that the 1990s will be the decade when parent involvement in education becomes a reality.

Throughout most of the 1960s and 1970s parents were encouraged to stay out of their children's education and their local school. "Leave education to the professionals—to those who are trained to understand what is happening in schools and what is best for children," they were told.

Many parents who found their lives already busy with family and work were delighted to leave education to the teachers and principals and school board members. Then came *A Nation At Risk* and a whole series of scathing reports on our schools. These were followed by an equally long series of studies that show that students learn better if their parents are involved in their education and that schools are better if parents and other community members take an active role in those schools.[1] So by late in the 1980s, parents were being invited back into schools, school personnel began to seek ways to work most effectively with them, and many government leaders claimed that more parent involvement rather than more funding for education would be the key to improving our schools.

The National PTA did not need to rediscover the importance of parent involvement. Our members and leaders have always been anxious to help their own children at home as well as all children in their school, community, state, and across the nation. That is what makes the PTA different from other parent groups. PTA members are part of a nationwide network that has set as its primary goal to get parents actively involved in their children's education.[2]

Nowhere is it more important to have parents involved in education than in the education of young children. Everyone recognizes that parents are children's first teachers. What parents do at home can vastly improve their children's chances of doing well at school. If parents do little to help their children learn, then schools and teachers are going to find it very difficult to provide what children have failed to get at home.

What is it that parents can provide their children? It is early stimulation, a loving introduction to learning, a delight in reading, the self-confidence and feeling of self-worth that are necessary for children to do well in school and in life and the knowledge that education is important.

PARENT INVOLVEMENT—NOT YET A REALITY

Are parents today deeply involved in their children's education? A recent *Newsweek* survey commissioned for the National PTA and Dodge found that most parents do help their children with homework and talk to them about school, but that relatively few are actively involved in their children's school.[3] Even those who help their children at home are often unsure if what they are doing is correct or if they are doing enough. They want guidance on what to do for their children and they need encouragement to get more involved at school. Therefore teachers and schools need to reach out to parents. Kindergarten and preschool teachers usually do this fairly well. Parents value the newsletters that many kindergarten and preschool teachers send home and the opportunities to visit class for special events and on other occasions.

I know of kindergarten teachers who each school year recruit a dozen or more parents to help in the classroom weekly, monthly, or whenever the parents can. Not only does this help the teacher and the students, but it also makes parents feel that they are a vital part of their children's education. It shows them what their children are doing in school. It gets them to know school personnel and the daily routine at school. It gives parents and children something to talk about and it builds parents' commitment to that school.

Sadly, though, in too many schools by first, or at most second, grade much of that reaching out to parents has ended. Parents are no longer invited to school for holiday celebrations. They are not asked or in many cases allowed to help in the classroom even if they volunteer. They receive a couple of information sheets a year and a short overview of the school from the principal at back-to-school night, and that is about all. They can talk to the teacher at one or two parent-teacher conferences a year, but those are short, formal meetings between people who don't know each other well and who, too often, are wary of each other. The only other times most parents talk to teachers is when problems have surfaced.

Why do schools and teachers who often say they want more parent involvement not reach out more actively to parents? I think in most cases it is because they don't know how. Principals need to take the lead and help their teachers find ways to involve parents more in their children's education. Teachers need to be more active and more creative, too. All school personnel from the superintendent on down have to decide that they truly want more parent involvement—more genuine involvement, not just parents who attend concerts, games, and school functions, and who support bond levies. Then school staff, particularly teachers, need to encourage parents to be more involved.

Most parents need teachers to motivate *them* as well as their children. Teachers need to make clear to parents how vital their role is in their children's education. They need to show them the benefits of volunteering at school. They need to guide them in the best ways to help their children with their homework. Parents often think they don't have time to help their children, but even the busiest parents can find two half-days or more a year to volunteer at school if their children's teachers ask them to. Even the most harried parents can read to or with their children for 10 minutes every night. And if teachers encourage them to, parents are more likely to turn off the television and help their children do their homework, play a game, read a story, or paint a picture.

What a difference it would make in the education of America's children if all teachers would ask each parent to volunteer in the classroom at least twice a year. I would also love to see all teachers send home a weekly newsletter with information on what the students are studying, updates on special projects, tips on homework, lists of books parents and children might like to read together, and suggestions for how parents can work with their children at home. I know that teachers are busy, but the hour or so it would take to put together such a newsletter each week would pay great dividends for students by creating a warm parent-teacher working relationship and producing a classroom full of motivated, enthusiastic, and ready-to-learn students.

PARENTS OF YOUNG CHILDREN NEED HELP

It has always been difficult to be a parent. It seems that you only start to understand your children when they grow out of one stage and into the next one. Just when you have finally figured out how to deal with an infant, that infant becomes a toddler and you have to learn how to deal with a toddler. It is the same with school. When you and your child get adjusted to preschool, it is time to go to kindergarten and when you both begin to feel comfortable with kindergarten, it is off to first grade. Therefore early childhood educators, whether preschool teachers or those in the primary grades, can help parents a great deal with understanding their children's development and their children's school.

Among the areas with which early childhood educators can help parents is the confusing matter of whether a child is "ready" for school. Over the last decade, more and more schools have begun to use so-called readiness tests to determine whether a child should start school. Given the current trend, we can expect that even more schools will adopt such tests in the future. Most parents who expect that their children will automatically be starting school at age five find the whole concept of "readiness" confusing. How, they wonder, can a test tell if their child should start school. Here is where a well-trained early childhood educator can help. The educator can explain to parents what the test their child takes means and help the parents decide whether to start the child in school or to hold that child out for a year. Many parents facing this decision find that a preschool teacher is much better able to help them gauge a child's readiness than any test. Also, parents who are unsure of the decision often find that a discussion with a kindergarten teacher will confirm their own feeling about their child's readiness.

Early childhood educators are well aware that individual children develop on their own schedule. Such teachers can do a lot to relieve the anxiety of parents who notice that Johnny or Mary seems slower than the child next door. Early childhood teachers also can help remind parents not to put too much pressure on their children. Many of today's parents, in an effort to give their children a "leg up" on the competition, push their children into academics before these children are ready. Preschool teachers can assure parents that most young children will benefit more by being allowed to play and explore the world in their own way than by being rushed into formal education at an early age.

Often it isn't only parents who are pushing children into too early academics: many schools are, too. Parents from all around the nation have told me that they see clear signs that what was once taught in second grade is now being taught in first; that where once first grade was a transition time that allowed children to adjust to school as well as learn, it is now much more intensely academic; that where kindergarten was once a gentle introduction to formal education, it is now highly structured with much more desk work than in previous years; and that what was once taught in kindergarten is now standard fare for many three- and four-year-olds in preschool. I was particularly struck recently by a parent who told me that her daughter came home from first grade and said, "Mommy, it is so sad! Kindergarten was fun but now all we do is work, work, work!" I hope that early childhood educators can help convince schools as well as parents that in education as in so many other facets of life, too much too soon can truly be a problem.

I would hope that in the 1990s both parents and schools would recognize the importance of letting children be children and that a more flexible curriculum would be developed that would adapt to children rather than force children to adapt to it. But, frankly I doubt that this will happen. Instead I fear that we will see more schools and more parents pushing children faster into formal learning. If that is the case we will undoubtedly see even more kindergartners and first graders flunking and more children deemed "unready" for school. I hope that this is not the case, but the pendulum is clearly moving in that direction. As we approach the 21st century, the National PTA will continue to remind parents that play and learning at their own speed are crucial to the development of young children and that school children should not be pushed faster than they can tolerate. We will be delighted to work with childhood educators to try to hold back the rush to teach children too much too fast.

AT-RISK CHILDREN HAVE SPECIAL NEEDS

Much of the PTA's attention in recent years has focused on helping parents of young children give their children a good start in life in order to prepare them for school and for a lifetime of learning, while still cautioning parents about the need to allow children to be children. Much of our concern also has been to get help for those children whose parents cannot or do not help them get ready to learn.

Everyone knows the statistics on children at risk—the high percentage of children who fail at school, who can't function well in English, who don't learn enough to get a job, who drop out, who ruin their lives with alcohol, drugs, and too early parenthood. Those statistics are only going to worsen unless steps are begun immediately and continued throughout the 1990s to help at-risk children at home and school.

The National PTA firmly believes that the best way to help these children is to start early to prevent the problems that will cause them to fail. For that reason we have long supported full funding for Head Start. We are encouraged by programs such as Missouri's "Parents as Teachers Program" and other efforts to help children and their parents break the cycle of ignorance, poverty, and failure. Despite the shining example of such projects, too little is still being done to help at-risk children. We intend to work to make the 1990s the decade when we stop talking about helping *all* children and start to do it.

If we are going to succeed, schools and teachers must have a major role in efforts to help these millions of children who are receiving too little assistance at home and school. Schools are going to have to be more active in reaching out to these children and their parents. Once children have "graduated" from programs such as Head Start, our schools and teachers are going to have to do much, much more to help them build on the improved start they have received. There is nothing more disappointing than to see bright, motivated kindergartners start sliding back into lethargy and failure because their schools and their parents failed to continue to provide the assistance they needed.

Schools are going to have to provide special services to needy children throughout their entire school career. It isn't enough to give them a good start and then to let them sink or swim on their own. Schools can't wait, either, until children have failed in middle or upper elementary grades and then try to step in and provide remediation. By that time it is usually too late. At-risk children need assistance at every step of the way to prevent them from falling behind and failing. Much more time, effort, and money must be spent trying to bring children who have fallen behind back to grade level than to keep them there in the first place. That is one of the lessons that must be put into practice in the 1990s if we are going to provide a good education for all children.

Another lesson is that it isn't enough just to help at-risk children. Schools, teachers, social service agencies, and all realms of society are going to have to work together to help these children's families, too. Studies of Head Start have shown that assistance to children is most effective when it involves parents. Studies of other programs have made it clear that children can't be helped unless their families also are helped. Over the last decades, school officials and teachers have often complained that they have had to take on more and more responsibilities that were once handled by families. I believe that in the 1990s schools will have to take on even more responsibility—this time it will be responsibility for the families of their young children as well as for what happens during the school day.

NOTES

1. See Anne Henderson, *The Evidence Continues to Grow: Parent Involvement Improves Student Achievement* (National Committee for Citizens in Education [10840 Little Patuxent Pkwy., Suite 301, Columbia, MD 21044], 1987) for more than 50 studies on the importance of parent involvement.

2. For more information on how the National PTA has been helping parents be more involved in education, see Melitta J. Cutright, *The National PTA*

PTA

Talks to Parents: How to Get the Best Education for Your Child (Doubleday, 1989).

3. For more information about the National PTA/Dodge survey on parent involvement that was commissioned by *Newsweek*, see *Newsweek*, March 12, 1990.

25. The Reality We Share in Common: An Afterword

by David Elkind

In his writings, Jean Piaget argued that our knowledge of reality is always a construction of human intelligence. Fortunately, commonalities in the functioning of our human sensory apparatus and in the laws that govern the external environment regardless of our place on earth ensure an underlying similarity in the realities we construct. Nonetheless, variation in our cultural, social, ethnic, professional, political, and familial backgrounds ensures that each of our realities has a uniqueness and individuality over and above the commonalities we share with others.

The force of that argument was brought home to me as I read the many contributions that make up this volume. Each author, or set of authors, is talking about early childhood education—the reality we all share in common. Yet, because each represents a different organization, each author or combination of authors sees early childhood education from the unique vantage point of the represented discipline. Put differently, each organization constructs early childhood education in a different way.

Some approach it from the standpoint of curriculum, what young children need to learn. Fortunately this is a broad rather than a narrow view, and the importance of art and movement are emphasized as much as reading and mathematics. Others see it from the perspective of the teacher and his or her training, role. Still others see it from the standpoint of parents and the importance of their involvement in the early educational process. Some writers are concerned with children of poverty, of color, or with children who have special needs.

Each of these positions has value and importance. Because we construct reality differently does not mean that one reality is right and another wrong. In education, as in science, we are presented with part-whole problems, not right-wrong issues. In science, theories that

Afterword

deal with isolated specific phenomena—say, gravitation—have to be incorporated within a broader more comprehensive theory—say, relativity. Both the specific and the general theories are valid, one is just more general than the other. In the same way, each of the many different perspectives presented here can be looked upon as a conception or theory of one part of early childhood education. Each has merit and is the groundwork for a larger theory that will encompass the more specific ones.

Although we are far from having a comprehensive theory of early childhood education at this point, one general conclusion is quite easy to draw from the contributions in this volume. This conclusion is that early childhood education must be regarded as a legitimate and full-fledged member of the educational enterprise. Early childhood education is not a preparation for later schooling; it is a form of schooling in its own right. Each of the contributions in this volume makes that point in a different way, but makes it nonetheless. Forward-thinking educators like Pestalozzi, Froebel, and Montessori always saw early childhood education in this way. It took a social revolution in our society for the rest of us to reconstruct our realities in such a way to accord early childhood education its rightful and legitimate place on the educational stage.